The Stage as
'Der Spielraum Gottes'

# Studies in Modern German Literature

Peter D. G. Brown
*General Editor*

Vol. 98

PETER LANG
Oxford · Bern · Berlin · Bruxelles · Frankfurt am Main · New York · Wien

Olivia G. Gabor

# The Stage as
# 'Der Spielraum Gottes'

PETER LANG

Oxford · Bern · Berlin · Bruxelles · Frankfurt am Main · New York · Wien

**Bibliographic information published by Die Deutsche Bibliothek**
Die Deutsche Bibliothek lists this publication in the Deutsche National-
bibliografie; detailed bibliographic data is available on the Internet at
‹http://dnb.ddb.de›.

British Library and Library of Congress Cataloguing-in-Publication Data:
A catalogue record for this book is available from *The British Library,*
Great Britain, and from *The Library of Congress,* USA

ISSN 0888-3904
ISBN 3-03910-268-0
US ISBN 0-8204-7197-6

© Peter Lang AG, International Academic Publishers, Bern 2006
Hochfeldstrasse 32, Postfach 746, CH-3000 Bern 9, Switzerland
info@peterlang.com, www.peterlang.com, www.peterlang.net

Printed in Germany

# Contents

# Chapter One
## *Das Moderne*

The present study will argue that its central topic, even if visible in the works of many individual writers over the centuries, essentially stems from historically unique aspects of the 'modern' period. The problem stems from several developments that can be accepted as leading to modern literature and reappears in the larger philosophical and theoretical attempts to clarify the 'modern'.

This study will examine a break with a religious tradition and the subsequent dilemma of language in the modern age. It will furthermore undertake to reveal, through an analysis of theatrical language, that a divine presence makes itself detectable in specific works of literature at exactly the place where the linguistic breakdown occurs.

The modern age is characterized by a lack of direction that stems not only from its break with a religious tradition and a set historical frame but also from a subsequent problem of speech and articulation. Most literary histories discuss the advent of Naturalism in the later part of the nineteenth century as the beginning of the 'Moderne' in Germany. The trends listed above culminate in this movement. But if anything truly distinguishes this epoch from the preceding ones and makes it truly 'new', it can be found in the open denial of the metaphysical and, more particularly, of God, as relevant to literature.

Naive acceptance of the Judaic and Christian holy writings as unique, infallible, and divinely inspired was no longer possible for most educated citizens of Europe after about 1875. Yet by the Age of Enlightenment, it was already widely assumed that human reason, natural law and progress were sufficient to create a perfect society. For the supporters of the Enlightenment, the world resembled a giant machine whose functioning had been impeded because the machine was not properly understood or because it had been left in the hands of metaphysical forces. Charles Darwin's work in natural history then provided a scientific validation of the middle-class conviction that the universe and nature could be understood without recourse to theological or metaphysical intermediaries. Yet Darwin's was no new denial of fundamentalist beliefs, for natural scientists had for over a century been publishing works that flatly denied the doctrine of God's creation. By the late eighteenth century, however, secularism had become a leading force in the revolutionary movements of workers and bourgeois against church supporters. Without these earlier developments, integral to the socioeconomic and political history of the West, the transition to modernity that occurred in the nineteenth century would clearly have been impossible, and Western civilization would still be Christian.

The turning of the balance from pre-modern to modern occurred for the Western world as a whole during the nineteenth century. Traditional religion in Europe in the nineteenth century came under attack not only from Darwinism but also from other directions, most notably the so-called 'higher criticism', which used modern methods of scholarship to study the Bible. French Positivists such as Ernest Renan (1823–92), and German Hegelians or post-Hegelians such as David Friedrich Strauss (1808–74) and Ludwig Feuerbach (1804–72), assisted this development.[1] A generation later, Friedrich Nietzsche claimed in his *Also sprach Zarathustra* (1883–85) that God was dead. Nietzsche views life and the world as an aesthetic spectacle that requires no further justification. Although, as we shall see in subsequent chapters, he exalts the man who recognizes higher values as solely aesthetic ones, he sees no religious goal for humanity – no divinity. With a spirit of fanaticism (that was 'religious' in its absoluteness, albeit in the service of a radical negativity), he pursued the quest for meaning without the benefit or necessity of the divine. This is plain even in Nietzsche's first book. *Die Geburt der Tragödie* (1872–86) maintains that 'nur als aesthetisches Phänomen ist das Dasein und die Welt ewig gerechtfertigt' (47). The preface added in 1886 declares:

> Hier kündigt sich, vielleicht zum ersten Male, ein Pessimismus 'jenseits von Gut und Böse' an, hier kommt jene 'Perversität der Gesinnung' zu Wort und Formel [...] eine Philsophie, welche es wagt, die Moral selbst in die Welt der Erscheinung zu setzen, herabzusetzen und nicht nur unter die 'Erscheinungen' (im Sinne des idealistischen terminus technicus), sondern unter die 'Täuschungen', als Schein, Wahn, Irrthum, Ausdeutung, Zurechtmachung, Kunst. (18)

This mood reflected the arrival of modernity, the condition of a European civilization that was becoming increasingly mechanized and dehumanized. The crisis of faith, Nietzsche's proclamation of God's death, the often anguished search for a viable substitute for religion, something that would retain purpose, plan and hope in the universe while sloughing off the discredited fable, are familiar features of the later-nineteenth-century intellectual landscape. This substitute for religion was mainly found in science, which, in turn, led to Naturalism.

Naturalism may be said to best reflect this collapse of the traditional value structure of Western civilization. The narrow focus of Naturalist literature stems from a real crisis of human values, a recurrent thematic of disintegration, of spent energies, of crumbling moral and social structures. Emile Zola, the godfather of German Naturalism,[2] much impressed by the achievements of science in the age of scientific progress, proclaimed that literature had to become as scientific as medicine; man is a creature determined by physical laws and is subject to verifiable investigation exactly as material objects and animals are. Yet perhaps the greatest of the cultural phenomena of late-nineteenth-century Europe is Naturalism's self-imposed confinement in a godless universe. For example, Zola states in his 1880 *Le Roman expérimental* (1902) that the metaphysical man is dead and only the physiological one remains. He passes over the spiritual source of life, that is, the soul, to concentrate on physiology and sociological processes. One of his most ardent German disciples, Wilhelm Bölsche, then claims in his 1876 influential book *Die naturewissenschaftlichen Grundlagen der Poesie* (1976, 27):

> Die Zeiten sind herum, wo die Menschheit einen Gott in Donnerwolken oder Knechtsgestalt zur Erklärung ihrer Sittengesetze brauchte: die Frage des ewigen Looses nach aller Zeitlichkeit fordert auch heute noch den kühnen Flug über die Grenzen des Erkannten, und wenn all dogmatische Religion sich sonst zersetzen sollte, so wird ihre letzte lebenskräftige Ranke sich immer wieder emporwinden an der festen Säule des Trostes am Grabe unserer Toten.

To be 'naturalistic' means, in one important sense, to explain all things without recourse to supernatural power, and, when faced with a lack of an explanation, to fall back upon a strong emphasis on chance, 'Zufall'.

9

The rise of modernity in Western literature stems, at least in terms of its rejection of the supernatural, from a new concept of what determines personal identity and freedom. The view that the individual should try to assert his freedom from the dictates of events and material reality shifts to one that the individual is subject to, and therefore understandable only in terms of, the influences of heredity and environment. The emphasis is now on how the intersections of a unique set of worldly relations define one's personal identity and center (a center that consequently cannot stand independently). In the pre-Copernican view of the universe in which all the spheres revolved around the earth, man was accorded a correspondingly central place. But man's centrality was not anchored in the physical properties of the cosmos but in his religiously determined significance. What made this planet important was not just its astronomically central position but the fact that it was inhabited by rational creatures whose destiny depended on an omniscient and omnipotent God in whose image they had been created. The astronomical systems of Copernicus and Kepler pushed back the boundaries of the medieval universe so that the physical universe was infinite space. In the light of these discoveries, and also due to the powerful influence of the Enlightenment's belief that reason would enable humanity to discover the natural laws regulating existence and thereby assure progress without any need for the metaphysical, Christian theology would, in some of its details, have to be *brought up to date*.

The twentieth century seems to acknowledge the death of God. Modern writers not only distrust, as did Nietzsche, the validity of their 'God-given' intelligence, but also begin to doubt the value of pure aesthetic resolution and dedication to art. They have come to feel that they have lost the tragic sense of life and art. Their metaphysical passion has become uncertain and destructive as it fights in vain against the fatalism of the religion of nothingness. The rise of science, therefore, has made it impossible to describe parts of the world or any of the things that happen in it in terms of the supernatural. The supernatural, thus drained of its empirical content, is revealed as void of meaning.

The universality of this process, however, is not simply accepted without challenge. For example, Albert Camus (1913–60), probably the most-cited exponent of 'absurdism', believes that the dynamic that sustains Christian belief has not disappeared. Far from it: Christian experience underlies the thinking of the West. Culturally speaking, Christianity may be suffering an eclipse.

Given the great discoveries of applied science in the twentieth century, with their dual promise of emancipating humanity from the drudgery of labor and the possibility of a happier, freer, more humane future, one must, like Max Horkheimer and Theodor W. Adorno, nevertheless ask in *Dialektik der Aufklärung* (1969, 1), 'warum die Menschheit, anstatt in einen wahrhaft menschlichen Zustand ein-zutreten, in eine neue Art von Barbarei versinkt'. The modern unbelief – welcomed by some and bemoaned by others – seems in any case to have created the situation that T. S. Eliot (1888–1965), a poet and critic who is sensitively aware of these traumatic changes in the spiri-tual climate of the twentieth century, describes in *On Poetry and Poets* (1957, 15):

> The trouble of the modern age is not merely the inability to believe certain things about God and man which our forefathers believed, but the inability to feel towards God and man as they did. A belief in which you no longer believe is something which to some extent you can still understand; but when religious feeling disappears, the words in which men have struggled to express it become meaningless.

This is the spiritual dilemma of the modern writer. Modern writers wrestle with the religious problem, yet God has become an empty word. He has become a promise that will never be kept. At the same time, however, science has not been able to replace Him. As a consequence, the image of God that some writers invoke is composed of negations while others indulge, like Bertolt Brecht, in self-conscious blasphemy. In either case, what they attempt to express is their feelings in a desolate world without God. In his recent book on Franz Wedekind, Fred Whalley (2002, 10) correctly identifies the condition of the modern writer:

> Thus the renewed interest in religious issues did not betoken a return to trad-itional beliefs; rather, religious imagery was reinvented in such a way as to point toward a spiritual world that existed in the mind of the artist and in

contrast to the strictly empirical, materialistic world-view. It also had the advantage of its potential to offend the reactionary and the traditionally religious.

Over the past centuries, the purveyors of Christianity have resisted the call to accommodate theological and ecclesiastical practices to changes in the world outside of church and monastery walls, and Christianity itself has, as a consequence, become a religion of the oppressors, an ideology of social conservatism in the service of the preservation of prevailing social forms. Such changes have been accompanied by a countercurrent that has always been conditioned and nourished by a fundamental aspect of religion. Max Horkheimer describes religion as the record of the wishes, desires, and accusations of many generations. According to the assertions of Horkheimer, 'true' religion basically undermines the authority and validity of social and political institutions. What characterizes the religious impulse is a longing for 'perfect justice' that, in contemporary times, often gives rise to many freedom struggles. This religious impulse, however, has been seized by nonreligious political pressure groups that have long forgotten their visionary source in original Christianity. Horkheimer writes in *Kritische Theorie* (1968b, 376):

> Die Menschheit verliert auf ihrem Wege die Religion, aber dieser Verlust geht nicht spurlos an ihr vorüber. Ein Teil der Triebe und Wünsche, die der religiöse Glaube bewahrt und wachgehalten hat, werden aus ihrer hemmenden Form gelöst und gehen als produktive Kräfte in die gesellschaftliche Praxis ein [...] In einer wirklich freiheitlichen Gesinnung bleibt jener Begriff des Unendlichen als Bewußtsein der Endgültigkeit des irdischen Geschehens und der unabänderlichen Verlassenheit der Menschen erhalten und bewahrt die Gesellschaft vor einem blöden Optimismus, vor dem Aufspreizen ihres eigenen Wissens als einer neuen Religion.

In the case of Christianity, its inherently revolutionary character was soon lost from sight. One did not have to wait for Karl Marx's condemnation of religion as the 'opiate of the masses'. One could scarcely say that the role of the Church as suppressing revolutionary or anti-establishment trends is just a 'modern' view. In fact, by the middle of the third century, Christianity had already lost its original impulse and was turned by the rulers of the Roman Empire into a means to manipulate the masses. As a consequence, Christianity then

12

became but another ideology in the service of the preservation of prevailing social forms. The patriarchal universe of Christian theology, with its accompanying doctrines and ecclesiastical power structures, is today still aimed at eliminating any liberating tendencies. To the degree that Christianity is forced to accommodate its doctrines about immutable truths to the fluctuations of the real world, it loses its redemptive power, for this redemptive power is in direct relationship to its willingness to protest against the suffering and oppression inflicted on humanity by the real world.

Nonetheless, most critics of modern society lament that theological authority and traditions, and the Church as their political expression and patron, do not function as the true representatives of the Christian religion with its message of liberation and hope demanded for a more humane world. Herbert Marcuse (1966, 64), in *Eros and Civilization*, speaks of a similar loss of religion: 'with the transubstantiation of Jesus, his gospel too was transubstantiated; his deification removed his message from this world. Suffering and repression were perpetuated.' Horkheimer's view of religion restates the Marxian notion that describes the central impulse of religion as a protest and longing for better conditions. The 'vital reality' at the heart of religion, he asserts, became repressed and weakened through the historical process of theology's accommodation to the prevailing power structures and political forces within which the churches sought and still seek their institutional self-preservation. With this historical accommodation to the social status quo, the Church 'spiritualized' completely Christ's liberating message that once encompassed material evils like the money-changing in the temple. As a result, Christianity was compelled to forfeit its counterforce to the experience of misery and suffering that marks the material and spiritual condition of most of humanity.

If Christianity is to reclaim its original purpose, it must, Horkheimer believes, transcend the traditional theological forms in which it has been imbedded, forms that have exhausted their capacity to motivate and support efforts for social and personal transformation. As he specifies in *Kritische Theorie* (1968b, 375), 'Es ist eine vergebliche Hoffnung, daß die aktuellen Diskussionen in der Kirche Religion erwecken werden, wie sie in ihrem Anfang lebendig war.' In this context we note that, in his analysis of religion, Horkheimer claims Christianity's inherent potential for overcoming the malaise of modernity with an *irdisches Schicksal* ('worldly destiny'). Christianity's very idea of a radically supreme divinity implies a criticism of all political and social arrangements: 'Im Gottesbegriff war lange Zeit die Vorstellung aufbewahrt, daß es noch andere Maßstäbe gebe als diejenigen, welche Natur und Gesellschaft in ihrer Wirksamkeit zum Ausdruck bringen. Aus der Unzufriedenheit mit dem irdischen Schicksal schöpft die Anerkennung eines transzendenten Wesens ihre stärkste Kraft' (374). In turn, the implied presence of the divine represents, as it were, not only a crack in the supposedly impenetrable world of strictly physical reality, it also implies a questioning of the tools and fundamental methods used to grasp the world and communicate either its meaning or its alleged lack of it. In short, an invocation of the divine became a problem for the modern period, not least because its reintroduction would call into question what supposedly constitutes the very essence of modernity, 'das Moderne'.

Marx and Nietzsche both viewed contemporary society as deluded by mystification and illusion. However, whereas for Marx this constituted a description of the development of a crisis in a revolutionary situation, for Nietzsche it described the total decadence of modernity with its lack of genuine passions, its false truths, its empty historicism, its eternal recurrence of the 'ewig-gleich' that did not veil or mask anything lying beneath it. Rather, modernity is this present, this inversion of all values, in a world of masks and illusions. What is left is an empty shell of convention and appearance: representation. The phenomenon of modern man has become wholly appearance; he is not visible in what he represents but rather concealed by it. This is expressed by Nietzsche in 'Unzeitgemäße Betrachtungen'. Not only is human perception forged in long historical experience, but also the objects we confront in the external world are themselves products of socialized and historical processes. With each historical epoch, domination reformulates and reinforces itself on higher levels established by the prevailing social conditions.

If one accepts Nietzsche's view, the progress of history is reduced to an illusion; advances in science and technology that are capable of realizing human happiness are transformed into their negation so that domination is reinforced. Man becomes an abstract category of a self-creating, commanding self, made in an equally alienated image of God. According to Horkheimer and Adorno (1969), Enlightenment becomes myth in the perpetual and inescapable cycle of intensified domination of technology over man. In such a society, people would be characterized only by a drive to maximize satisfactions. Hegel and Marx attacked such a picture of 'civil society', and later Max Weber feared that modernity was developing in precisely this direction. Horkheimer and Adorno shared Weber's fear. They saw a 'Dialektik der Aufklärung' whereby differentiation paradoxically develops into a homogeneous society where all life is subordinated to the rationality of production and efficiency. For Horkheimer and Adorno, as well as for Marx, a society is not free as long as injustice, exploitation, and suffering constitute the given condition of certain social groups whose oppressed condition is perceived as a prerequisite of the well-being of those other groups for whose service the exploited work and live. Individual autonomy becomes completely restricted. In order to make the functioning of the market smoother, the individual has been standardized to fill the needs generated by the machinery of the culture industry: 'In der Kulturindustrie ist das Individuum illusionär nicht bloß wegen der Standardisierung ihrer Produktionsweise. Es wird nur so weit geduldet, wie seine rückhaltlose Identität mit dem Allgemeinen außer Frage steht' (163). Conversely, what an individual thinks, feels or needs is created by the culture industry.

As a consequence of the modern predicament, much of modern literature shows, in the words of Eckhard Lobsien (1988, 12), 'daß, keinerlei akzeptierten Garantien, Normen oder Vorbilder mehr in Anspruch genommen werden können'. The lack of direction that characterizes the modern age arises from its break from tradition, a predetermined historical frame, and the traditional understanding of language's relationship to reality. The tendency of the modern age is to express itself in a literature that is motivated by iconoclasm yet suffers self-doubt due to its need to question its own medium.

Along with the historical atheism, one notices an increasing concentration, especially in drama, on the limits of language. Language, as seen by modern theory in terms of signifiers and signifieds, breaks down. As a consequence, 'Sprachnot' occurs, a condition that characterizes modern literature.[3] Through such 'Sprachnot', which has, for modern theorists, become the central problem in language, signification suspends itself. Silence becomes the only recourse left us as viewers. In this context, silence, however, goes beyond capitulation before a mute universe because it refuses to declare itself to us. For such silence, in keeping with Spinoza's old truth in the *Ethics* that 'nature abhors a vacuum', cries out to us to fill it like a vacuum. On this very idea of 'Sprachnot' the present study will be based. It will examine the resultant vacuum of silence as a lacuna so universal the reader feels obligated to look to the most universal concept available as the sole possibility to close it. This silence then becomes the 'Spielraum Gottes'.

Since the present study deals with a phenomenon that runs counter to a general historical trend (toward atheism), it must also constantly touch on different discourses of social and historical moments, so as to suggest the particular directions history has taken, in order to reveal the changing possibilities for, and limits of, transformations independent of prevailing attitudes. In turn, this will substantiate Paul Tillich's assertion that 'der Grund des Seins, auf den alles endliche Sein verweist, weil es die Tiefe seiner Bedeutung erst sucht, ist der Geschichte entzogen.'[4] For many, modern civilization has become part of a meaningless and disordered world that has managed to eradicate the individual's identity. The proposed study will seek, through a distinct critique of the present society and its methods of communication, a presence of the divine within as well as outside the boundaries of language.

Christianity has such a subversive potential in the modern age of the Western world because the very idea of a radically supreme divinity implies a criticism of political and social arrangements and because it questions the tools used to grasp the world and communicate its meaning. When one recognizes that established theology and ecclesiastical power have degenerated into the representatives of the social order, we accept that the task of reclaiming the autonomous and liberative dimension of Christianity must fall to individuals. Horkheimer asserts in *Kritik der Instrumentallen Vernunft* (1968c, 228) that in a period of masses, the liberative work is left to the individual: 'Als Hoffnung bleibt die Arbeit daran, daß in der anbrechenden Weltperiode der Blöcke verwalteter Massen noch einige Menschen sich finden, die Widerstand leisten wie die Opfer der Geschichte, zu denen der Stifter des Christentums gehört.'

This study contends that individuals have their most effective medium in literature. Writing about Charles Baudelaire, Nägele argues in *Echoes of Translation* (1997, 77):

> In contrast to a powerful aesthetic tradition Christianity does not threaten art, but its denial is posited as the deadly threat. While Marx declared religion (above all, Christianity) as the opium for the people, Baudelaire declares that new paganism as the opium of the writer 'cette déplorable manie, qui tend à faire de l'homme un etre inerte et de l'écrivain un mangeur d'opium'.

If we understand modernity in the sense proposed above and in Jürgen Habermas's *Philosophischer Diskurs der Moderne* (1986) as the radical project of Enlightenment, secularization, and immanence, then aesthetics play a central role in modernity. Habermas argues:

> In der Moderne verwandeln sich also das religiöse Leben, Staat und Gesellschaft, sowie Wissenschaft, Moral und Kunst in ebensoviele Verkörperungen des Prinzips der Subjektivität. Deren Struktur wird *als solche* erfaßt in der Philosophie, nämlich als abstrakte Subjektivität in Decartes 'Cogito ergo sum', in der Gestalt des absoluten Selbstbewußtseins bei Kant. Es handelt sich um die Struktur der Selbstbeziehung des erkennenden Subjekts, das sich auf sich als Objekt zurückbeugt, um sich wie in einem Spiegelbild – eben 'spekulativ' – zu ergreifen [...] Bis zum Ende des 18. Jahrhunderts hatten sich Wissenschaft, Moral und Kunst auch institutionell als Tätigkeitsbereiche ausdifferenziert, in denen Wahrheitsfragen, Gerechtigkeitsfragen und Geschmacksfragen autonom, nämlich unter ihrem jeweils spezifischen Geltungsaspekt bearbeitet wurden. Und diese *Sphäre des Wissens* hatte sich insgesamt von der *Sphäre des Glaubens* einerseits, von der des rechtlich organisierten *gesellschaftlichen Verkehrs* wie des *alltäglichen Zusammenlebens* anderseits abgesondert. (29–30)

According to Nägele in *Theater, Theory, Speculation* (1991, xii),

> The aesthetic sphere becomes the priviliged sphere of the reconciliation of interiority and exteriority [...] But if we understand Modernism (as distinguished from modernity) as that phenomenon that begins paradigmatically with Baudelaire's *Fleurs du Mal* and is marked by the texts of Nietzsche, Flaubert, Mallarmé, Kafka, Proust, Freud, Brecht, Benjamin, Joyce, and Beckett, among others, the reconciliations of the aesthetic sphere are radically undercut. It is

> Modernism [...] that undertakes the radical critique of modernity. If modernity, as it emerged in the late eighteenth century, is characterized by a move from poetics to aesthetics and by a systematic process of secularization, then Modernism moves back from aesthetics to poetics and insists on the traces of an otherness that could not be erased by secularization.

In Nietzsche we read that art, because it contains positive force, can serve as a counter movement to the *historical* 'forms of human decadence'. As early as his 1873–76 *Unzeitgemäße Betrachtungen* (1988d), Nietzsche spoke of the redemption of art as the only hope in the modern age. Art's positive force can be encountered most powerfully in the transitory moment as long as we are able, 'das Vermögen, während seiner Dauer *unhistorisch* zu empfinden. Wer sich nicht auf der Schwelle des Augenblicks, alle Vergangenheiten vergessend, niederlassen kann [...] der wird nie wissen was Glück ist' (1988d, 250). Such an attitude against the past and tradition has taken on various expressions, one of which was theater. Criticism of the Church and organized religion was hardly something new, but beginning with modern times, one could finally, so to speak, institutionalize the attacks on established institutions like the Church and the state it supports. The theater could, in short, become the establishment to attack the religious 'establishment', a role it has come to relish.

Modern German drama is the genre best equipped to take on the responsibility of implying divine presence in modern Western civilization. In terms of their content, plays, like any literature, can and frequently do present as false many moral and ideological values of society: religion, capitalism, socialism, fascism, and similar values that repress and destroy the individual.

Of all artistic genres, plays are unique because only in a play can the presence of a god or several gods be asserted in viable form. One might, of course, be tempted to ascribe a like capability to films, especially since films with a plot are based, as it were, on a 'screen-play'. Through double exposures and various relatively simple devices, films have, almost from their inception as an art medium, proven their ability to give the invisible and intangible a form that is just as visible and tangible as every other image on the screen. But that is the very point! The characters and settings in a film never have the same claim to a tangible existence in the world of the viewer as that exercised by everyone and everything on the stage of the so-called legitimate theater. In fact, today's computerized images of the creatures in the once existent but never viewed world of the Jurassic or of the inhabitants of a necessarily imaginary world of other planets during 'Star Wars' can no longer be distinguished from the 'real' ones of our world. In turn, the audience in the cinema can and often does distrust its senses to a far greater extent than the theatergoer has the freedom to do. Ultimately, what distinguishes a play from a film is, among many things, the unique need and capability of the former to evoke a feeling of trust in the existence of a 'Spielraum Gottes' that may well transcend the sensory world we have brought with us into the theater yet does not openly conflict with it. But the Judaeo-Christian God has seldom been permitted to appear on the stage, and least of all in an age in which God has been declared dead. There is, however, one remarkable exception.

The Greeks and Romans had felt no discrepancy in their use of machines because they had anthropomorphized their deities. Heinrich Heine's use of the human aging process to portray the gods' situation in 'Die Götter im Exil' seemed but another step along a well-known path, and his intent would scarcely have been considered esthetically or theologically revolutionary or more than humorously disrespectful. But Oskar Panizza's humanized God in the play *Das Liebeskonzil* (1894)[5] evoked, as he had intended, a scandal. Separating Wolfgang Borchert's portrait of God grown old and feeble from Panizza's humanized *God* is, among other things, the salient difference in tone. To be sure, they vent their antagonism through abundant use of the discordant and grotesque (albeit with the distinction that Panizza is drawing on the tradition of the *Fastnachtsspiel* and Borchert on that of Expressionism). Both playwrights implied authority stemming from their fates as victims of the evils caused or permitted by God. Nonetheless, Panizza's bitterness betrays the mocking superciliousness of a Naturalist expressing disdain for everything without scientific foundations, especially religion. Paradoxically, Panizza's portrayal of God implies that He does not exist for the author.[6] Borchert, as we shall see, displays a gallows humor that implies the victim's inferior position in the chaotic and therefore apparently illogical course of world events.

Previous representations of a god or gods, because their existence was not questioned any more than that of any scenery or characters, could be satisfactorily achieved with stage machinery and other artificial constructs. Yet such ethical abstractions, once they have been revealed to be untrue, often negate themselves and disappear. Such godly and divine images had therefore already become outdated and been reduced to the abstract values of our world. Our thinking is thereby liberated and becomes receptive to the possibility that the divine is not merely another abstraction. Instead, one has to think in terms of tangibles, and where there are none one envisions an opening. The opening that reveals emptiness is just as much a part of the real world and everyday life as any thing or person. Because this emptiness is comprehensible as part of our lives, it becomes a summons for us, the audience, to accept the possible presence of the divine as an essence that was previously 'nichtdarstellbar' but has now become 'vorstellbar'.

At other times, even though the world subject to the limits of representation does not negate itself, the limits of representation that characterize a dramatic performance make room for the inference that the supernatural exists. In both cases, it is a matter of language. The presence of God in modern German theater becomes evident when the limits of language are reached. The 'Sprachnot' of the age and the 'Sprachskepsis' of a selective group of dramatists creates an opening in which the divine can be found. Through the suspension of signification, silence occurs, which, in turn, creates the 'Spielraum Gottes'.

The present study will demonstrate why drama is the only genre that can suggest the physical presence of the metaphysical in a way that makes the viewer aware of the existence of the divine. While drama avails itself of those qualities of language common to all literary genres, it also encompasses the performer's body as well as the speech of sign, gesture, song and articulation. Understanding drama's physical potential has been emphasized only relatively recently. Western dramatic criticism for most of its history had dealt mainly with the texts as static. Then Antonin Artaud, writing in the 1930s against this trend and against the kind of performance it tended to produce, came

20

to see in theater the potential for a kind of surgical operation on the audience. In *Le Théatre et son double* (1964, 18) he writes: 'Briser le langage pour toucher la vie, c'est faire ou refaire le théatre; et l'important est de ne pas croire que acte doive demeurer sacré, c'est-à-dire réservé. Mais l'important est de croire que n'importe qui ne peut pas le faire, et qu'il y faut une preparation.' Artaud considers most, if not all, European theatrical forms to be *dead* forms of art because the constrictive nature of language has led to a general collapse of their moral, mythic centers. He continues: 'Si le signe de l'époque est la confusion, je vois à la base de cette confusion une rupture entre les choses, et les paroles, les idées, les signes qui en sont la représentation' (12). In turn, in determining the limits of language consideration must be removed from the sign and placed on what is not signified.

A second criterion unique to drama as a literary genre must also be considered. Narrative prose has a narrator, who, even in third-person stories and novels, makes his presence known and felt because most descriptions are in *his* words. In short, the reader has an identifiable individual who is relating the story. What happens to his language has implications for what must be accepted as true for the entire novel or story. Much the same can be said of lyric poetry with its 'lyrischer Sprecher'. In most instances, however, drama presents us with an entirely different situation. Only seldom do we have a case in which the words spoken by characters and heard by the audience are all demonstrably those of one real or invented author. The closest one comes to this phenomenon is the one-man show in which the words of one famous or less famous but unique person are presented. Only this person is comparable to the 'Erzähler' or lyrical speaker, whose words signal the representational limits of the piece itself.

In most plays we hear not the words of the playwright but those of characters. The plays that have most completely divorced themselves from their creator are the naturalistic or radically realistic ones that treat the audience as the stage's 'fourth wall'. In his notes on his play *Vor Sonnenaufgang*, Gerhart Hauptmann (1922, 753–57) writes:

Schon oft hat man die alte Forderung wiederholt: die Bühne sei kein Katheder! Und ich unterschreibe diese Forderung. Ich stellte sie auch an mich, als ich mein Stück begann (und vermied irgendwie und irgendwo, in das Publikum hineinzupredigen) und schrieb es durch, ohne an das Publikum zu denken, als ob die Bühne nicht drei, sondern vier Wände hätte. Auch Alfred Loth redet nirgend zum Publikum. Er redet zu Hoffmann von Dingen, wie man sie nach einer langen Trennung notwendigerweise zur Sprache bringt, er redet unter dem Essen im Kreise einer Tafelrunde ohne Prätention – und zwar nur für diesen Kreis – von Angelegenheiten, die der Gang der Unterhaltung ihm aufdrängt.

Between these plays, the popularity of which was confined mainly to the heyday of Naturalism, and the one-man productions, most modern plays can be found; in them, as one might well expect, the voice of the playwright can be discerned, albeit merely as one voice among many through an obvious spokesman – e.g., Akki in Friedrich Dürrenmatt's *Ein Engel kommt nach Babylon* or in the 'unrealistic' tone or form of the dialogue – e.g., the verse in Hugo von Hofmannsthal's *Jedermann* or the 'Telegrammstil' of all characters in Wolfgang Borchert's *Draußen vor der Tür*. This is inescapable, despite what Peter Szondi, in his influential *Theorie des Modernen Dramas* (1978b, 17), writes on this subject:

> All dies zeigt, daß das Drama eine in sich geschlossene, aber freie und in jedem Moment von neuem bestimmte Dialektik ist […] Das Drama ist absolut. Um reiner Bezug, das heißt: dramatisch sein zu können, muß es von allem im Äußerlichen abgelöst sein. Es kennt nichts außer sich. Der Dramatiker ist abwesend. Er spricht nicht, er hat Aussprache gestiftet. Das Drama wird nicht geschrieben, sondern gesetzt. Die im Drama gesprochenen Worte sind allesamt Ent-schlüsse, sie werden aus der Situation heraus gesprochen und verharren in ihr; keineswegs dürfen sie als vom Autor herrührend aufgenommen werden.

For our part, we can concede only that drama is obviously a genre completely distinct from all others.

The presence of God in modern theater becomes evident when the limits of language are reached: the 'Sprachnot' of the age and the 'Sprachskepsis' of the writers create an opening, a lacuna. The divine is to be found within this lacuna. By its very nature the divine refutes all signification as well as its role as a signifier. Its presence becomes that of a non-signifier to the extent that it emerges as an all-encompassing presence. The critique of language that refers to that which must remain within the individual, that is, the feelings and perceptions that can never be expressed, already had significance for mysticism and in pietism, but it moves to the forefront during the age of Goethe, as an age of sentiment and feeling, an age that understands the soul as the place of revelation of truth. The individual cannot be represented; nor can he be defined: 'Individuum est ineffabile.' The self as a totality is constantly undermined by language. Christian Hart Nibbrig (1995, 201) considers this same idea when discussing Friedrich Schiller's formulation, '*Spricht* die Seele, so spricht, ach! schon die *Seele* nicht mehr': 'Ach!' – this sound makes a caesura that expresses the impossibility of further expression through words. The ability of poetic language to speak is therefore denied and dislodged in the 'ach!' and transferred ('übersetzt') into the non-verbal dimension of the divine. At the place and moment of such a caesura, therefore, a lacuna could be perceived on the stage – as 'der Spielraum Gottes' – through which God can enter to fill the emptiness.

While 'Sprachnot' has a long history as a literary theme or personal lament of writers, it has, as we have seen, become for many modern theorists the central problem in language itself. A brief summary of a few pertinent thoughts of three leading theorists of language is necessary in order to explain and better illustrate the suspension of signification of language and the subsequent potential for the sacred to assert itself within profane texts.

Ludwig Wittgenstein's understanding of meaning and language in his early works is of major importance for this argument. For the early Wittgenstein there is no skepticism about meaning. Language represents the world. Words, and accordingly language itself, function merely as names or designations of pre-given realities. The clearest and most consistent presentation of this view is to be found in his 'Tractatus Logico-Philosophicus' of 1922. As Wittgenstein asserts in his 'Tractatus' (1984), a great deal of stage-setting in the language is presupposed if the mere act of naming is to make sense. Even as late as 1931, Wittgenstein argues in the *Philosophische Bemerkungen* that the meaning of any single word in a language is 'defined', 'constituted', 'determined', or 'fixed' by the grammatical rules in that language. As mere sounds or marks on paper, words, Wittgenstein explains, are lifeless and dead. In order to discern an understanding of words, it is best to see how they are actually used rather than trying arbitrarily and theoretically to come up with a definition:

> 18 [...] Die Frage 'was ist ein Wort?' ist ganz analog der 'was ist eine Schachfigur?'
> 19 Ist denn nicht Übereinstimmung und Nicht-Übereinstimmung das Primäre, so wie das Wiedererkennen das Primäre und die Identität das Sekundäre ist? Wenn wir den Satz verifiziert sehen, an welche andere Instanz können wir dann noch appellieren, um zu wissen, ob er nun wirklich wahr ist? [...] Die Übereinstimmung von Satz und Wirklichkeit ist der Übereinstimmung zwischen Bild und Abgebildeten nur so weit ähnlich wie der Übereinstimmung zwischen einem Erinnerungsbild und dem gegenwärtigen Gegenstand. (62)

Wittgenstein (1960b) concludes in his 'Tractatus' that such traditional areas of supposed meaning as ethics, metaphysics, and religion are, strictly speaking, quite meaningless in that the propositions that are advanced in these fields cannot possibly picture any factual state. His judgment that ethics, metaphysics, and religion are meaningless follows from the basic premise that meaning is mere signification. In Wittgenstein's view, the reason why these problems of philosophy are posed in our society is that the logic of our language is misunderstood. Our language about God, like our language about everything else, has to start from our life in the material world in which we live. The expressed purpose of the 'Tractatus' is to show that those areas about which we cannot talk, which do not lend themselves to discussion, we must pass over in silence: 'Wovon man nicht sprechen kann, darüber muß man schweigen' (7). Wittgenstein was, however, anticipated by Kierkegaard, who called the method that he used in a similar situation 'indirect communication'. He distinguished between the appropriate methods for communication in science and art and concluded that science or specific knowledge of content must be communicated directly. Art, on the other hand, is already within the subject and hence must be taught in another way. It is a question of 'luring the ethical out of the individual rather than beating it into him'. Indirect communication does not impart any new knowledge; instead it brings something out in the other. Kierkegaard (1962, 269) asserts in *Die Tagebücher* that 'the object of the communication is [...] not a knowledge but a realization.'

In a letter to the publisher Ludwig von Ficker about his book *Philosophische Bemerkungen*, Wittgenstein (1984, 35) writes:

> Und da ist es Ihnen vielleicht eine Hilfe, wenn ich Ihnen ein paar Worte über mein Buch schreibe: Von seiner Lektüre werden Sie nämlich – wie ich bestimmt glaube – nicht allzuviel verstehen […] Ich wollte nämlich schreiben, mein Werk bestehe aus zwei Teilen: aus dem, der hier vorliegt, und aus alledem, was ich *nicht* geschrieben habe. Und gerade dieser zweite Teil ist der Wichtige. Es wird nämlich das Ethische durch mein Buch gleichsam von Innen her begrenzt; und ich bin überzeugt, daß es, streng, nur so zu begrenzen ist. Kurz, ich glaube: Alles das, was viele heute schwafeln, habe ich in meinem Buch festgelegt, indem ich darüber schweige.

Since logical form, as the form of propositions and of the world, does not exist in the world, it cannot be expressed in words. Thus Wittgenstein (1960b) writes in paragraph 6.13 of the 'Tractatus', 'Die Logik ist keine Lehre, sondern ein Spiegelbild der Welt.' Only as such does it make the whole scheme of language possible. As a consequence, he continues in paragraph 4.0621, one must search for a possible meaning through indirect communication, within the non-positive, the negative, 'daß […] in der Wirklichkeit nichts entspricht'.

Something of a Kierkegaardian stance runs through Wittgenstein's comments on ethics, to the effect that ethics cannot ultimately be a matter of the reasoned development of an argument but rather a matter of indirect expression, communication and finally, realization. Thus there is a redoubled indirectness in communication. The ethical purpose is hidden behind the logical appearance of the work. The logical apparatus is incapable of carrying its own weight. The foundations of logic too must therefore be indirectly communicated. In a late entry in *Culture and Value*, Wittgenstein (1980) makes an interesting contribution to ethics, brief though it is, in discussing the effects of circumstances and (modern) environment on ethical character. He asks: 'How could a man, the ethical man, be coerced by this environment? […] No human being has to give way to compulsion' (84). Yet perhaps his most fundamental assertion here argues that 'what is good is also divine. Strange as it sounds, that sums up my ethics. Only something supernatural can express the Supernatural.' The irony and paradox of these remarks is that, in leaving so much unsaid, they say so much. To try to say anything about absolute value or about reality or the world as a whole is to attempt to say the unsayable, to go beyond the boundary of language.

In *Wittgenstein und der Wiener Kreis*, Friedrich Waismann (1967, 68) recounts a conversation with Wittgenstein had in Vienna in 1929, in which Wittgenstein linked his own ideas with those of the philosopher Martin Heidegger:

> Ich kann mir wohl denken, was Heidegger mit Sein und Angst meint. Der Mensch hat den Trieb, gegen die Grenzen der Sprache anzurennen […] Alles, was wir sagen mögen, kann a priori nur Unsinn sein. Trotzdem rennen wir gegen die Grenzen der Sprache an. Dieses Anrennen hat auch Kierkegaard gesehen und es sogar ganz ähnlich (als Anrennen gegen das Paradox) bezeichnet. Dieses Anrennen gegen die Grenzen der Sprache ist die Ethik.

In a somewhat similar manner to Wittgenstein's, Heidegger (1985) is of the conviction that only an altered philosophical relationship to language can free thinking from the exhausted categories of the Western tradition. He wants to reform that tradition which was in accord with the Kantian 'Ding-an-sich'. In his view, one could eliminate the 'Ding-an-sich' with no discernible epistemological loss. Objective reality has become completely inaccessible to thought. As a consequence, one is left only with empty representations. Yet, necessarily, Heidegger also speaks of an altered experience of language in 'Unterwegs zur Sprache' and wants to read the history of ontology backwards. Accordingly, the destruction of the history of ontology, which in *Sein und Zeit* means looking for what went wrong somewhere back in the tradition in order to *repeat* and *redo* it ('wiederholen'), is reconceived as a work of *recollective* thought ('an-denken') that tries to recover something that has dropped out of sight. By a 'going back which destroys' ('destruirender Rückgang') into the history of ontology, Heidegger's aim is to loosen the grip of post-archaic ideas that tend to block off a discovery that is breaking through in modernity. He resists all rule-referenced explanations of our linguistic competence: 'Wir wollen die Sprache nicht überfallen, um sie in den Griff schon festgemachter Vorstellung zu zwingen. Wir wollen das Wesen der Sprache nicht auf einen Begriff bringen, damit dieser eine überall nutzbare Ansicht über die Sprache liefere, die alles Vorstellen beruhigt' (10). He wants to go behind such 'accounts' of language to discover what makes them possible. He hopes to experience language preconceptually, to get behind all current theories about it. The authority of our practices is given by the primal authority of language itself: 'die Sprache spricht,' (10) says Heidegger, and all human thought and action is grounded in that speaking. Certainly we speak, but at the same time and before all else, language speaks. Heidegger's attack is on the Enlightenment picture of the self; it is an attack founded on his radical experience of language as the original Logos.

In a 1944 lecture course on logic, Heidegger exploits his conviction that only a new relationship to language – he speaks of this as an altered experience of language – can liberate thinking from the depleted categories of the Western metaphysical tradition and simply get back to what is spoken.[7] *Aletheia*, Heidegger argues, is no longer translatable as 'Wahrheit'. Instead, *aletheia* functions like a hidden clue for anything that is spoken purely and is not limited to a manifest theme. *Aletheia* is what something is when it is not to be found, that is, when it constitutes the silence of the opening. That means, Heidegger (1984, 201–21) writes in *Grundfragen der Philosophie*, that *aletheia* must in a certain way be overlooked. *Aletheia* itself cannot appear; it can only be pointed out subsequently as the element within which a given historical form unfolds. In Heidegger's understanding, what is merely spoken is a poem. Literature can be that pure speaking of language to which the philosophers must listen. He writes in *Unterwegs zur Sprache* (1985, 26–27):

> Im Gesprochenen des Gedichtes west das Sprechen. Es ist das Sprechen der Sprache. Die Sprache spricht. Sie spricht, indem sie das Geheißene, Ding-Welt und Welt-Ding, in das Zwischen des Unter-Schiedes kommen heißt […] Der Unter-Schied enteignet das Ding in die Ruhe des Gevierts. Solches Enteignen raubt dem Ding nichts. Es enthebt das Ding erst in sein Eigenes: daß es Welt verweilt. In die Ruhe bergen ist das Stillen. Der Unter-Schied stillt das Ding als Ding in die Welt […] Was ist Stille? Sie ist seineswegs nur das Lautlose […] *Die Sprache spricht als das Geläut der Stille.*

Heidegger's *Sein und Zeit* (1949) can be seen to harbor a distrust of modernity, of liberal institutions, of the Enlightenment ideals of cosmopolitan universalism and egalitarianism, and, generally speaking, of life in the bourgeois world. Man stands in the accomplishments of the technological world. But there is one point at which this distrust of modernity is not in place, and this must not be overlooked. *Sein und Zeit* contains no eschatological and anti-modernist warning about the present time as an ominous end time into which the European world has been driven, an extremity of decline defined by the technical world. On the contrary, Heidegger is in agreement with those advances of modernity that have made it possible to perceive the temporal meaning of *Dasein*. However much he may have been opposed to Emmanuel Kant's Enlightenment ideas in ethics and politics, Heidegger is very much indebted to his transcendental philosophy of time.[8] Heidegger's destruction of the history of ontology is meant to loosen the grip that the tradition exerts upon us. Regardless of what is said about *Dasein* overtly, every historical ontology is covertly committed to a temporal account of *Dasein*. The tradition to which *Dasein* has fallen prey must be destroyed down to its original experiences. The destruction is to be carried out backwards, beginning with Kant, because Heidegger believed that it is only lately, in modern times, that one begins to search for the clue to the 'meaning' of *Dasein*.

Writers and thinkers of modern Europe still lived in societies Ernst Bloch had described as filled with 'non-synchronous time'. Ernst Bloch (1977, 22–38) affirms in 'Nonsynchronism and the Obligation to Its Dialectics' that such time is marked by the co-existence of different temporalities that reassure that what has passed was still available to them as an aura, still accessible as a model to the negativity of daily life under capitalism. Like Heidegger, Walter Benjamin (1977, 261) proposes in *Illuminationen* the necessity of bringing to light the new as present in the repeatedly same, for only so can one project a revolutionary program that produces a consciousness of the present and explodes the continuum of history. He too finds historicism guilty of directing historians to receive the narrative of historical progress passively rather than 'die Geschichte gegen den Strich zu bürsten' (254), and he too shows a deep concern with the linguistic being of truth.

Benjamin's critique of language distinctly illustrates the suspension of signification of language in order to release the potential for the sacred within profane texts. Nägele (1997, 47) describes in *Echoes of Translation* Benjamin's understanding of language in terms of the Baroque:

> Language, pure Language, does not exist, cannot be grasped and perceived, but it 'is' there in the tangible effects between languages and in the crevices within languages (between sound and meaning, for example) where it can be 'felt', in what Benjamin calls the *Gefühlston*, the mode of meaning which is specific to every language and every time. Thus the abyss between sound and meaning is specifically the baroque *Gefühlston* and its stylistic bombast.

The use of biblical and theological history functions as a critique of historicism.[9] Despite their pronounced esotericism, Benjamin's early philosophical writings are consistent with this program and offer telling proof for an indissoluble connection between the religious and language in much of modern theory. The foundation of philosophy in its search for religious truth is to be sought in terms of the philosophy of language. Benjamin (1977b, 168) writes in his 'Metaphysisch-geschichtsphilosophische Studien':

> Die große Umbildung und Korrektur die an dem einseitig mathematisch-mechanisch orientierten Erkenntnisbegriff vorzunehemen ist, kann nur durch eine Beziehung der Erkenntnis auf die Sprache wie sie schon zu Kants Lebzeiten versucht hat gewonnen werden. Über dem Bewußtsein daß die philosophische Erkenntnis eine absolut gewisse und apriorische sei, über dem Bewußtsein dieser der Mathematik ebenbürtigen Seiten der Philosophie ist für Kant die Tatsache daß alle philosophische Erkenntnis ihren einzigen Ausdruck in der Sprache und nicht in Formeln und Zahlen habe völlige zurückgetreten [...] Ein in der Reflexion auf des sprachliche Wesen der Erkenntnis gewonnener Begriff von ihr wird einen korrespondierenden Erfahrungsbegriff schaffen der auch Gebiete deren wahrhafte systematische Einordnung Kant nicht gelungen ist umfassen wird. Als deren Oberstes ist das Gebiet der Religion zu nennen.

The secret of redemption is encoded in language. At issue in Benjamin's argument is the 'fallen' character of a human history that takes on the appearance of 'natural history', of a history that is consigned to a fate of decay and decline. Such a fate results in an inescapable web of guilt that originated with man's expulsion from Paradise and provides affirmation that a seemingly infinite distance separates historical man from the state of grace. From his lowly position in the historical world, fallen man sorts through the ruins of previous ages for traces of redeemed life in the hope that these traces can be renewed in the present. It is Benjamin's fear that the excessive Enlightenment biases of Kant's theory of knowledge wish to produce a concept of experience that remains dependent on the scientists' prejudices of his age; and that the highly rationalized concept of experience which results from this epistemological standpoint resembles too well a mechanical modern world in which the values of technical reason reign supreme.[10]

Adorno (1955, 291), in *Prismen*, characterizes Benjamin's idea of sacred text as follows:

> Die Idee des heiligen Textes transponierte er in eine Aufklärung, in die umzuschlagen nach Scholems Aufweis die jüdische Mystik selber sich anschickte. Sein Essayismus ist die Behandlung profaner Texte, als wären es heilige. Keineswegs hat er an theologische Relikte sich geklammert oder, wie die religiösen Sozialisten, die Profanität auf einen transzendenten Sinn bezogen. Vielmehr erwartete er einzig von der radikalen, schutzlosen Profanisierung die Chance fürs theologische Erbe, das in jener sich verschwendet.

Although he grasps the driving force of Benjamin's philosophy, Adorno misunderstands Benjamin's sacred–profane distinction. Rather than imposing standard notions of the sacred on seemingly profane texts, Benjamin tries to demonstrate the relation of all texts to a model of language as self-communication of spiritual being.[11] In his 1916 essay 'Über Sprache überhaupt und über die Sprache des Menschen', he writes that human language appears in its highest form as the completion and mirroring of the divine language of creation (1977d).

Benjamin's concept of language opposes the standard view of language as a means of communication. Far from being merely a medium for an outsider to communicate meaning, language communicates itself. This phenomenon is epitomized by the act of naming. Benjamin (1977d, 144) writes in 'Über Sprache überhaupt': 'Der Name ist dasjenige, *durch* das sich nichts mehr, und *in* dem die Sprache selbst und absolut sich mitteilt. Im Namen ist das geistige Wesen, das sich mitteilt, *die* Sprache.' This pure language of naming has nothing to do with meaning; it communicates only itself. Before the Fall, human language was linked closely to divine creation, naming, and 'geistiges Wesen' (142). The Fall marked the birth of the human word, in which name no longer lived intact. Only after the Fall do languages multiply, words lapse into 'Mittel', 'bloße Zeichen', and things become 'übernannt' (342). Abstraction occurs, which entails a loss of communicative immediacy, the multiplicity and confusion of languages, and the condition in which nature mourns its objects as over-named (329–30). The human word communicates something other than itself.

The main objective of Benjamin's essay entitled 'Die Aufgabe des Übersetzers' (1987, 57) is to establish the original language of naming as the theological foundation of the ultimate relationship of all languages, which should in turn provide the divine basis for the translation of any one language into another. Instead of defining language as the expression of thought, Benjamin calls it the communication of the spiritual/intellectual contents ('geistige Inhalte'). Language expresses more than just the thought of an individual speaker but rather the thought/spiritual essence of the language itself. In 'Über Sprache überhaupt', Benjamin (1977d, 142–43) writes: 'Das Mediale, das ist die Unmittelbarkeit aller geistigen Mitteilung, ist das Grundproblem der Sprachtheorie, und wenn man diese Unmittelbarkeit magisch nennen will, so ist das Urproblem der Sprache ihre *Magie*. Zugleich deutet das Wort von der Magie der Sprache auf ein anderes: auf ihre Unendlichkeit.' The mention of magic as a synonym for the immediacy of language is central to Benjamin's argument. It suggests that the same linguistic phenomena can be viewed from a rational, philosophical standpoint or from an 'irrational', magical one; this move reflects Benjamin's deeper conviction that linguistic philosophy coincides with metaphysical and religious thought. Magic also suggests to Benjamin that language is infinite, for precisely because nothing is communicated through language, what is communicated in language cannot be externally limited or measured.

Benjamin's philosophy begins and ends with a theory of language that sets the pure language of naming as a counter to the bourgeois language of mere signs. Modernity represents a transformation of experience by new technological phenomena. Benjamin (1987, 51) asserts in 'Die Aufgabe des Übersetzers' that the development of language from the pure name to the mere sign suggests a linguistic theory of history in which individual works and languages literally have lives of their own. Biblical narrative and magic thus function initially as critical alternatives to prevailing theories of language. At the same time, the use of biblical and theological history functions as a critique of historicism. Adorno (1955, 294), in *Prismen*, observes of Benjamin:

> Seine Anschauung von Moderne als Archaik bewahrt nicht Spuren eines vorgeblich alten Wahren auf, sondern meint den realen Ausbruch aus der Traumbefangenheit der bürgerlichen Immanenz [...] So gedachte er der Entfremdung und Vergegenständlichung zu entgehen, in der die Betrachtung des Kapitalismus als System diesem sich anzugleichen droht.

The theories of language and history are more critical than constructive; they develop alternative forms of inquiry and discourse about language and history. Benjamin never claims to retrieve linguistic purity or to impose an objectivist model of history on the developmental theory of language. His theory of language represents not a historical analysis of language, but rather a linguistic theory of history[12] in which this fallen linguistic state corresponds to modernity. Against the continuity and progress of prevailing historiography, Benjamin defines history as 'Stillstand' and 'Stillstellung des Geschehens'.[13] He sees historical epochs, for the most part, as a succession of failed human efforts to recover the pure language of the past. In opposition to the typical celebration of the modern in terms of progress, Benjamin's notion of modernity emphasizes tradition. History is defined in terms such as 'Dialektik im Stillstand' and 'Jetztzeit', which focus on the momentary and illuminating suspension of time.

German historiography around the turn of the century was deeply concerned with the problems of modernity and historicism. Philosophers and historians, including Weber, addressed questions about the status of historical understanding as well as the status of the modern period. For Benjamin, modernity represents a complete transformation of experience by the new urban and technological phenomena. Instead of describing these changes in terms of profane secularization, he links them to a subtle view of the sacred–secular opposition. Therefore, the linguistic theory of history takes shape as history writing, which, like translation, aims at the restoration of language through the concept of the sacred text.

The present survey will make evident that various modern German plays are indeed able to bring forth a presence of the divine on their stage by capitalizing on the communicative potential of silence as it is implied by the above approaches to language as a historical phenomenon. This, in turn, will indicate that the limitations imposed by the secularization of the modern age and its subsequent 'Sprachnot' are not binding on all modern literature. Instead, secularization, industrialization and the ensuing 'Sprachnot' themselves can allow room for a divine presence to make itself known. Hofmannsthal's theater, by attempting to fulfill the form, attains a moment of a vision of a new creation. Through contrast, as well as through archaic forms of presentation, such as verse, rhythm, expression, representation and tone, he creates a 'Gewebe', an 'Ensemble' that frees the individual from the 'Sprachnot' of the age. While Borchert's belatedly expressionistic form displays the despair of a slogan-dependent society, as well as society's need to allow the ensuing silence to speak of the divine, Brecht's 'epic' theater distances the spectator by presenting him with unresolvable contradictions, destroys his passive behavior and confronts him with a need for change at the moment of the caesura. Within that moment an implication of the divine arises. Dürrenmatt's theater is a grotesque presentation of 'Zweifel' in ideology that destroys the prevalent accepted beliefs and that ultimately brings into being a new belief in the divine.

Objectively, one may agree with the social theorists who, from Hegel and Comte to Weber, have pointed out that modern society is 'rationalized' and the modern mind 'positivistic'. This is true of modern society to the degree that it drives art into the margins of society along with religion and other often nonrationalistic modes. This is one of the great themes that define modernity. The growing belief in the twentieth century that God must be dead was bound to bring about a transformation in consciousness, sensibility, and ontological values more revolutionary than that which took place when Copernicus overthrew the Ptolemaic system or when Newtonian physics triumphed and the laws of Nature supplanted the laws of God.

Yet the works of all four of these playwrights with their textual as well as non-textual representations allow for an otherwise-un-accounted-for presence of the divine. 'Sprachnot', the dilemma of the modern age represented on the German stage by Hofmannsthal, Borchert, Brecht and Dürrenmatt, allows the stage to open up and to be transformed into 'der Spielraum Gottes'.

# Chapter Two
## Hofmannsthal's *Jedermann*

When we speak of the 'modern' period in German literature, we mean the advent of Naturalism in the 1880s, at the latest 1889, when 'Die Freie Bühne' was established in Berlin. The productions of this organization would initiate the dominance of the naturalist style of acting, as this was developed by Otto Brahm, for the next ten years. It might therefore appear somewhat surprising that this investigation begins with Hugo von Hofmannsthal's *Jedermann: Das Spiel vom Sterben des reichen Mannes*, which was first published in 1911 and premiered in Berlin on December 2, 1911.

The following considerations, however, make this decision far more compelling. First of all, we consider the basic tenets of Naturalism, that is, the scientific faith in language as reducible to a strictly denotative function and the ability of the individual to distance himself from the external world in order to describe it 'objectively'. The forces that challenged these notions almost from the beginning arose in Vienna. Thus Hermann Bahr published his *Überwindung des Naturalismus* in 1891, even before the appearance of such unchallenged masterpieces of Naturalist dramaturgy as Gerhart Hauptmann's *Biberpelz*, *Die Weber*, and *Hanneles Himmelfahrt*. In fact, Hauptmann's *Ratten* – which, if not dogmatically naturalist, certainly shows its heritage as inseparable from Naturalism – appeared in 1911, the same year as *Jedermann*. But while one might smile about Hermann Bahr's reckless announcement of Naturalism's passing, his call for a new psychology and an elimination of the distinctions between the individual and the external world proved prophetic:

> Spuren des Neuen sind manche vorhanden. Sie erlauben viele Vermutungen. Eine Weile war es die Psychologie, welche den Naturalismus ablöste. Die Bilder der äußeren Welt zu verlassen um lieber die Rätsel der einsamen Seele aufzusuchen – dieses wurde die Lösung [...] So kam man von der Psychologie, wie ihren Trieben nachgegeben wurde, notwendig am Ende zum Sturze des

Naturalismus: Das Eigene aus sich zu gestalten, statt das Fremde nachzubilden, das Geheime aufzusuchen, statt dem Augenschein zu folgen, und gerade dasjenige auszudrücken, worin wir uns anders fühlen und wissen als die Wirklichkeit [...] Wenn der Klassizismus Mensch sagt, so meint er Vernunft und Gefühl; und wenn die Romantik Mensch sagt, so meint sie Leidenschaft und Sinne; und wenn die Moderne Mensch sagt, so meint sie Nerven. Da ist die große Einigkeit schon wieder vorbei. (86–87)

But Bahr had already been anticipated by Ernst Mach (1922, 58), an Austrian professor who had established the indistinguishability of the internal and external worlds:

Es gibt keine Kluft zwischen Psychischem und Physischem, kein Drinnen und Draussen, keine Empfindung, der ein äußeres von ihr verschiedenes Ding entspräche. Es gibt nur einerlei Elemente [...] die eben nur, je nach der temporären Betrachtung, drinnen oder draussen sind. Die sinnliche Welt gehört dem physischen und psychischen Gebiet zugleich an.

The reluctance of playwrights to allow God on the stage began with Naturalism. Thus Hauptmann has Hannele obviously 'dream' about Christ. Otherwise, however, Naturalism had a rather naive attitude toward language that is the antithesis of a 'Sprachskepsis'. Obviously, Hofmannsthal was a product of a culture that not only shared many attitudes with Germany, but was also already developing the principal objections to these notions.

Furthermore, we shall see how Austria already manifested the signs of the political and social disintegration that would contribute to 'Sprachskepsis'. By contrast, Germany was still enjoying the euphoria evoked by the establishment of the Second Reich in 1871. Epigrammatically speaking, one could say that Germany was now relishing its new role as the monolith that the Habsburg monarch had once been. In turn, Hofmannsthal, in a sociopolitical context as well as in an epistemological-aesthetic one, lived in a culture ripe for the emergence of 'Sprachskepsis'.

Finally, while most of the dramatists to be studied here consciously sought to be revolutionary (which also applied to the Naturalists), Hofmannsthal's success with *Jedermann* can be attributed to this piece's link with the past. Referring to the Berlin premiere of *Jeder-*

*mann* on December 2, 1911, Jaron, Möhrmann and Müller (1986, 710) observe:

> Daß der Abend ein Erfolg und ein gesellschaftliches Ereignis war, dem sogar der Hof beiwohnte, und daß ein gewaltiges Beifallsbrausen das Unternehmen beschloß, wurde zwar überall bestätigt. Nur wurde dies kaum auf das Konto von Reinhardt verbucht. Es wäre mehr 'die Neubelebung einer entschlafenen, vergessenen Schauspielgattung aus der Urgeschichte unseres modernen, deutschen Theaters', die das Interesse 'erweckte und fesselte' (Landau). 'Der Stoff mit seiner ungeheuren Fülle erlesener Regiekniffe' würde ihn nur 'belasten' und 'überfrachten' (Keller). Auch sei 'der mächtige Apparat', die alte dreistufige Mysterienbühne, mehr aus 'Stockwerken' als aus 'Absätzen' bestehend, 'fast zu schwer' für 'die einfache Allegorie' (Landau) und 'das Auf- und Abbauen während der offenen Szene von störender Wirkung' (Buchhorn).

This corresponds, of course, to the wish expressed by Hofmannsthal in his 1911 preface to *Jedermann*. After emphasizing the long history of the story, Hofmannsthal (1923, 33) concludes:

> Alle diese Aufschreibungen stehen nicht in jenem Besitz, den man als den lebendingen des deutschen Volkes bezeichnen kann, sondern sie treiben im toten Wasser des gelehrten Besitzstandes. Darum wurde hier versucht, dieses allen Zeiten gehörige und allgemeingültige Märchen abermals in Bescheidenheit aufzuzeichnen. Vielleicht geschieht es zum letztenmal, vielleicht muß es später durch den Zugehörigen einer künftigen Zeit noch einmal geschehen.

It seems, therefore, most fitting to consider first Hofmannsthal, who shows the greatest interest in carrying past accomplishments over to his own time and thus manifests most clearly the involuntary break with traditional language as well as the 'modern' attempt to overcome the resulting lacuna.

The development of technology and industry in the Austro-Hungarian Empire in the years before and at the turn of the century, the negative changes in the relations between European nations, as well as the mixture of cultures and languages in the imperial city, significantly influenced society. This especially affected the lifestyle of the 'Großbürgertum', a social class to which Hofmannsthal and the majority of his readers belonged. Insofar as it found itself alienated as a completely separate and distinguished class, the upper-middle class was in danger of being overpowered by a middle-class mentality. It therefore became necessary for the nobility and the upper-middle class individual to resort to exterior methods of gratification as a means of masking a vacuous interior life. As a consequence, the 'Groß-bürgertum' increasingly expressed a latent subjectivism through an outward display of satisfaction. This class was driven by a sense of decline to the most ephemeral pursuit of pleasure and loved the solid elegance of its aristocracy and the lighthearted atmosphere of the city. The loss of the war in 1866 and the consequent economic crash in 1873 brought Austria great difficulties that had their consequence many years afterwards and that led to an ever stronger 'österreich-ischen Selbstgefühl'.[1]

The political collapse of the Austro-Hungarian Empire after 1918 completed an ongoing process of internal dissolution that had intensi-fied over decades, if not centuries, a dissolution conditioned by the disharmony between the Habsburg state and its many national and cultural components. As the rational communication that constitutes the basis for society came to be viewed as more elusive, if not totally impossible to attain, the very foundations of language itself were con-demned. Consequently, the popular notion of Vienna as the crucible of modernity found its meaning here.

*Fin de siècle* Vienna, most scholars and cultural historians agree, is indeed the birthplace of Modernism. The death of God so clearly displayed in the works of Naturalist writers influenced by Emile Zola's determinism had already found its allies among intellectuals of that time. Picking up on Naturalism's presentation of the brutal con-temporary realities of poverty, moral decadence, and religious hyp-ocrisy, all of modernism now rejects religion, and an escape into anthropocentric individualism becomes a central issue among writers at the end of the century.[2]

However, many of the accomplishments and intellectual ad-vances were greatly influenced by Friedrich Nietzsche's philosophy of modernity and the death of God. According to critics, Nietzsche played a central role in shifting the focus away from strictly social concerns.[3] In the same vein, Jens Fischer, in *Fin de Siècle* (1978, 39), provides a cogent summary of Nietzsche's success in winning people away from the fold of Naturalist concerns: 'Bereits 1891 hatte Her-mann Bahr es wieder einmal als erster gemerkt und die Überwindung

38

des Naturalismus proklamiert. In Deutschland führte die Entwicklung zu einem individualistischen Zerbröckeln der naturalistischen Bewegung, deren Autoren ihre zunehemende Isolierung nietzscheanisch überhöhten.' Nietzsche's contribution to the intellectual climate was clearly manifold, yet the one major factor that could be traced back in a large part to Nietzsche's influence and that is of crucial importance in the development of literary history at the turn of the century was the increasing strength of antireligionism. Roy C. Cowen, in 'Der Naturalismus' (1994, 105–06), explains:

> Daß Nietzsche als Gewährsmann des anwachsenden Atheismus im 19. Jahrhundert immer wieder zitiert wurde und selbst manche darwinistischen Implikationen übernahm, muß hier nicht gezeigt werden. Erwähnenswert ist gleichwohl, daß Nietzsche der Bourgeoisie insbesondere im Zusammenhang mit den Maximen christlicher Moral Heuchelei und Verlogenheit vorwirft und dagegen den Trieb im Menschen betont.

The 'gehobene Bourgeoisie', as Hofmannsthal referred to the upper class, attempted to replace the Naturalist's portrayal of the oppressive and external reality of the state and culture as immanent with a contemplation of subjective values. C. Magris (1975) explains the root problem of this age as the 'Auflösung des Subjekts als Ordnungsprinzip der Wirklichkeit'. He associates this subjectivity with the nobility:

> Im Unterschied zu anderen europäischen Literaturen fällt in der österreichischen der Untergang der individuellen Werte [...] nicht mit dem Ende der bürgerlichen Kultur zusammen sondern mit dem der aristokratischen [...] Von Anfang an betrachtet die österreichische Kultur die bürgerliche Kultur als Unordung, Anarchie, horizontale Verflechtung, Bruch der organischen Totalität, als Reduktion. Hofmannsthal besteht auf dieser aristokratischen Dimension, auf der Vornehmheit und der feinen Zurückhaltung dieses Abschieds des Schriftstellers vom Wort. (61–62)

Hermann Bahr, a prominent member of the literary group named 'das junge Wien', while admitting to the obscure nature of the concept, delineates at the beginning of the 1890s what lies at the core of 'das Moderne' for the young Viennese intellectual and literary generation:

Die Jünglinge wissen es nicht zu sagen [...] Sie haben kein Programm. Sie haben keine Aesthetik. Sie wiederholen nur immer, daß sie modern sein wollen. Dieses Wort lieben sie sehr, wie eine mystische Kraft, die Wunder wirkt und heilen kann [...] In allen Dingen um jeden Preis modern zu sein – anders wissen sie ihre Triebe, ihre Wünsche, ihre Hoffnungen nicht zu sagen. Sie sagen es [...] ohne jenen Hass der jüngsten Deutschen gegen die Vergangenheit. Sie verehren die Tradition. Sie wollen nicht gegen sie treten. Sie wollen nur auf ihr stehen. Sie möchten das alte Werk der Vorfahren [...] auf die letzte Stunde bringen. Sie wollen, wie Jene, österreichisch sein, aber österreichisch von 1890. (144ff.)

The upper stratum of Austrian society developed a liberal culture in its ethical and moral orientation, an apolitical attitude and an esthetic modern culture. On the literary scene, the Habsburg metropolis witnessed the emergence of a circle of young poets who became known as the authors of 'das junge Wien' and whose work provides a reflective background for the growing moral and ethical decline of the Second Empire. Bruno Hillebrand, in *Nietzsche und die deutsche Literatur* (1978), writes in respect to Stefan Zweig, Rilke, Heym, Musil, Benn, Stadler, Hesse, the Mann brothers, Hofmannsthal and George, among others: 'sie wurden ausgebildet an Schulen und Universitäten, die vom Gründergeist geprägt waren: gewinnmaterialistisch, utilitarisch-optimistisch, nationalistisch. Sie alle glaubten zu ersticken in dieser Luft [...] Nietzsche, der Europäer, verkörperte für sie die Befreiung von solcher Enge' (5). Vague and unidentifiable in a pure and undiluted form, 'das Moderne' became the rallying point for the young intellectuals who viewed themselves as leaders of the art of the future.

Nietzsche's critique of modern ideology is in all basic respects a critique of modernity. Modern culture symbolizes the fleeting, transitory, and fortuitous nature of modernity. All modern culture, Nietzsche argues, requires an inward grasp and exploitation of the momentary, and absolutely nothing else. A general apathy towards creative, original effort drove the young Viennese intellectuals into a despondent isolation and brought about the atmosphere that the *fin de siècle* produced in Vienna. The age of the Baroque had, by its emphasis on constant endeavor, symbolized the Austrian sense of mission to achieve unity and synthesis out of a multitude of free forms, but it had long since given way to the values of the complacent, unheroic Biedermeier period. In this new middle-class climate of material prosperity and shifting social foundations, the new generation of literati felt itself drifting in a spiritual vacuum, yet constrained by the narrow aspirations of the 'Gründergeist'. Their sense of non-attachment either led them to what was also called a 'culte du moi', or left them in a permanently perplexed and despondent crisis of self-confidence, both of which proved detrimental to their development. In the now prevailing mood of frustrating impotence, intellectuals evolved into an introspective, esthetic culture and acquired a belief in art that, according to Carl Schorske, suggested, so to speak, a *religious* longing for what was missing in their culture. Although Schorske (1961, 934–35) does not admit to the class need for the metaphysical, he does suggest an 'implied [...] withdrawal of its devotees from a social class; in Vienna alone it claimed the allegiance of virtually a whole class, of which artists were a part. The life of art became a substitute for the life of action. Art became almost a religion, the source of meaning and the food of the soul, as collective action proved increasingly futile.'

Christianity bears much of the indictment of Nietzsche's criticism of modernity, since this *fin de siècle* contemporary and revolutionary sees the 'self' as suppressed by the Christian mentality and through the Christian tradition. In his view, the more altruistic a religion is, the more it distorts the self of its follower. Zarathustra finds the greatest challenge to the modern person's achieving selfhood in Christian morality. In 'Ecce Homo', Nietzsche (1988b, 1158) collectively refers to Western morality as 'die Entselbstungs-Moral'. He points out that because this 'unselving morality' is the only one that has been taught and learned, it has enjoyed its success as an unchallenged code and achieved a corresponding longevity. Yet to the extent that the meaning of life has previously been tied to religion or to any other exclusively dominant ideal, if we accept and follow Nietzsche's criticism, the retreat of the ideal leaves us in a vacuum, similar to the value vacuum experienced by the elite society of Vienna.

Hofmannsthal's theater, particularly his play *Jedermann*, has the potential of filling the void of his age. What the author himself wishes to accomplish socially through his form and style opens up room for the presence of the divine in literature, thus refuting the claim that God is dead. Hofmannsthal's early work subtly reflected this ethically barren mood at the end of the century. The youthful Hofmannsthal was very preoccupied with the artistic problems of the young European elite and with the dangers of estheticism. Many of Hofmannsthal's statements about the loss of values and ethics echo Nietzsche's criticism of modernity. In our period this yearning is expressed by the indiscriminate reading of the intellectually fragmented masses. As a substitute for religion, art reached its pinnacle toward the end of the nineteenth century. Its practitioners lived in splendid isolation, occupied with their 'holy' rites, and disdained everything that seemed ugly or commonplace. Naturalism, which served as spokesman for the nonexistence of God by emphasizing the factual and often hideous, no longer attracted the attention of the esthete who had already rejected realism and its reliance on the commonplace. A new mystical experience was necessary, an 'Ersatzreligion'. *Jedermann* offers spectators and readers the possibility of an encounter with a metaphysical presence through a mystical experience that no 'Ersatzreligion' could evoke.

Hofmannsthal's literary production must be seen against a dispiriting, chaotic, isolated and religiously and ethically void background. As a product of the older Viennese culture, Hofmannsthal was very aware of what Broch called 'das Wert-Vakuum der Welt'. Broch (1974, 36–49) writes: 'Warum erweckte aber dann die sogennante Gründerzeit Deutschlands, das ist die Zeit von 1870–1890, den Eindruck einer völligen geistigen Öde? […] hätte also das "Wert-Vakuum", wie man den Zustand dieser Dezennien recht wohl nennen dürfte, eigentlich zum Verschwinden bringen können.' Hofmannsthal's early diary entries already suggest oppositions and contrasts that will reappear later in his work. We read in 'Aufzeichnungen aus dem Nachlass 1894' (1980b, 381):

Mit Poldy in der Abenddämmerung in Schönbrunn. 2 Alleen, sternförmig ausgehend: In der linken fast Dunkelheit, auf dunklem Gewölk ein blasser Regenbogen; in der rechten heller metallisch blauer, leise grüner Himmel, mit mattsilbernen Wolken und über Wipfeln purpurn untergehende Sonne. In diesen 2 Alleen zweierlei Epochen, zweierlei Schicksale.

Wir glauben die Seele dieses Wiens zu spüren, die vielleicht in uns zum letzten Male aufbebt; wir waren triumphierend traurig.

Hofmannsthal found it difficult to conform to the contradictory atmosphere on which his society's rules and ethics were predicated and doubted the possibility of expression through words, an idea subsequently termed 'Sprachskepsis'. By the time he was in his twenties, he had become so skeptical of the polygamy of languages and cultures in his city, that he could no longer find satisfaction in the articulation of poetry and shifted to theater.[4] Hofmannsthal's letters reveal how gravely bewildered and threatened he felt by a stagnation of his creative powers that was aggravated by corroding doubt about the efficacy of language. Benjamin Bennet (1988) in his work on Hofmannsthal, however, detects a more than formal interdependence between the two genres during this period in Hofmannsthal's transition from lyric to drama, and attributes to drama the task of dealing with those unresolvable tensions that lyrics could not resolve. According to Bennet, literature must both '*be* the metaphysical action by which world is spoken into being and [...] a resolute turning away from the metaphysical toward the mimetic' (12).[5]

Hofmannsthal's *Jedermann* is constructed in such a way that it conveys to us more than the author or characters could ever intend to voice. To borrow the key Wittgensteinian concept introduced in the 'Tractatus', the letter must 'show' more than its author is able to 'say'. In paragraph 4.21 we read:

> Der Satz kann die logische Form nicht darstellen, sie spiegelt sich in ihm. Was sich in der Sprache spiegelt, kann sie nicht darstellen. Was *sich* in der Sprache ausdrückt, können *wir* nicht durch sie ausdrücken. Der Satz *zeigt* die logische Form der Wirklichkeit. Er weist sie auf.

The distinction between 'saying' and 'showing' is among the most important elements, perhaps the most important, in the theory that Ludwig Wittgenstein develops in the 'Tractatus' (1960b). Wittgenstein's 'sagen/zeigen' differentiation delineates the dual capacity of linguistic communication. In paragraph 4.1212 he writes: 'Was ge-

zeigt werden kann, kann nicht gesagt warden.' There are definite
limits to what one can consciously, that is, intentionally, state through
language. And, in keeping with what Walter Benjamin also understood the function of poetry to be, its ultimate goal is not to investigate
the utilitarian or communicative functions of linguistic creations, but
rather to understand them in their crystallized and thus ultimately
fragmentary form as intentionless and noncommunicative utterances
of a world essence.

Hofmannsthal's poetic language is not self-expression primarily,
but rather a mirror in which language *as such* is reflected. One reads
in 'Aufzeichnungen aus dem Nachlaß' (1980b) that reality is a 'fable
convenue der Philister', in which 'bürgerliche' individuals exist 'mit
überreichem Selbstbeobachtungsvermögen, mit wenig Willen'. For
them, 'alle anderen Objekte [sind] Akkumulationen von Stimmung
oder zur Rührung' (247). *Jedermann* is capable, instead, of allowing
the spectator to attain an 'Augenblick' of a 'Vision einer Schöpfung'.
The realization of an 'Augenblick' can occur only when words begin
to fail. The moment of skepticism about the adequacy of language
provides an awareness of the vacuum inherent in language. At the
moment when language can no longer function as a tool for communication, one reaches an area of 'Nichtigkeiten'. Overwhelmed in
such unpredictable moments by the resulting emptiness, the reader/
spectator reveals his own openness to new experiences. Such an
occurrence consists in the subordination of the self so that the self can
no longer manipulate or be manipulated by worldly things. At this
place of 'Nichtigkeiten', the vacuum allows for the possibility of
a uniquely supernatural interaction. Hofmannsthal wished to create a
'Gewebe' and to bring an awareness of the possibility of attaining a
new perception of order and harmony. The text, however, was heading
toward a realization of an 'Augenblick'.

Hofmannsthal longed for the homogeneity in language and nation that he believed once existed in the age of the Baroque. In *Ein
Brief* (2000, 10) he writes: 'Mir erschien damals in einer Art von
andauernder Trunkenheit das ganze Dasein als eine große Einheit:
geistige und körperliche Welt schien mir keinen Gegensatz zu bilden'.
Such unity of spirit and matter precedes the divisive effects that
language has on man's being. The pre-linguistic state of mankind

has traditionally been considered a state of experienced grace;[6] a number of early theories on the origin of language proposed in the Classical and Romantic periods (particularly those by Johann Gottfried Herder,[7] Friedrich Schlegel,[8] and Jean-Jacques Rousseau)[9] argue that when language becomes necessary in the evolutionary model of man's history, the loss of perception of an original universal language is of greater concern than the gain of language as a tool for the articulation of thought. Contemporary society's situation holds no tying bonds to a great unity simply because the bond which once existed has disappeared with the arrival of modernity. The tying bond offered by the materialism of the age was only an illusory one, under which was masked a speechless emptiness. In his forward to 'Wert und Ehre deutscher Sprache' (1980e, 129), Hofmannsthal tries to explain this:

> Die mittleren Sprachen der anderen besitzen eine glatte Fügung, in der das einzelne Wort nicht zu wuchtig noch zu grell hervortritt. An den Hörer soll gar nicht das Wort herandringen mit seiner magischen Eigenkraft, sondern die Verbindungen, das in jedem Wort Mitverstandene, das mimische Element der Rede [...] Nicht so sehr das, was er für sich ist, soll in seiner Sprache sich ausprägen, als das, was er vorstellt [...] Es herrscht in einer solchen Umgangsrede *zwischen den Worten ein Etwas*, dass sie untereinander gleichsam Familien bilden, wobei sie alle gleichmässing verzichten, ihr Tiefstes auszusagen. Ihre Anklänge und Wechselbezüge kommen mehr zur Geltung als ihr Urlaut.

Despite the chaos and inefficiency of language, one begins to sense in Hofmannsthal's work that 'ein Etwas' is indeed in control of the situation. The 'mittlere Sprachen', with their 'Anklänge' and 'Wechselbezüge', allow something more in the original sounds and words to surface. Like Chandos in Hofmannsthal's *Ein Brief* (2000), who realizes that he is controlled by the tradition of words and that he must lose them before he can entirely deconstruct and reconstitute his perceptions of the world, the individual must become aware of a disintegration of the binding framework of subject and object: 'Die abstrakten Worte, deren sich doch die Zunge naturgemäß bedienen muß, um irgendwelches Urteil an den Tag zu geben, zerfielen mir im Munde wie modrige Pilze' (13). Benjamin, whose philosophical interests concentrated on the philosophy of language, found that as a consequence of the modern predicament, naming through quoting has become the only possible and appropriate way of dealing with the past without the aid of tradition. He writes in 'Über Sprache überhaupt und über die Sprache des Menschen' (1977d) of a pure, original language that relates humans to God, not words to objects. Language expresses not the thought of an individual speaker but rather the spiritual or magical essence of the language itself, which he terms 'geistige Inhalte' (40ff). The allusion to 'magic' is common in discussions of Hofmannsthal's work, for example in those of Karl Pestalozzi in *Sprachskepsis und Sprachmagie* (1958), and Manfred Hoppe in *Literatentum, Magie und Mystik* (1968). Pestalozzi associates magic with the idea of a 'language of life'. In language as we use it, the immediacy of life has petrified into a system of concepts. But Mauser (1977) argues that poetry finds a way out of the world of concepts. The poet, he maintains, breathes life into things petrified by conceptual thought. Pestalozzi writes of a 'Stimmung' where 'dieses Ineinander von aussen und innen, von Ich und Welt zeichnet den Augenblick aus […] In diesem mystischen Vorgang werden Ich und "Leben" eins' (74). The problem arises, however, when one considers that the magic and the mood of a certain text inevitably belong to the words of that text. How can we be sure that the 'Stimmung' that Pestalozzi and Mauser write of, the suspension of the opposition between ego and world, is not, in fact, merely an emotional state of the author or reader? It is poetry itself, not the poet, that can bring 'life' into the text. The play *Jedermann* reveals these 'geistige Inhalte' and this 'Etwas' as the divine.

Hofmannsthal, throughout his poetical career, remained the pure artist, pure creator, unhindered by philosophical dogmas. Yet his own being depends on his creation because, through the process of writing, it is possible that the creation separates itself from its creator and achieves the greatness that the creator was unable to attain. Despite the impossibility of a successful active and intentional involvement, the poet is very present. Yet he remains part of the play as the creative and self-productive character of poetic language continues to inspire and motivate an inward transformation and revelation of the text.

The play *Jedermann* attains the 'Augenblick' that Hofmannsthal advocated. Consequently, this achievement yields to a presence of the divine on the stage. This is achieved in two ways. First, the presence of the divine becomes possible for the viewer as soon as he recognizes the deficiency of language of the play, which manifests itself in the internal contradictions and negations symptomatic of the 'Sprachnot' crippling the *fin de siècle* society. Second, the divine exists to the same degree that the audience is receptive to its representations and negations on the stage.

In 'Die Idee Europa' (1979b, 50), Hofmannsthal speaks philosophically about money and closely cites Georg Simmel's book *Philosophie des Geldes*:

> Hat das Geld, frage sich jener, der es ins Auge faßte, nicht die Kraft, sich an Stelle Gottes zu setzen? – und ihm tat sich ein seltsamer Gedanke auf, der abschreckend durch die Blasphemie und verlockend durch die Folgerichtigkeit war: der Gottesgedanke hat sein tieferes Wesen darin, daß alle Mannigfaltigkeit und Gegensätze der Welt in ihm zur Einheit gelange, er ist die Ausgleichung aller Fremdheiten und Unversöhntheiten des Seins: daher umschwebt ihn Friede, Sicherheit, allumfassender Reichtum.

This assertion clearly shows Hofmannsthal's conception of money and brings to light the antithesis in society between religion and money.

Hofmannsthal implies that the medieval story of *Jedermann* deserves retelling because it portrays a similar inability of the rich upper-middle class at the turn of the century to understand itself. This inability to understand itself leads to a 'Sprachnot' when it tries to communicate with its world. Man can recognize neither his true identity nor true reality:

> Wer bin ich denn: der Jedermann,
> Der reiche Jedermann allzeit. (77)

Man is a split and deceived being. Like a coin without a face, he has no identity.

> JEDERMANN. Ich glaub – ich glaub –
> GLAUBE. Die Red' ist arm! (85)

His *Ich* is in fact an illusion – a useless metaphor. The deceitful nature of language and things with its restrictive boundaries has left Jedermann poor.

Hofmannsthal is keenly aware of the all-pervasive power of money in society. In 'Die Idee Europa' (1979b, 48–49), he characterizes man in the years before the war as 'maximale Zuspitzung und Ausbreitung des Verlangens nach Geld'. Hofmannsthal calls money 'den Knoten des Daseins' (49), the knot that binds together man's existence. Because his entire existence is characterized by his possessions, Jedermann symbolizes the world of the 'Großbürgertum'. Jedermann feels that through the invention of money, 'unsere ganze Welt [ist] in ein höher Ansehen gestellt.' Money has the power to create the 'ungequälten Ort'. It is a god-like power, a 'kleine Gottheit' (47) that men make in their image. The subsequent appearance of Mammon makes it all too clear that gold has replaced God in this society and offers a feeling of easiness, mobility, and versatility in all aspects of life.

Nonetheless, money has no symbolic significance unless it can be traded/exchanged for services or goods of a different physical constitution. Money is 'Währung'. Since its first introduction into society, money has been a commodity of exchange, 'Tausch': one receives goods for money and money for goods. Yet money, the means of exchange, is also 'Täuschung', since it deceives by not representing itself. The definition of money and what money in fact represents are two different things. Money only represents something through an exchange and has no equivalent meaning outside of this exchange. Consequently, 'das Wahre' becomes 'das Falsche'. Nietzsche, in an early essay in 'Die Geburt der Tragödie' (1988c, 881), writes:

> die Wahrheiten sind Illusionen, von denen man vergessen hat, daß sie welche sind, Metaphern, die abgenutzt und sinnlich kraftlos geworden sind, Münzen, die ihr Bild verloren haben und nun als Metall, nicht mehr als Münzen in Betracht kommen.

Jedermann's power and authority depend on money. As long as he has money, he is represented by it. At the same time, however, as long as he has money he is deceived by what it represents. The master–servant relationship has been inverted:

> MAMMON. Ich steh gar groß, du zwergisch klein.
> Du Kleiner wirst wohl sein der Knecht. (79)

Language is also a means of exchange. Heraclitus understood even the entire function of the world as an exchange of equivalents. As C. L. Hart Nibbrig writes in *Übergänge* (1995, 87): 'Alles ist Austausch des Feuers und das Feuer Austausch von allem, gerade wie für Gold Waren und für Waren Gold eingetauscht werden.' In his studies on language, 'Philosophische Untersuchungen', Wittgenstein (1960a) writes of the commercialization of the mind in paragraph 120:

> Man sagt, es kommnt nicht aufs Wort an, sondern auf seine Bedeutung, und denkt dabei an die Bedeutung wie an eine Sache von der Art des Wortes, wenn auch vom Wort verschieden. Hier ist das Wort, hier seine Bedeutung. Das Geld und die Kuh, die man dafür kaufen kann. (Andrerseits aber: das Geld und seine Nutzen).

In the same manner, a word and its meaning have become two separate and distinguishable ideas that depend on an exchange with one another. Language is both 'Tausch' and 'Täuschung'. Hegel simlarly argues in *Phänomenologie des Geistes* (1907, 33), that 'true' and 'false' are also misconceptualized independent concepts that barter with one another:

> Das Wahre und Falsche gehört zu den bestimmten Gedanken, die bewegungslos für eigene Wesen gelten, deren eines drüben, das andre hüben ohne Gemeinschaft mit dem anderen isoliert und fest steht. Dagegen muß behauptet werden, daß die Wahrheit nicht eine ausgeprägte Münze ist, die fertig gegeben und so eingestrichen werden kann. Noch gibt es ein Falsches, so wenig es ein Böses gibt.

In order to further develop the dialectic of 'wahr' and 'falsch', Hegel inserts the 'Münze' at exactly the place where the exchange takes place. The two are then fixed against one another and only thus are able to be opposites.

Language as 'Tausch' is communication, the means of exchange for understanding. It consequently becomes 'Täuschung': language attempts to represent something through this exchange, yet the meaning it offers is not that which it in fact represents. By its nature, 'Währung' implies 'Tausch', but it is also 'Täuschung'. The same is true for Jedermann's self and language. He has depended on money for his personal appearance, definition, and authenticity in society. We read in *Jedermann*:

> Dein Reichtum bin ich halt, dein Geld,
> Dein eins und alles auf der Welt. (78)

When he is ultimately confronted with the 'halt[ing]', restrictive boundaries of his society and with the insufficiency of his words and things, what Jedermann perceived to be an all-encompassing unity in his life reveals itself as a confining and controlling hold. Only at the moment when he is finally silent can Jedermann become aware of the deception he had been living.

The failure of language belongs to the very character of the age and goes hand in hand with the failure of the individual. At the turn of the century in Europe, the examination of language developed into a much-discussed topic. Fritz Mauthner argued in *Erinnerungen* (1918, 213ff.) that even the language we use to speak and write about language is subject to investigation:

> Der kann das Werk der Befreiung von der Sprache nicht vollbringen, der mit Worthunger, mit Wortliebe und Worteitelkeit ein Buch zu schreiben ausgeht in der Sprache von gestern oder von heute oder von morgen, in der erstarrten Sprache einer bestimmten festen Stufe. Will ich emporklimmen in der Sprachkritik, die das wichtigste Geschäft der denkenden Menschheit ist, so muss ich die Sprache hinter mir und vor mir und in mir vernichten von Schritt zu Schritt, so muss ich jede Sprosse der Leiter zertrümmern, indem ich sie betrete.

In 'Corona', Hofmannsthal (1979a, 672) quotes Goethe's poem 'Sprache' as a way of describing the word: it is a 'vegrabne Urne' and 'Schwert im Arsenal'. Similar ideas follow from Mauthner's understanding of Nietzsche who wrote that the action and the will are man's true contact with reality. Words, therefore, cannot produce knowledge.

In *Erinnerungen* Mauthner (1918, 213ff.) asserts: 'Wissen ist Wortwissen. Wir haben nur Worte, wir wissen nichts.' Hofmannsthal continues in *Buch der Freunde* (1929, 84): 'Wahre Sprachliebe ist nicht möglich ohne Sprachverleugnung.' Jedermann speaks, yet he cannot communicate:

> JEDERMANN. Mein Freund!
> GESELL. Sprich frei, tu auf den Mund
>      Muß alles mir werden offenbart
>
>      .....................................................
>      *Jedermann will den Mund auftun.*
> GESELL. Dein Jammer geht mir mächtig nah
>
>      .....................................................
>      Es geht dir um dein Geld und Gut
>
>      .....................................................
> JEDERMANN. Nein, lieber, nein!
> GESELL. Braucht nit viel Wort
>      Bei mir ist dein Vertraun am Ort
>
>      .....................................................
> JEDERMANN. Nein, Lieber Guter hör mich an.
> GESELL. Spar dir die Reden Jedermann
>      Bist ohne viel von mir verstanden. (67–68)

Language can only be the means for achieving understanding. Hart Nibbrig (1995, 201) refers to language in *Übergänge* as an 'Übersetzungsinstrument'. Jedermann's situation intensifies:

> Ist alls um nichts dein Handausrecken
> Und hilft kein Knirschen und Zähnebläcken,
> Fährst in die Gruben nackt und bloß,
> So wie du kamst aus Mutter Schoß.
> JEDERMANN *ohne Sprache, eine lange Stille.* (80)

At this most crucial point, neither money nor language can give consolation and satisfaction. Every man begins to understand that he can rely on neither for existence. He finally comes face to face with the reality of a world without any meaningful reality. Nothing can be experienced as long as the 'Schein' has dislodged 'das Wahre' of things.

This crisis of language ('Sprachkrise') is the crisis of a consciousness that has lost its structural identity. In other words, it is the result of the impossibility of establishing a formal constancy and cohesion of meaning in life. Jedermann's self, being in opposition to unity, can grasp neither the 'Unmittelbarkeit' of things and words nor the 'Unmittelbarkeit des Lebens'. Only when he is able to achieve complete silence can realization and comprehension take place. For Jedermann, this moment lies outside of language, although, as Wittgenstein observes, what language can never 'say' directly still belongs to language, for it achieves existence precisely by the futile mechanism of verbal communication.[10] At the beginning of *Jedermann* we are told:

> Der Stoff ist kostbar von dem Spiel
> Dahinter aber liegt noch viel. (35)

The possibility of an experience behind language stresses, paradoxically, the priority of language. Martin Heidegger carries out an adequate argument on this very point in 'Unterwegs zur Sprache' (1984, 151), where he maintains that an impossible naming is necessary in order to bring us face to face with a possibility of undergoing a thinking experience with language:

> Wo aber kommt die Sprache selber als Sprache zum Wort? Seltsamerweise dort, wo wir für etwas, was uns angeht, uns an sich reißt, bedrängt oder befeuert, das rechte Wort nicht finden. Wir lassen dann, was wir meinen, im Ungesprochenen und machen dabei, ohne es recht zu bedenken, Augenblicke durch, in denen uns die Sprache selber mit ihrem Wesen fernher und flüchtig gestreift hat.

The early Nietzsche, in 'Über Wahrheit und Lüge im außermoralischen Sinne' (1988f), is concerned with the question of reality and our understanding of it. Is the reality ('Wirklichkeit') that is accessible to man's perceptions in fact the reality that we actually assume in our consciousness? Can we recognize 'die Wahrheit'? As Kant and Schopenhauer have done, Nietzsche also denies that the human intellect can recognize the 'Ding an sich'. We deceive ourselves and therefore live in a world of 'Täuschung', in a 'Lüge im aussermoralischen Sinne'. Nietzsche also includes language in this argument: 'wie steht es mit jenen Conventionen der Sprache? [...] Ist die Sprache der adequäte Ausdruck aller Realitäten?' (878) He denies this later in 'Die Geburt der Tragödie' (1988c, 880–81):

> Was ist also Wahrheit? Ein bewegliches Heer von Metaphern, Metonymen, Anthropomorphismen kurz eine Summe von menschlichen Relationen, die, poetisch rhetorisch gesteigert, übertragen, geschmückt wurden, und die nach langem Gebrauch einem Volke fest, canonisch und verbindlich dünken: die Wahrheiten sind Illusionen, von denen man vergessen hat, daß sie welche sind [...]

Hofmannsthal's style clearly exemplifies this.

In *Jedermann* we are presented in several places with the paradoxical situation of a beautiful and highly stylized form that exposes the insufficiency of language. For example:

> WERKE. Hättest erkannt in deinem Sinn,
>     Daß ich nit völlig häßlich bin,
>     .............................................
>     Komm näher, *meine Stimm ist leis* – :
>     Bei Armen wärest eingegangen
>     Recht als ihr Bruder, heiliger Weis,
>     .............................................
>     Und ich, wie ich gebrechlich bin,
>     Ich wär, *verklärt* vor deinem Sinn,
>     Dir worden ein göttliches Gefäß,
>     Ein Kelch der überströmenden Gnaden
>     Dazu deine Lippen waren geladen. (82)

The voice of Works is soft, yet had Jedermann's lips not already been 'geladen', Works, in her wavering and seemingly submissive tone, would have offered Jedermann a 'Kelch der überströmenden Gnaden'. A similar display of incongruity occurs again later:

> TEUFEL.
>     ...........................
>     Beweis! Gib eine einzig Red,
>     Die vor Gericht zu Recht besteht!
> GLAUBE. Vor dem Gericht, vor das er tritt,
>     Bestehen deine Rechte nit,

Die sind auf Schein und Trug gestellt
[…] Und bleibt in solchen Schranken stocken,
Wo aber tönet diese Glocken,
*Man hört von Innen das Sterbeglöcklein, Glaube und Werke fallen auf die Knie.*
Hat angehoben Ewigkeit.
TEUFEL. *hält sich die Ohren zu*
Ich geb es auf, ich kehr mich um […] (93)

One cannot overlook the representational use of language here. The Devil's demands for a physical representation and Faith's refutation thereof as mere appearances are interrupted by the sound of a passing bell. In response to this sound, Faith and Works fall down to the ground while, in an upward movement, eternity lifts up/begins ('hat angehoben Ewigkeit'). The devil cannot bear this indeterminable tone. His gesture, as well as his figural expression in response to the sound of the bell, turns his theatrical character around and upside down. At the same time, he also hints at a conversion that is about to take place as death approaches.

The paradoxical gesture of using language to point behind it raises inversion to a major technique in *Jedermann*. In turn, the individual inversions negate or invert words and symbolic representations to produce new directions and invalidate limiting concepts. This process goes behind abstractions and ultimately renders these concepts null and void. The 'Wahre' quality of 'Währung' is inverted. By exchanging places, 'Tausch' becomes 'Täuschung'. Words lose their 'Schein' character and leave Jedermann 'schuldig'. At the center of the *x* that is the 'Augenblick', limiting words cancel themselves out and limitless potentials of new values become apparent: the moment of nullification is the moment of the presence of the divine. In this 'Augenblick', the most personal convictions of an individual are not communicated through words.

Jedermann's appearance after an encounter at the crossroads ('Kreuzweg') acknowledges this suspension. The journey that Jedermann is undertaking is in fact, in Hofmannsthal's words,

kein wirklicher Weg mit Anfang und Ziel, sondern er hat viele Kreuzwege, ja er besteht wohl eigentlich nur aus Kreuzwegen und jeder Punkt ist der mögliche Ausgangspunkt zu undendlichen Möglichkeiten. (20)

54

The roads that run through Hofmannsthal's text, together with their inversions, lead to individual crossroads. In turn, only at the intersection of these 'Kreuzwege' can restrictive boundaries disappear and give way to endless possibilities. At such a crossroad, the suspension taking place between Jedermann and his language is expressed through the spiritual essence, the 'geistige Inhalte' of language: 'Jedermann tritt oben hervor [...] sein Angesicht ist totenbleich aber verklärt' (94). This consequent encounter at the 'cross' with the divine can occur neither literally nor visually. It happens behind concepts, 'backstage', so to speak. It devalues the relationship of words to objects or representations and relates instead individuals to the divine. Due to his encounter at the 'Kreuzung', Jedermann is transfigured ('verklärt'). But how does this backstage *transfiguration* that renders representations and things as invalid take place?

In order to overcome the authority of representations, Jedermann must first arrive at an understanding of his present self and finally overcome it. One's individuality plays a crucial role in this context. It is the very justification for a person's existence. Jedermann's possessions have always represented his very being and self. As long as the empirical world controls his life and as long as he tries to express the deep experience that is within him, he is incapable of reaching true individuality. Jedermann believes that he can express literally his deepest feelings:

> JEDERMANN. Ich glaub – an Gottes Langmut
> Wenn einer bei Zeiten Buß tut.
> Aber ich bin in Sünden zu weit
> Dahin reicht keine Barmherzigkeit.
> GLAUBE. *tut einen Schritt auf ihn zu*
> Bist ganz in Wollust denn ertrunken
> In Lastern völlig versunken,
> Daß dir nit auf die Lippen kommt
> Was ewig deiner Seelen frommt? (86)

Words gave him position/standing in society in the past, and he assumes he can use the same method to save his soul. When faced with death, however, he realizes that the self cannot be represented or defined. The critique of language that refers to that which is within the individual – the feelings and perceptions that can never be expressed – and that has been called by Fritz Mauthner 'sentimentale Sprach-kritik', had significance already in mysticism and in pietism but becomes significant during the age of Goethe, an age of sentiment and feeling that understands the soul as the place of revelation of truth.

At the place of this turn, using Hofmannsthal's words in 'Die Briefe des Zurückgekehrten' (1953b, 565) 'aus dem Abgrund der Wesenlosigkeit', the self is able to encounter 'die eine Substanz'. The general human experience with transitoriness extends into a question of existence in *Ad me ipsum* (1980a, 613): 'Ohne Glauben an die Ewigkeit ist kein wahrhaftes Leben möglich' (396). Jedermann, at a certain moment, recognizes the deceitful nature of appearances and acquires the ability to perceive the eternity of that vacuous moment:

JEDERMANN *auf den Knien.*
> O ewiger Gott! O göttliches Gesicht!
> O rechter Weg! O himmlisches Licht!
> Hier schrei ich zu dir in letzter Stund,
> Ein Klageruf geht aus meinem Mund. (88)

The worldly subject begins to lose itself into that immeasurable instant. In the 'Aufzeichnungen' (1980b, 538), Hofmannsthal cites Baudelaire: ''Il est de certaines sensations délicieuses dont la vague n'exclut pas l'intensité, et il n'est pas de pointe plus acérée que l'Infini'.' The cry 'O' flows over into the eternal and divine as the adjectives 'ewig', 'göttlich' and 'himmlisch' that follow Jedermann's indescribable sigh 'O' declare what he cannot grasp or see. This ex-perience of 'Unendlichkeit'[11] expressed by Jedermann at this moment while he lies 'im tiefen Gebet auf seinem Angesicht' (88) reaches deep into his subjectivity and goes beyond the limits of appearance and reality. The last lines of Baudelaire's well-known poem 'Ele-vation' in 'Fleurs du mal' (1961b) speak of such an experience of a metaphysical expression: 'Qui plane sur la vie et comprend sans effort / Le language des fleurs et des choses muettes' (10). The flowers and the mute things are themselves a part of an 'existence brumeuse'. Exactly for this reason, only he who can rise above the 'miasmes morbides' of everyday life and speech is able to understand such an unexpressed language.

Yet even the silence itself can be mere appearance and 'Täuschung' for the one who is unable to recognize the immense depth of the chasm or to become aware of the metaphysical significance of this silence. Hofmannsthal writes:

GLAUBE.

.............................................................

Die Red ist aus dem Munde kommen,
Der keine Lügen reden kann.
Glaubst du daran in diesem Leben,
So ist der deine Sünd vergeben
Und ist gestillet Gottes Zorn.
JEDERMANN. O, deine Worte sind gelind,
Mir ist, als wär ich neugeboren. (87)

Jedermann is not yet completely beyond words at this stage in his experience with God and is consequently still bound to concepts. A certain effect must first be achieved before he can fully encounter the divine:

GLAUBE. Ja solches wirkt die tiefe Reu,
Die hat eine lohende Feuerskraft,
Da sie von Grund die Seel umschafft. (93)

The realization of the conceptual character of the world *transforms* or, rather, turns upside down the mundanity of Everyman. Consequently, this powerful and active revolution of the soul out of the 'miasmes morbides' to a higher spiritual level creates an inexplicable essence of the divine, transformed and reshaped by its own fire. The devil is unable to grasp such a transformation:

Ha! Weiberred und Gaukelei!
.............................................................
Ein Wischiwasch! Salbaderei!
Zum Speien ich dergleichen haß!
Beweis! Gib eine einzig Red,
Die vor Gericht zu Recht besteht! (93)

The Devil builds his argument to fit the rhetorical style of the verse on which he, in turn, also relies. His correspondingly hollow words are meant to keep Jedermann from experiencing the conversion mentioned above. In their emptiness, however, these words provide evidence for just such a transformation.

The moment of the 'Augenblick' is the moment Jedermann is forced to encounter death. Death is an interruption. When Jedermann wishes to carry his 'haben' with him as a representation of what he is, he is interrupted:

> *Tod tritt in etlicher Entfernung hervor.*
> ERSTER KNECHT. Dort steht ein Teufel und winkt uns Halt. (76)

Death is a 'Halt' in the road. Before the appearance of death, Jedermann was caught in the contradictory state of being in two places at once. He was both object and subject. On the one hand, he is still part of the world and had not yet entered into the openness of nothingness. On the other hand, he is already heading away from the world:

> STIMMEN. Jedermann! Jedermann! Jedermann!
> JEDERMANN. *springt angstvoll auf*
>    Mein Gott wer ruft da so nach mir?
>    Von wo werd ich gerufen so?
>    Des werd ich im Leben nimmer froh. (62)

It is clear that he is communicating between two worlds because he hears voices not heard by others. They are unearthly voices calling out his mundane name 'in fürchterlicher Weis [...] Ganz fremd und doch bekannt zugleich' (62). Jedermann replies with the words 'Mein Gott'. These words, a common exclamation of surprise, lose their traditional meaning here for two reasons. First, the contradiction in the accepted definition of the two terms 'mein' and 'Gott' invalidates both terms. God cannot be the possession of anyone and Jedermann is not yet in a position to speak of his self as a valid one. Second, the conventional statement 'mein Gott' is here not separated from the rest of the question by a comma. Jedermann asks the question, but by implying an answer he turns the contradictory statement into a possibility. It is God who is calling his name. Paradoxically, not only do his words reveal confusion, fear, and lack of understanding (he is confused because he cannot know whose voice this is) but also this same appellative supplies the reason for his being called. He, however, cannot yet see the reason. He can only hear it in the voice that calls his name. As a result, the following two lines hint at the transition that will ultimately begin with dying: the object 'mir' of the anxious inquiry turns into the subject 'ich' in the next line and arrives at the reason in the third line: 'Des werd ich im Leben nimmer froh.' Without yet realizing the gravity of his words, he consciously exclaims over the stark opposition between 'im Leben [...] froh' and 'ich'. He now finds himself between two worlds. He realizes that he must begin a journey toward God, but he cannot grasp the full significance of such a journey:

> JEDERMANN. Nun, wollen wir die Reis angehen,
> Ganz in der Still, heimlicher Weis
>
> .......................................................
>
> Ach Gott, wie graust mir vor dem Tod. (76–77)

Hofmannsthal understood well the significance of Jedermann's experience. In the fourth of his 1907 'Briefe des Zurückgekehrten' (1953b, 560), he writes how ill he felt 'von innen heraus', yet not from a bodily illness, rather from 'die Krise eines inneren Übelbefindens [...] Verkehrtheiten und Unsicherheiten des Denkens oder Fühlens' that left an impression of earthly things as 'so nicht-wirklich'.

Through its 'position/posture', death does not allow the continuity of the same. His encounter with death forces Jedermann to sacrifice everything by which he has previously defined himself. Only so can a shift from 'having' to 'being' redefine him. What Jedermann owned in the world before his death is the very essence of his being. Yet he must experience dying in order to acquire a complete identity. At the moment of death every man is reduced to what he is by being stripped of all things that constituted his being up to this point. The dialectic of reaching the highest moment in self-consciousness is found at the moment of being *equal* to every man. Jedermann as subject ('mir') shudders when faced with death. Yet the cry 'Ach Gott' separates itself from the rest of the sentence. It expresses much more than fear of the mysterious 'Tod'. What he could not comprehend earlier through his own words 'mein Gott' comes to being in the uniting of 'ach' and 'Gott'. In other words, the transition occurs from 'expressing' ('mein') to a 'naming', in a Benjaminean sense ('ach'). The inexpressible part of the soul and the unnamable divine come together for a brief moment in the notion of death. Perhaps Claudio, in Hofmannsthal's 1898 *Der Tor und der Tod* (1979c), already perceives it best: 'Erst, da ich sterbe, spür ich, daß ich bin.' A radical individualization takes place: through a turn at this moment of intersection between opposing ways, the former 'Knoten des Daseins' is undone and we are able to inwardly experience another 'Vision einer Schöpfung'.

As the reader has experienced it through the stylized form of *Jedermann*, 'Sprachnot' is a problem of society. In the openness created by the text's crossroads, its 'Kreuzwege', and their subsequent encounters, the 'Not' of 'Sprache' consequently breaks. In this elevated moment of the 'Augenblick', the 'Knoten des Daseins' also comes undone, and everyman is able to see through the distress and deception:

Schein und Trug
.......................................
Auf Hie und Nun und diese Welt,
[d]ie ist gefangen in der Zeit. (93)

By means of negation of the elements of language as bearers of meaning, Jedermann transforms his entire existence into a personal gesture that ultimately does accomplish what it is intended to do. His utterance becomes a kind of inverted performative. In this way, Jedermann succeeds in 'showing' what it is not possible to 'say'.

At this point in the reading of Hofmannsthal's *Jedermann*, a question inevitably arises: Why should a member of the audience consider the language as more than a text? How can he be induced to embrace it as not only the author's and characters' experience of the divine, but also as his own? Drama is poetry as action on the stage and is able to govern the spectator's response in ways that a written text cannot do alone. One must also address the problem of how to maintain the spectator's status as a listener, how to ensure that one is addressing a true 'listener', not a mere theatergoer, hence the problem of how to maintain the metaphysical quality of the action.

Peter Szondi, in an essay on Hofmannsthal's early work in *Satz und Gegensatz*, 'Lyrik und lyrische Dramatik in Hofmannsthals Frühwerk' (1978a), argues that poems inherit a new 'objectivity' from plays. Lyrical dramas, he continues, represent a criticism of earlier poetry and a preparation for later poetry. He writes:

> Der eigentliche Unterschied, der qualitative Sprung, der von dem novellistischen Drama, vom lyrischen Einakter, zur großen Form (deren Sprache freilich immer noch lyrisch ist) führt, liegt auf dem selben Weg, der von der frühen Lyrik zu Gestern ging und der als Objektivierung des eigenen als problematisch erlebten Ich zu verstehen ist. Die große Form stellt eine neue Etappe auf diesem Weg dar, und zwar dadurch, daß die vom lyrischen Ich zunächst auf andere projizierten und in der Projection schon bis zu einem gewissen Grad objektivierten und der Kritik ausgelieferten Gefühle nun noch stärker entfremdet werden [...] (253–54)

This, in turn, is not inconsistent with this lyrical text's origin as part of a medieval 'lebendige Bühne'. The play as part of the 'lebendige Bühne' sheds light on the text as a timeless and autonomous work of art. Consequently, this combination of qualities situates the listener/spectator within a discourse of the sacred that can no longer accept the *fin de siècle* belief that God is dead.

*Jedermann* is based on the morality play of *Everyman*. In a letter to Elsa Bruckmann-Cantacuzène on August 31, 1911, Hofmannsthal writes: 'Wenn ich sage: *mein Jedermann* so mein ich nichts anderes als eine Erneuerung des alten Spieles "vom Sterben des Reichen Mannes" dessen englische Version *Everyman* Ihnen gewiß bekannt ist.'[12] Hofmannsthal continues:

> Dieser Erneuerung des alten Spieles liegt für den Aufbau vornehmlich der anonyme englische Text des fünfzehnten Jahrhunderts zugrunde. ('Everyman, a Morality Play' gedruckt zu London um 1490.) Aus des Hans Sachs 'Comedi vom sterbend reichen Menschen' wurde manches einzelne herübergenommen, zumeist in den Anfangsszenen. In der Szene der Mutter ist ein gereimtes Gebet eingeWoben, das von Albrecht Dürer stammt. Das Tanzlied und die übrigen Lieder sind einer neueren Sammlung der Minnesänger des dreizehnten Jahrhunderts entnommen. (291)

Hofmannsthal's *Jedermann* is 'loosely' based on the old supposition that the sinner, isolated from the community by death, is confronted with his solitary, personal responsibility and can only lay hold of it by accepting the offer of the Christian 'faith', which, in turn, draws its entire power from God's redemptive act in the Cross of Jesus Christ. This is immediately highlighted to an exaggerated degree by the prologue of 'Gott der Herr', who looks down on mankind.

The play was first produced on December 2, 1911, by Max Reinhardt in the Berlin Zirkus Schumann before an audience of thousands. Subsequently, Hofmannsthal felt obliged to describe it in *Jedermann* as a 'Märchen', yet '[ein] allen Zeiten gehörige[s] und allgemeingültige[s]' one (33). When the critic Bodenhausen expressed his dissatisfaction with the allegorical figures, which left him cold, Hofmannsthal pointed out in *Briefe der Freundschaft* (1953a, 136) that it is the religious context which gives the play its invigorating third dimension, as was the case in ancient drama and in the mystery play.

However, this 'Nachdichtung' represents more than a mere revival of a mystery play as a forgotten genre. It is noteworthy to mention that Hofmannsthal's first attempt at a revival of the mystery play was unsuccessful. In 1910, through the advice and support of Max Reinhardt, Hofmannsthal began working intensively on *Jedermann* and completed an almost perfect translation of the medieval English *Everyman* by the end of the year.

Hofmannsthal's reworking and rewriting of the old medieval theme had a lasting effect. The playwright clearly intended his new version of *Jedermann* (1911) to be more than the admonitory voice and pointing finger of the Church with its religious dogma fixed in a bygone epoch and space. He writes: 'Sein eigentlicher Kern offenbarte sich immer mehr als menschlich absolut, keiner bestimmten Zeit angehörig, nicht einmal mit dem christlichen Dogma unlöslich verbunden [...]' (115). While his version repeats the medieval theme of a wasted life that is judged by God and saved through the intervention of death, Hofmannsthal uses a system of coordinates that is entirely new. *Jedermann*, he writes in 'Aufzeichnungen' (1980b, 262), is 'Nach-dichtung':

Es muß einen Stern geben, auf dem das vor einem Jahr Vergangene Gegenwart ist, auf einem das vor einem Jahrhundert Vergangene, auf einem die Zeit der

Kreuzzüge und so fort, alles in einer lückenlosen Kette, so steht es dann vor dem Auge der Ewigkeit alles nebeneinander, wie die Blumen in einem Garten.

Hofmannsthal implies a conviction that, just as language strives to return to its original pure state, so, too, theater must attempt to overcome tradition and representation. As Rölleke (1996, 105) asserts, 'die Traditionslinie der *acedia*, der Langeweile, Melancholie, gesteigert bis zum Lebensekel' also needed to be overcome. *Jedermann* is 'belated' literature as it attempts to go backwards into tradition to locate what has been forgotten and give new direction to what is missing and to what has become 'Not' in modern society.

*Jedermann* is also '*Ver*dichtung'. It is a rewriting of the original as 'Fälschung'. Wolfgang Matz (1989, 57–58) explains this through the relationship between Benjamin and Hofmannsthal:

An einem anderen Punkt begegnen sich beide Autoren indes noch einmal: in der Form der Übersetzung. In seiner Ankündigung des 'Angelus Novus', stellt Benjamin deren Aktualität direkt als Folge der zeitgenössischen Sprachkrise dar, und in der von von Hofmannsthal geschätzten Vorrede an seinen Baudelaireübertragungen begründet er ausdrücklich die These, Übersetzungen dienten nicht dem Zweck, Literatur dem der Originalsprache Unkundingen zugänglich zu machen. Hofmannsthals eigene Übertragungen und Bearbeitungen entsprechen diesem Program [...] Wenn er [...] Hofmannsthals Werk in exzentrischer Weise unter dem Begriff der 'Fälschung' diskutiert, so um dessen poetisches Verfahren als ein sich Beziehen auf 'Urbilder' zu deuten, als ein Verfahren 'äußerster und sublimiertester Verdichtung'.

The negation of images, the intersection of movements, as well as their place of pivot, is the location of the divine. It is a matter of 'Conversion', of 'Umkehr'. Representations, traditions, time, and place lose their earthly significance as boundaries between beginning and end dissolve and as the stage opens up at the point of the cross.

Like the God of the Old Testament, Hofmannsthal's 'Gott der Herr' wishes to impose his power by use of justice upon a people that has forgotten him and that has made idols to replace him. He is a God of the stage, a deus ex machina who ultimately decides the fate of the characters. All but one of the representations 'stand' for something. 'Gott der Herr', who appears on stage only at the beginning of *Jeder-*

*mann*, is sitting. His posture is a representation of a forgotten God who no longer stands for anything:

GOTT DER HERR. *wird sichtbar auf seinem Thron und spricht*
  Führwahr mag länger das nit ertragen,
  Daß alle Kreatur gegen mich
  Ihr Herz verhärtet böslich,
  Daß sie ohn einige Furcht vor mir
  Schmählicher hinleben als das Getier. (35)

The eyes of the people have become blind and 'kennen [ihn] nit für ihren Gott' (35). This God is not the God found in the moment of the 'Augenblick'.

The God of the 'Augenblick' cannot be designated through words or representations. Instead, His presence becomes apparent through the negation of the very representations and words that attempt to represent Him. In 'Die Aufgabe des Übersetzers' (1987, 18), Benjamin quotes the words 'En arche en ho logos' of the beginning of the Gospel according to John in Greek, and he translates them into German: 'im Anfang war das Wort'. As Rainer Nägele states in *Echoes of Translation* (1997, 117–18),

> the logos of John's Gospel goes through a sequence of qualifications and translations. Like the 'himeros' of the Sophoclean chorus, he is placed at the beginning with the highest principle [...] with God ('pros theon') in the text of John. This being of the logos with God seems first of all to displace God from himself, when the text continues 'kai theos en ho logos', God was the logos. From the beginning, then, God did not become logos, but was it already. It is now this being of the logos that is declared the principle of all genesis, of all becoming: 'werden'. 'Panta di'autou egeneto, kai choris autou egeneto oude hen, ho gegonen.'

The seated position of God at the beginning of the play portrays the opposite of such 'werden'. It is an essentially static image of the God of the Old Testament prepared to have mortals pay the price for their forgetting.

Not only has *God* become a worldly image of religion, but also the majority of the religious aspects of this drama are replete with 'secular', financial metaphors. Jedermann is summoned before God to settle his spiritual account. The Lord issues specific instructions that Jedermann bring along his 'Rechenbuch' (36), the record of his spiritual credits and debits. Since Jedermann is guilty of having erected his entire existence on money without concern for its deceitful nature, his eventual trial before God is also treated as a financial transaction. Furthermore, much of God's language is couched in financial vocabulary. The purpose of Death's mission is announced as 'Abrechnung' (49). The reference to Jedermann's earthly life and goods as 'geliehen' is no doubt an allusion to the New Testament parable of the talents.[13] At the time of his repentance, it is in keeping with his and the other characters' materialism that Jedermann views the achievement of salvation as but another purchase:

> Durch gute Werk und Frommheit eben
> Erkauft er sich ein ewig Leben. (81)

Finally, even Faith's theological refutation of the devil's claim is cloaked in financial parlance. Christ's death has

> Jedermannes Schuldigkeit
> Vorausbezahlt in Ewigkeit. (92)

Mammon has replaced Gott – one allegorical representation has replaced another:

> dem Mammonsbeutel Ehr,
> Als obs das Tabernakel wär.

Not even priests are spared, for, according to Jedermann:

> Das ist nun einmal ihr Sach in der Welt,
> Ist abgesehen auf unser Geld.

Jedermann's calling, however, does not come from the stage. The voices he hears are unlike the voice of 'Gott der Herr'. They are not earthly voices:

> Mein Gott wer ruft da so nach mir?
> Von wo werd ich gerufen so?
> Des werd ich im Leben nimmer froh. (62)

As we have previously seen, Jedermann's statement 'Mein Gott' expresses much more than it appears to. So often used to express bafflement at something unsettling, these words here paradoxically not only show his confusion and fear, but also supply the purpose for his calling. The purpose, however, is not within the range of the representable. The space of the stage consequently departs from the visible and tangible, and approaches the solely audible. As a result, we no longer, so to speak, see God in 'our mind's eye'; now we hear in 'our mind's ear' a silence that speaks of a divine presence. Jedermann hears this silence, yet he cannot identify the 'wer' nor locate the 'wo'.

This question-word 'wo' appears repeatedly throughout the play. In one instant, Mammon asks Jedermann: 'Ich bleib dahier und wo bleibst du?' (79). Jedermann's response is silence: 'Ohne Sprache, eine lange Stille' (80). Werke answers this question later for Jedermann: 'wohin es auch sei' (89). Whereas Mammon remains stationary and temporal, the response to his 'wo' question shows Jedermann acquiring a direction. As a result of having heard strange voices, he is literally moved in his innermost being. Melancholy and fear after the realization of the indebted condition of his soul damn Jedermann as long as he chooses to remain within the 'wo', to remain 'im Leben nimmer froh'.

The representations of Glaube and Werke must also be treated as allegorical theatrical representations. Faith and good works have become useless and outdated in modern society. Yet paradoxically, the ability of these characters to save Jedermann's soul lies in what they stand for, in their gestures. Through their upright posture, they support Jedermann's internal struggle and final confrontation with death. They are Jedermann's companions at the crossroads to death and pray 'mit gefalteten Händen' (91). On the other hand, the devil's posture and words are grotesquely exaggerated and comical when he attempts to interrupt the journey:

> TEUFEL *kommt angesprungen, schreit und winkt von weitem.*
> Halt Jedermann! Aufhalten Jedermann!
> ...........................................................
> GLAUBE. Halt da! (90)

Faith stands as a foil to the Devil's intention. A few lines later, the Werke do the same. A 'Kreuzweg' consequently develops on the stage between the various 'Haltungen'. The Devil himself expresses what occurs at the point of this intersection:

Seit wann? seit wo? wie geht das zu?
Geschiehet das in einem Nu? (92)

'Nu' is the eternity inherent in the present moment, 'Gegenwart des Unendlichen'.[14] It cannot be located, knows no time, and has no beginning and no end. 'Nu' is described in *Grimms Deutsches Wörter-buch* as the 'Augenblick, der Moment, überhaupt ein sehr kurzer Zeit-raum'.

The 'Nu' is a moment between all space and time, between here and now ('Hie and Nun') and illusion and deception. It is space and openness. Hart Nibbrig, when discussing 'betweenness' in languages in *Übergänge* (1995, 10), writes: 'Zwischen: [...] eine Grenze, die, versucht man sie festzuhalten, zu wachsen beginnt, zum Zwischen-raum sich weitet, wo Platz ist für alles und Nichts.' This betweenness connects that which is divided, as well as divides that which is con-nected. The voices that accompany the descent of the curtain at the end of the play are an audible expression of such an absence. The intersection of the highest moment of the self-consciousness, of death, and of time, triangulated in one another, all takes place in the 'Nu'.

This moment between space and time is emphasized even more through the unidentifiable presence of a 'Jetzt' that cannot be fixed as an object, location or precise time. Paradoxically, however, Jeder-mann, through his exclamations 'Ach Gott' (53, 77), 'Mein Gott' (62), 'Hilf Gott' (80) still calls out to an unknowable, to what Hugo von Hofmannsthal refers to as a 'Hauch' and 'Ahnung des Blühens, ein Schauder des Verwesens, ein Jetzt, ein Hier und zugleich ein Jenseits, ein ungeheures Jenseits' (110). The voices speak of an unidentifiable place and time. Throughout the whole play, an ambiguity of time alludes to a certain necessary forgetting in the play. At the very beginning, 'Gott der Herr' refers to a certain 'Bund' constructed long ago between humans and their God. Over time, these humans have forgotten their ties. As a consequence, they no longer know their God nor do they believe in or fear anything beyond. We read in *Jeder-mann*:

> In Sünd ersoffen, das ist was sie sind,
> Und kennen mich nicht für ihren Gott,
> Ihr Trachten geht auf irdisch Gut allein
> Und was darüber, das ist ihr Spott
> ........................................................
> Des geistlichen Auges sind sie erblindt
> ........................................................
> So han sie rein vergessen den Bund
> Den ich mit ihnen aufgericht hab. (35)

As Nägele points out, Augustine understood time as moving from vanishing point to vanishing point, each tense of time then disappearing. In the eleventh book of the *Confessions*, Augustine (1914, 14) starts an investigation of time with the question 'Quid est enim tempus?' Nägele writes in *Reading after Freud* (1987, 175):

> The past is no more, the future is not yet; and when Augustine wants to hold on to that which seems to be, the present, it dissolves under the analytical gaze into points without extension of time. It is a non-time. And yet Augustine, like Hegel and Freud after him, insists that what is said is true, that language does not lie. We do say that the past was, the present is, and the future will be. The question is, how and where *are* they: what is the being of time? Here Augustine makes the decisive move from presence to representation which articulates the correct form of the tenses as *praesens de praesentibus, praesens de praeteritis, praesens de futuris* (20, 26): the presence of something which *itself is not*, and which is yet the foundation of presence.

A certain 'Nachträglichkeit', or 'belatedness', becomes necessary. Nägele continues:

> *Nachträglichkeit* touches upon the fundamental relationship between event and history [...] It designates the transformation and rewriting of experiences, impressions, and memory traces on the basis of later experiences [...] all phenomena of *Nachträglichkeit* are marked by a period of *latency*, of *forgetting*. (175)

The progression of time has caused forgetting. The act of forgetting is necessary, in our context, because it allows us to understand the

'Bund', of which the stage God speaks, in a different context. As Bennet (1988) argues in his essay on Hofmannsthal, the stage enacts self-consciousness as a quasi-divine capability to which Hofmannsthal later gives the name 'pre-Existenz'. As memory it renders past and present mysteriously simultaneous, overcoming time. Our existence, however, no sooner begins to make sense to us, as a 'glorious' taste of eternity, than it turns out to be senseless. Our existence, to be viewed as a totality, must in some sense have been terminated. We must do what the actor does, the good actor, when, after having thought about his role as a totality, he takes a firm grip and places himself in the midst of it, no longer outside as knower and creator but now somehow inside, as the character himself (70–71). We are no longer 'bound' to culture and narrative.

Walter Benjamin has a similar understanding of history. As Wolfgang Matz (1989) writes,

> Der Geschichtspessimismus, den Benjamin im *Ursprung des deutschen Trauer-spiels* formuliert, ist 'die elementare Naturgewalt im historischen Geschehen' (308) die auch Hofmannsthal zu gestalten sucht, und kein Zufall, daß beide ihre Gedanken am gleichen Gegenstande, dem barocken Trauerspiel und Mär-tyrerdrama entwickeln.

The power of the progress of history is disrupted. Yet Hofmannsthal would never actively accomplish what his text does on its own: 'Hofmannsthal war das Illusionäre seines Entwurfes bewußt' (53–54). Significantly, and in agreement with Nietzsche's understanding of history, the individual must be posited *against* his time and tradition rather than in it. In 'Unzeitgemässe Betrachtungen II' (Nietzsche, F. 1988d, 247) we read:

> So viel muss ich mir aber selbst von Berufs wegen als classischer Philologe zugestehen dürfen: denn ich wüsste nicht, was die classische Philologie in unserer Zeit für einen Sinn hätte, wenn nicht den, in ihr unzeitgemäss – das heisst gegen die Zeit und dadurch auf die Zeit und hoffentlich zu Gunsten einer kommenden Zeit – zu wirken.

The temporality and rigid framework of the play prove to be in fact unreliable.

Yet the spectator, who is watching the play from beginning to end and is, perhaps, looking at his watch from time to time, remains conscious of the play's limits in terms of outside time. Nonetheless, the open beginning and the open end render these limits meaningless in the world on stage. The play begins with 'Jetzt' and ends with 'Nun'. The former immediately situates the spectator within the present moment. The word declares itself to us now, but, as we have seen, the temporality of it is now obscure. The date of conception is not adequate for describing the now of the text. Aside from explicit reference to the present imperative, the 'Jetzt' at the beginning of the play also points to its importance by comparing the past, present, and future with it:

> SPIELANSAGER. Jetzt habet allsamt Achtung Leut
> Und hört was wir vorstellen heut!
> ......................................................
> Darin euch wird gewiesen werden,
> Wie unsere Tag und Werk auf Erden
> Vergänglich sind und hinfälling gar....
> GOTT DER HERR.
> ......................................................
> Und wie ich sie mir anschau zur Stund
> So han sie rein vergessen den Bund. (35)

Furthermore, the importance of the 'now' is established not just by the multiple appearances in the text (as 'jetzt' and 'nun'), nor by the use of the present tense, but also by the obvious significance of what happens during those repeated occurrences. For our own purposes, the one who actively enters into the depth of the boundless 'Augenblick' at the critical time understands the speech of those things that cannot be uttered and ultimately encounters the presence of God. The propitious moment or 'der erfüllte Augenblick' is the moment in which the divine re-appears as the place of origin and as the beginning. In his essay on Hölderlin's 'Feiertage', *Erläuterungen zu Hölderlins Dichtung* (1971), Heidegger writes of a connection to the holy. He concentrates on Hölderlin's words that indicate the limits of temporality. Thus, he says of Hölderlin's 'Jetzt aber tagts!' that the 'jetzt' speaks of the approach of the holy. The holy approaches as a distinctive now, but this now is not a temporal now in the conventional sense. Heidegger writes of the temporality of the now by illuminating Hölderlin's 'Ist eine Weile das Schiksaal' (105). According to Heidegger, 'weilen' has a distinctive constancy: 'Wenn dieser gar noch auf Anfang und Ende verzichten kann, erhebt sich die anfang- und endlose Dauer zum Schein des reinsten Bleiben' (106). Thus, the past as past, the present as present, the future as future, all remain in a constancy which destines itself as, according to the speaking of the poet, a peculiar and distinctive 'weilen'. This illumination of Hölderlin's word 'Weile' is Heidegger's highly condensed attempt to think through past, present, and future time as a unity which lingers and thus shows the nature of being as presence.

The audience is urged to understand this at the very start of the play. Merely closing the textbook or lowering the curtain does not suffice to 'end' the play: that is, for the play to truly end it must return to its origin, its source or essence. For us, the source of origin is its definition as a mystery play, as well as its beginning with the raising of the curtain. The end takes us back to the beginning once again and, as we encounter the same again yet differently, through the repeated 'Umkehr', we arrive at this higher, holy presence. In his same letter to Elsa Bruckmann-Cantacuzène, Hofmannsthal (1990, 292) writes:

> Man macht halt, wozu man sich getrieben fühlt, lernt daran, kommt weiter und hoffentlich nicht im Kreise herum, sondern in einer Spirale nach oben. Da berührt man scheinbar den gleichen Punkt, aber auf einer höheren Windung [...]

Jedermann is able to do so at the end of the play: the moment of the 'Augenblick' is the moment Jedermann enters into the grave. Already the title of the play emphasizes the importance of actively dying above Death: *Jedermann: Das Spiel vom Sterben des reichen Mannes*. Just as 'Schweigen' implies more than just *not* speaking, 'sterben' means more than merely *not* living. It is an action. As Jedermann comes closer to this moment of this 'action' of 'sterben', his appearance changes as well: 'Sein Angesicht ist totenbleich aber verklärt' (94). Unlike a play such as *Der Tor und der Tod*, *Jedermann* portrays the high moment of progression in self-consciousness that is ultimately followed by the highest moment attainable:

> JEDERMANN *schließt die Augen.*
> Nun muß ich ins Grab, das ist schwarz wie die Nacht,
> Erbarm dich meiner in deiner Allmacht. (95)

As Jedermann begins to believe actively without seeing, Glaube acquires a new role.[15] Werke also achieves a new purpose as Jedermann consciously climbs into the grave.[16] Jedermann experiences new faith and works at the cross, where he 'goes into' a final knowledge of the divine:

> WERKE *hilft ihm ins Grab, steigt dann zu ihm hinein.*
> Herr laß das Ende sanft uns sein,
> Wir gehen in deine Freuden ein. (95)

'Eingehen in', to go into (accusative) something, to perish into something or to arrive into something, fulfills all three definitions in Jedermann's *act* of going into the grave. His works speak for him in the plural 'wir' once he has lost his former identity. Furthermore, Death as a character sent by the stage character God to call Jedermann before the judgment seat has lost its power to death: '*Der Tod ist hervorgetreten und geht hinter ihnen einher*' (94). Death loses its meaning and the audience experiences an active interaction with the theater.

Jedermann is every man. The play *Jedermann* about a 'reicher Mann' intends a criticism of the materialism of every individual and his belief that riches make happy. Therefore, Jedermann's 'Sprachnot' is every person's 'Sprachnot'. The spectator realizes that the same will happen to everyone seated in the audience as has happened to Jedermann. As the play progresses, each person begins to recognize his individual responsibility for his own 'ich' in that final moment of death, as Jedermann sinks and the angels sing, when the individual must decide what his actions will be. Writing about the self and its necessary separation from itself in order to reach authenticity, Heidegger (1989, 88) states in *Beiträge zur Philosophie*:

> Das Auseinandertreten selbst, das scheidet und im Scheiden erst in das Spiel kommen läßt die Er-eignung eben dieses im Offenen als der Lichtung für das

Sichverbergende und noch Unentschiedene, die Zugehörigkeit des Menschen zum Seyn als des Gründers seiner Wahrheit und die Zugewiesenheit des Seyns in die Zeit des letzten Gottes.

Such an understanding of the decision is circular. Confrontation with the decision brings forth the division that allows for something to be outstanding and 'not yet decided'. It is not only a matter of 'das Treffen einer Wahl'. The 'Ent-scheidung' is also a chasm between the stage and man. By this splitting, the 'Ent-scheidung' allows things to step forward as matters for decision. The decision is not decided ('getroffen') in the normal sense as much as it is made through a 'leap' into Being.

The spectator must also decide whether he is willing to allow the transition from *having* to *being* to take place and to take this leap of faith into the 'Augenblick' as a constant recurring of the original. He is not forced to do so. The ending turns, however, into a calling to the audience to be conscious of what occurs at the moment of death. Jedermann sinks into the grave and angels sing from beyond the stage. We are soon back at the beginning, called by the 'Spielansager' to make a decision 'Jetzt' that ultimately leads to a 'conversion',[17] which, in turn, will endlessly repeat itself. Consequently, a great openness comes together in the ending of the play. The gap between the stage and the audience is dissolved and the threshold between theater and life is crossed. The transition from stage to life has begun as God becomes present on the stage: 'O Herr und Heiland steh mir bei' (95), cries out Jedermann, as he enters into the 'Ewigkeit' of the grave. At this moment a transfer occurs from the inexpressible sigh 'O' to 'Herr' and 'Heiland', who emerges on the stage. Jedermann's last words remind us of the metaphorical expression of the sheep who will be reunited with their shepherd on that final day:

So wahre jetzt der Seele mein,
Daß sie nit mög verloren sein
Und daß sie am jüngsten Tag auffahr
Zu dir mit der geretteten Schar. (95)

Hofmannsthal's *Jedermann* offers a radically different theatrical closure: through a constant repetition of inversions and negations, the spectator is presented with an 'open' end in which he can now encounter the presence of the divine. Hofmannsthal's final words in the preface express the necessity of a repeated occurence: 'Vielleicht geschieht es zum letztenmal, vielleicht muß es später durch den Zugehörigen einer künftigen Zeit noch einmal geschehen' (33). In this manner, a 'modernization' of the 'Märchen' will continue to take place and a new version will be necessarily rewritten ('verdichtet') as the times change.

# Chapter Three
## Borchert's *Draußen vor der Tür*

Germany's unconditional surrender on May 9, 1945 brought an end to a dark political and social period but no immediate replacement of great promise. Hans Erich Nossack gives a vivid and factual description of life in Hamburg at the end of 1945:

> Vor allem ist da aber die Kälte, die Gedanken verwirren sich darüber [...] Die meisten Menschen laufen mit geschwollenen Fingern und offenen Wunden umher, und es lähmt alle Tätigkeit [...] Erst ab 3 Uhr gehen die Verkehrsmittel wieder, [und ich] bin dann aber auch so erfroren, zumal ich nur zwei Scheiben trockenes Brot mitnehmen kann [...][1]

As Heinrich Böll comments in an interview with Siegfried Lenz (1982), the chaotic circumstances had a leveling, almost anarchistic effect on society without creating a society that was more than conditionally 'new':

> Es gab ja eine neue Gesellschaft, eine andere, sagen wir nicht neu, das ist zu positiv, sondern von der Geschichte in eine bestimmte Situation hineingezwungene Gesellschaft, in der ich keinen Klassenunterschied festgestellt habe. Natürlich gab's irgendwo reiche Leute, für die dieser dreckige Alltag gar nicht existierte. Aber ich erinnere mich nicht, daß Unterschiede etwa zwischen einem Oberstudienrat oder einem Arbeiter oder mir bestehen, wenn's ums Fressen ging. (55)

Germans had to readjust themselves to their own traditions and accomplishments as well as to those of foreign countries.

The first theater production after the war took place as early as May 1945 in Berlin, and by the end of the year no fewer than sixteen theaters and opera houses were functioning in the old capital alone. Hungry for the art and culture that it had been deprived of during those years of the Third Reich, much of the public was willing to spend its money on literary events and articles. Yet fewer people were truly interested in hearing what the contemporary authors were writing. Heinrich Vormweg (n.d.) reports:

> Ich habe alles gelesen, was erreichbar war. Nichts von dem Neuen heilt, so schien mir [...] Ich entdeckte, daß die Zukunft für mich in der Vergangenheit lag, in der Literatur der Vergangenheit, die alles übertraf, so schien mir, was die Gegenwart hervorbrachte. Und in den Literaturen der anderen Länder [...] Die T. S. Eliot-Euphorie bekam ich schon direkt mit. Aber da war auch Rilke für mich noch etwas ganz Neues. Dann Thornton Wilder und Sartre und Gide und Heinrich Mann und Hemingway und so weiter. Sie blieben wichtiger als die Autoren der vorgeschützten wie der erlittenen inneren Emigration. Auch als die neuen jungen Autoren.

Both Wolfgang Borchert and Beckmann, the protagonist of Borchert's only drama, find themselves in 'Stunde null', an environment in which time and history have come to a standstill at the point where religion no longer offers consolation and the continuity of religious tradition has been ruptured.

With the onset of modernity man ceased believing in God. At the end of World War II, the modern German man no longer believes in anything. His newly found realistic and materialistic understanding of the world promises no insight into a greater meaning or context. Economical and political distress and World War II prompted Germany to repeat the 'question of Being' that Friedrich Nietzsche so polemically proclaimed in his philosophy at the end of the century. According to Martin Heidegger, Being appears in the existentialist philosophy after the war as 'verschlossen' and, according to Karl Jaspers, as penetrable only in certain aspects, and never completely. Man has become estranged from his self and feels surrounded by nothingness.

The expression 'Menschen zwischen Ruinen', attributed to one of the authors whose writing portrayed the reality of the situation after World War II, refers not only to a theme in such works, but also to the author's own mentality. The 'Heimkehrer', former soldiers and prisoners, could see reality only as it is because they no longer had the 'rosarote, blaue, schwarze Brillen' of earlier idealists. Returning from the war, these authors found it difficult to articulate experiences to which they could no longer apply the language of earlier generations and for which they had none of their own. In turn, their literature reminds society that the 'Zerstörung unserer Welt', because it went beyond the physical and therefore reparable reality, would not disappear in a few years.[2] Physical as well as mental hunger, cold, and death became such an all-consuming part of everyday life that society no longer saw any relevance in traditional morals.

Virtually overnight, Wolfgang Borchert, a mentally exhausted and physically sick returning soldier, achieved incredible success. Borchert wrote his only play, *Draußen vor der Tür*, in just one week in late 1946. It was first produced as a 'Hörspiel' on February 13, 1947, and in November of the same year on the stage. As a radio play, it made Borchert famous overnight by savagely portraying society's moral, political, and religious situation at the end of the war. As both a radio play and stage play, *Draußen vor der Tür*, which was premiered in Hamburg on the day after Borchert's untimely death, quickly became a central topic of discussion. Helmut Gumtau (1969, 71) attributes the immediate success of the play primarily to its timing: 'Die Wirkung, erinnert sich der erfahrene Rundfunkmann, war "ungeheuer: Ich habe so etwas noch nie erlebt." Borchert kam weder zu früh noch zu spät. Er hatte das Glück der rechten Stunde'. Although only 26 at the time of his death, Borchert was already famous. His play was not only soon discussed and performed in many theaters outside of Hamburg but was also filmed in 1948 under the title 'Liebe 47'.

Yet as time passed, society lost its initial enthusiasm and came to view this play, as Wulf Köpke (1984, 84) writes, 'als Übergang und Vorläufer'. Now seen as a literary work of lesser quality,[3] the play soon seemed forgotten. Gumtau (1969, 10–11) writes:

Unsere jungen Zeitgenossen empfinden die Fragen noch immer als ungelöst, die vor und nach dem ersten Zusammenbruch von 1918 die Jugend bedrängten. Wieder geht es darum, den Zustand des entstellten, gepeinigten, irregeleiteten Menschen aufzuheben und sicht- und denkbar zu machen, was wir sein und was wir tun sollten.

Today, the play's recognition and popularity are concealed by a certain reservation: it, along with all of Borchert's other works, must be taken as 'zeitgebunden' and relevant mainly for a certain group of

77

people as the experience of a brief period during a bygone time. Just two decades after the premiere, Borchert's work was only rarely mentioned. Even these critics found in Borchert, no less than in many other representatives of 'Nachkriegsliteratur', merely humanitarian pathos and self-pity.

Neither a religion nor any moral, social, or political ideology can possibly offer support and hope for the despairing and isolated individual in the apathetic world that Beckmann encounters. Borchert expresses his isolated stance clearly in the play's subtitle: *Ein Stück, das kein Theater spielen und kein Publikum sehen will.* This is indeed a play that emphasizes the ugliness of the present, while much of contemporary society struggles to deal with the present situation by remembering the grandeur of the past. While the post-war society attempted to fill the loneliness of the social, moral, religious, and intellectual vacuum by evoking the esthetical beauty of previous ages, Borchert's work fell under the category of 'Kriegs-, Trümmer- und Heimkehrerliteratur'.

The majority of critics have missed the point made in this play. For example, Wilhelm Duwe (1962, 430) sees the play as a Passion Play in reverse. Wilhelm Grenzmann (1964, 307) characterizes the play as a document of the hopeless frustration of the youth of post-war Germany. Anna Maria Darboven (1957, 5) sees in the hero Beckmann simply a tired soldier returning from the war. Joseph Mileck (1959, 333–34) feels that Borchert could not come to terms with his society because Beckmann remains an existentialist hero steeped in his guilt. Karl Weimar (1956, 155) feels that the end of the play portrays Beckmann refusing to accept death and forgetting in favor of a vacuous life in an existential hell. Despite the wide range of views and serious analyses of the play, critics, and perhaps Borchert himself, have not been able to grasp its full significance. I suggest that exactly this expressionist/realist representation of the 'Stunde null' with its seemingly existentialist or nihilistic characteristics allows a reappearance of the divine.

Wolfgang Borchert's *Draußen* comes across as an expressionist, even absurd, existentialist, nihilist, and antireligious portrayal of man's desperate situation when facing the most dehumanizing processes of modern life. In it, political and social generalities give way to a moving portrayal of man's inner struggle to find a substitute for God and, consequently, personal meaning in society. The religious zeal mixed with the feelings of hope of the Expressionists has given way in Borchert's writing to the mere sense of inwardness and hopelessness, to an emotional and cognitive factor that seems more significant than external and physical appearance. As we have already seen with Hugo von Hofmannsthal, it is indeed possible that the creation separates itself from its creator and achieves a greatness of its own through the process of writing. While the playwright is and remains the creator of his play, the self-creative and self-productive character of a particular literary text is able to inspire and motivate an inward transformation and revelation of something new within the text.

*Draußen* allows the emergence of an overpowering and omnipresent divine being on the stage and, consequently, a new reading of a seemingly nihilistic work of 'Trümmerliteratur'. It does not try to adjust existence to life's absurdity, nor does it celebrate a search for a new 'man'. As we shall see, the spectators of *Draußen,* like those of *Jedermann,* are provided an opportunity to experience the presence of the divine. This occurs as soon as they recognize the insufficiency of the God portrayed by Borchert on the stage and the deficiency of the play's language as manifested in the internal contradictions and negations characteristic of the 'Sprachnot' that cripples the returning soldier.

In the play *Draußen*, Borchert distinguishes the dominant metaphor of confinement by the symbol of the closed door which marks the main character as being excluded from instead of welcomed into society. Beckmann's situation is similar to that of Jedermann, who looks desperately for support in his time of need from his worldly friends. He, like Beckmann, becomes discouraged and terrified when he realizes on his solitary road to God that society refuses to be concerned. Weimar (1956, 153) also sees a resemblance between Borchert's Beckmann and Jean-Paul Sartre's figures in *Huis Clos*:

> Sartre's three are forever sealed within the walls of society in *Huis Clos*. The closed door of the original titles, *Draußen* and *Huis Clos,* is an unmistakable symbol of isolation and loneliness […] the one, despite his frantic drive, is

irremediably closed off from existence, and the other is ironically walled in toward existence.

The impenetrability of the doors and the physical finality of the conditions underscore the inability of the individual to rescue himself from his confinement. It is as if life were condensed to social circumstances that promise neither access to prior knowledge nor the possibility of a subsequent existence. The opposite understanding of confinement appears to underscore the situation of Beckmann. In fact, however, after returning from the war, he finds himself trapped inside a timeless vacuum with no connection to an interior life. Referring to Borchert, Stephen Spender (1952, v) writes: 'To read him is […] to study the sensibility of a man who is the victim of a machine which is itself destroyed, tearing his life down with it. His vision is entirely confined by this machine'.

Borchert's own progression toward the isolation that stems from entrapment by external social conditions is thematized by his characters' realization that they are imprisoned within the walls of the city and cannot perceive an order beyond their immediate surroundings. His short story 'Die Hundeblume' (1949e) provides an excellent example for the metaphor of a controlled prison environment in which people's interaction is reduced to a monotonous cycle of life and death, hate and alienation in an absurd society. Borchert captures the sense of imprisonment by describing the prison as a society of fellow sufferers, each suffering alone. Here, it is not a search for a way to enter society, but an individual's acceptance of his surroundings that provides personal salvation from the social confinement and thereby an escape, whether fleetingly or permanently, from the cycle of absurdity.

*Draußen* does not evoke a 'Vision' of the sort that Kasimir Eschmid ascribes to the Expressionists. The Expressionist writers desired to liberate their art from the enslaving effect of mimesis by actively searching for their vision behind limiting words and concepts. Their ability to objectify through abstraction makes them modernists. They shared a tendency to abstract through dream-like visualization. This, in turn, led to an inner spiritualization. In *Über den Expres-*

*sionismus in der Literatur und die neue Dichtung*, Edschmid (1919, 54) writes:

> So wird der ganze Raum des expressionistischen Künstlers Vision. Er sieht nicht, er schaut [...] Nun gibt es nicht mehr die Kette der Tatsachen: Fabriken, Häuser, Krankheit, Huren, Geschrei und Hunger. Nun gibt es ihre Vision.
>
> Die Tatsachen haben Bedeutung nur so weit, als, durch sie hindurchgreifend, die Hand des Künstlers nach dem fasst, was hinter ihnen steht.

There is no doubt in the spectator's mind that Borchert's hero is completely unable to transcend the immediate ugliness of reality:

> BECKMANN. Alles, alles kann ich nicht mehr da oben. Ich kann nicht mehr hungern. Ich kann nicht mehr humpeln und vor meinem Bett stehen und wieder aus dem Haus raushumpeln, weil das Bett besetzt ist. Das Bein, das Bett, das Brot – ich kann das nicht mehr, verstehst du!
> ELBE. Nein. Du Rotznase von einem Selbstmörder. Nein, hörst du! Glaubst du etwa, weil deine Frau nicht mehr mit dir spielen will, weil du hinken mußt und weil dein Bauch knurt, deswegen kannst du hier bei mir untern Rock kriechen? (137)

The spectator experiences neither the hope that the hero will somehow be brought out of his desperate state nor even the least reparation for Beckmann's fate. Beckmann must come to terms with the lasting impenetrability of the closed doors of society.

In the chaotic, godless, and desolate atmosphere of Germany during this time, everything that once gave society ethical form and meaning seems to have turned into formlessness and fragmentation. God, or at least a replacement for Him, seems to be desperately needed; there appears to be a need for, at the least, an 'Ersatzreligion' that can, if not fill the void, then at least offer a hope for limiting it. Yet the possibility of such a panacea seems remote. As we shall see, God, albeit a prominent figure in *Draußen*, finds that His common representative role as the all-powerful traditional God is now negated. His impotence, once discovered by the audience, brings into being an opening. In turn, this opening produces the presence of an omnipotent divine being or force. Beside allowing the presence of such a new God to appear on the stage, this opening also nullifies the importance of the closed doors of society and allows Beckmann, as he actively enters into the open 'nothingness' of the stage, to experience new religious values.

In *Draußen* God is 'ein alter Mann, an den keiner mehr glaubt':

> DER ALTE MANN *nicht jämmerlich, sondern erschüttert*. Kinder! Kinder! Kinder!
> BEERDIGUNGSUNTERNEHMER. Warum weinst du denn, Alter?
> DER ALTE MANN. Weil ich es nicht ändern kann, oh, weil ich es nicht ändern kann. (134)

The God on the stage is a helpless figure who, like man, must face the overwhelming inhumanity and nihilistic attitude of society. In Borchert's portrayal of Him, God appears not as timelessly youthful but as an old man, a fabrication of the theologians and other representtatives of the Church and now a mere symbol of the Christian religion, which has been reduced to a powerless ideology by the destructive consequences of the modernization of society. He is 'ein tintenblütiger Theologe [...] in den Kirchen eingemauert' who seems a bit 'zu theologisch' (182).

Christian theology, with its doctrines and ecclesial power structures, has over the centuries been transformed to eliminate any liberating ideas and is now completely devoid of its authority and control over the individual. As a stage character, Borchert's God represents religion and its false ideology of morals and values in society. In turn, the traditional view of man as made in God's image has become outdated. God's fate is one worse than death. He has become worthless.

As we have seen, the old man personifies the impotence of God. Yet he is also a personification of man. We find Beckmann reprimanding God for faults that apply equally well to Beckmann himself. For example, he reproaches God for having a soft voice. He also accuses God of allowing millions to die. Later Beckmann enjoins God to come alive with the others, while at the same time he himself begins to succumb to the death wish because he has allowed thousands to die. In short, he demands of God exactly what is missing in himself: the will to live and the absolution of guilt. Since God is merely a theological construct made in the image of man, once mankind falls apart, so does this image.

In Hofmannsthal's *Jedermann*, God, who makes His entry in the prologue of the play, is the angry God of the Old Testament, who punishes those who no longer keep His commandments. He comes as a deus ex machina and thunders his injured pride. Jedermann is no longer able or willing to accept such a representation. He therefore ultimately gains faith, not in the God of the stage, but in an unseen presence of the divine. This occurs at the moment he recognizes that sensually perceivable representations of, or material substitutes for, God are valueless. In that 'Augenblick', a God outside of man's construction or conceptualization of Him appears.

Belief and faith in God, in any God, seem impossible in *Drau-ßen*, however, as Beckmann, from the very beginning, shows awareness of his situation as hopeless. He does not accept anything, including the worthless theological representation of the Church, that is, God. This is clear already from the prologue. The meeting with God and death no longer takes place in heaven, but rather on the desolate earth. Furthermore, no longer is death sent by God to judge the world, as was the case in *Jedermann*. Instead, God has been replaced by a fat 'Beerdigungsunternehmer' and 'Strassenfeger, der gar keiner ist', both allegorical representations of 'der neue Gott' who underscores his grand entry by belching. This representation, of course, is well justified, for by the end of the war the Church found itself almost as bereft of esteem and stability as a defunct state. Death no longer provides an eternal haven but has been reduced to an allegorical representation of the seemingly eternal mortality and decomposition that alone constitute the history of mankind. Treated allegorically, Death devalues everything tainted by this-worldliness and turns it into lifeless representations. Paradoxically, these lifeless, meaningless signs have deceptively allegorical names but are little more than products of man's last attempt to retain command of an inverted world that has only generic designations.

In *Draußen* God, supposedly the answer to the 'sting' of Death, remains limited to society's traditional understanding of Him. As the individual desperately searches for some super-personal value in society and in himself, he finds only empty signs as remnants of society's understanding of religion.

At a time in his life when he realizes that contemporary society and individuals need God most, the desperate human being recognizes that the image of his youth, the traditional 'Gottesvorstellung', no longer satisfies his needs. Any hope for help is impossible since Beckmann, as just such a desperate person, can no longer see any reason to go on living. At this new time of need, the traditional, timeworn God cannot help. To the extent that all of the other characters in *Draußen* are no less mere projections of Beckmann's insights and reactions, they too have no other choice:

> DER ALTE MANN. Sie erschießen sich. Sie hängen sich auf. Sie ersaufen sich.
> (134)

In their despairing and desolate situation, the only sure way out for the hopeless and homeless and the only thing they can still believe in is His antithesis – death. Even the God on the stage recognizes this:

> GOTT. Der Tod? – Du hast es gut! Du bist der neue Gott! An dich glauben sie. Dich lieben sie. Dich fürchten sie […] (135)

Yet Borchert's understanding of God does not end here. His letter continues:

> Nun antworten Sie mir: Das Göttliche ist in uns und in allem Leben. Ja, wo sollte es anders sein! Aber sagen Sir mir auch: Wie soll ein junger Mensch unserer Zeit, der erkennt, daß seine kindliche Gottesvorstellung falsch war, der durch diesen Krieg und diesen Frieden hindurchgeht, wie soll er an das Gute, an das Göttliche glauben? Dazu bedarf es sicher einer großen inneren Reife und Festigkeit und – einer gewissen bürgerlichen Ruhe. Diese Eigenschaften aber kann und soll ein junger Mensch nicht haben. (118)

It follows then, that this play offers no fixed message or directive to which the young individual can clutch. Nor is such a message necessary or even desirable, since those who have 'bürgerliche Ruhe' cannot truly understand what it is like to have a heavy conscience, to be alone, desperate, cold, and surrounded by individuals with 'große innere Reife'. In turn, people with 'Reife' cannot know or understand what it is like to need God, nor can they ever know that the God they hold up will never be there for them when they need Him. In their complacency and arrogance, they have even dubbed this God 'lieb':

> BECKMANN: Ach, du bist also der liebe Gott. Wer hat dich eigentlich so genannt, lieber Gott? Die Menschen? Ja? Oder du selbst?
> GOTT: Die Menschen nennen mich den lieben Gott.
> BECKMANN: Seltsam, ja, das müssen ganz seltsame Menschen sein, die dich so nennen. Das sind wohl die Zufriedenen, die Satten, die Glücklichen,und die, die Angst vor dir haben. Die im Sonnenschein gehen, verliebt oder satt oder zufrieden – oder die es nachts mit der Angst kriegen, die sagen: Lieber Gott! Lieber Gott! Aber ich sage nicht Lieber Gott, du, ich kenne keinen, der ein lieber Gott ist, du! (181)

Beckmann belongs to neither the comfortable and satisfied 'bürger-liche' part of society, nor to the oppressed souls who have been indoctrinated to believe in and rely on the theological and oppressive God represented by the Church.

The voices that acknowledge the worthlessness of God in the play are the voices of those who have suffered and now find themselves faced with a great religious and social void. They cannot specify their need, nor are they willing to define and limit a presence of God within rigid concepts and empty assertions such as standing 'draußen vor der Tür'. For the moment, however, while they disavow the inverted order of the old theologian with ink in his veins, they are not aware of the presence of the divine. To their disavowals God answers: 'Ich bin der Gott, an den keiner mehr glaubt. Und um den sich keiner mehr kümmert [...] Meine Kinder haben sich von mir gewandt, nicht ich von ihnen [...] Ich kann es doch nicht ändern' (182). God has not abandoned mankind; mankind has forgotten God in the same way that the God in *Jedermann* has been forgotten.

However, this God on the stage is not intended to represent the same God for whom countless generations have been searching and whom only few individuals have found. He is merely a shade, a God without substance that society has constructed over the centuries. Many spectators may well belong to those seeking the God of substance, such as Michelangelo's Sistine Chapel ceiling portrays, but He can no longer be represented. Consequently, in order for the spectator to become free of the constricting character of text and stage representation, he must employ his 'Vorstellungskraft', an ability stimulated by the means of theatrical presentation and beyond the stage. God in modern society has become such a pitifully weak chimera that even his representation can no longer be used as a deus ex machina. He can no longer even open the doors in front of which Beckmann stands. When Beckmann accuses God of being too 'leise', it is because the God of the stage and His mediator, the Church, have lost their voices.

God's voice emerges precisely in the seeming nothingness of the stage. What we see, that is, the visible and the representable, *turns* into its opposite:

> BECKMANN. Geh weg, alter Mann. Du verdirbst mir meinen Tod. Geh weg, ich sehe, du bist nur ein weinerlicher Theologe. Du drehst die Sätze um. (182)

Beckmann denies and resents the image of God that society has constructed. Yet, paradoxically, this representation is necessary, for precisely this patently grotesque portrayal of God stimulates the audience to think in terms of its opposite. The powerful atmosphere of negativity, combined with Beckmann's obvious yearning for God, creates in the audience the necessary receptivity for a new voice, a new text, and ultimately a new life 'draußen vor der Tür'.

Contrary to a belief held by various critics[4] and against any tendency to oversimplify the play's patent symbolism, Borchert stresses the need for abstract words, images, and sounds. Critics have tried to explain the seemingly random form and style and frantic pace of the play by recourse to the short time, a week, in which the author wrote it with obviously heated, creative anguish. *Draußen* appeared first as a radio play and remained unchanged for the stage. Although many critics disagree, Wilhem Duwe (1962, 429) correctly states that the technical aspects have nothing to do with the fact that the play was written for the radio. Traditional and everyday descriptive statements yield to a new and dynamic style about which Borchert writes in 'Das ist unser Manifest' (1949a, 371):

> Für Semikolons haben wir keine Zeit und die Harmonien machen uns weich und die Stilleben überwältigen uns: Denn lila sind nachts unsere Himmel. Und

das Lila gibt keine Zeit für Grammatik, das Lila ist schrill und ununterbrochen und toll [...]

Borchert's sentences display a patent disregard for the correct use of grammar. His work recalls that of the Expressionists, for in it words are missing, punctuation is omitted or overused, and compounds vary. A plot does not develop through cause and effect relationships, but rather through the language. Edschmid (1919, 66) writes of *Draußen*: 'das Wort erhält andere Gewalt [...] Es wird Pfeil. Trifft in das Innere des Gegenstands und wird von ihm beseelt.' Consequently, the artist's metaphysical obligation is humbly acknowledged: 'Aber die Menschheit weiß noch nicht, daß die Kunst nur eine Etappe ist zu Gott. Die Ziele aber liegen nahe bei Gott' (66). Many critics mistakenly believe that Borchert's success lies not in the language, but in the timelessness of his theme. Among them is Gumtau (1969, 71), who writes of the radio premiere:

Der Erfolg war nicht im Dichterischen begründet [...] Als sprachliches Ganzes ist das Stück ein unbedenklicher Entwurf [...] von den lakonisch strengge-formten Texten sind literarische Wirkungen ausgegangen, die dem Drama nicht vergönnt waren.

Although this is a widely shared view and perhaps one of the contributing factors to the play's short-lived success, language and form in fact form the door. Once this door is opened, the presence of the divine can be intuited and the vacuum of the age envisioned as filled.

Unlike either the metaphysically inclined Expressionists or the politically driven ones, Borchert did not expect post-World War II literature to evoke new hope for fraternization, love, and a better world. Toward the end of World War I, the Expressionist Yvan Goll (1917, 599–600) understood the mission of the artist in far vaguer terms: 'Kunst ist kein Beruf. Kunst ist kein Schicksal. Kunst ist Liebe [...] Darum, Künstler, tritt ins Volk und zeige ihm dein grosses Herz. Deine Rufe und den Menschen, deine Volksreden, werden Gedichte sein. Du hast das äußerste Mittel der Liebe zur Verfügung: du hast Gott.' A generation later, modernist Borchert's motto for the radio play *Draußen* was:

Eine Injektion Nihilismus
bewirkt oft,
daß man aus lauter Angst
wieder Mut zum Leben bekommt.[5]

Existential fear is overcome by an injection of nihilism, not by adorning life with idealistic values. It is truly the 'Stunde null' for many writers, because nihilism has supplanted God. Paradoxically, however, one can claim this for Borchert's drama only to the extent that one admits that such nihilism allows room for a scarcely perceivable hope in a new life. For example, Borchert makes constant use of the symbol of the lantern, with which he identifies himself. In his small collection of poetry *Laterne, Nacht und Sterne: Gedichte um Hamburg* (1949i), he affirms the individual's perspective and reasserts the messianic claim of Expressionism. The last line of his poem 'Laternentraum' distinctly expresses the incongruity between a close, personal relationship of the individual, with a 'you', and a simultaneously insecure, nihilistic perspective – 'per Du' is juxtaposed with the despairing reading of the words as 'perdu':

Ja, ich möchte immerhin,
wenn ich tot bin,
so eine Laterne sein,
die nachts ganz allein,
wenn alles schläft auf der Welt,
sich mit dem Mond unterhält –
natürlich per Du. (16)

In fact, much in Borchert's collection is a perfect example of the recurring combination of nihilism and hope. For example, we read in another poem:

Ich möchte Leuchtturm sein
in Nacht und Wind –
für Dorsch und Stint,
für jedes Boot –
und ich bin doch selbst
ein Schiff in Not! (13)

Similarly, Borchert allows the language of *Draußen* to shift randomly from the enthusiastically lyrical but often bombastically abstract style of the early Expressionists to the banal, crude, and unambitious jargon of the war and everyday speech.

Far from just a scream of anguish and disillusionment, Borchert's style, at once lyrical and rhetorical, is rich in such self-consciously literary devices as alliteration, assonance, and repetition. If a spectator or a listener allows herself to consider closely the play *Draußen* from two perspectives based on the opposing poles of the variability of language and the demands of mimesis, she begins to sense through her new 'listening' and 'observing' another dimension of which she was not aware before. The play manages to acquire a power and energy of its own and a new voice through which God reveals His presence to us. Our task is to allow it to do so by using our 'Vorstellungskraft', our power of imagination/presentation.

In situations where the audience expects it to communicate information, the language of *Draußen* has been reduced to very simple phrases and words that serve, at best, to express only a character's feelings. Yet this very simplification imbues them with new energy and power:

> BECKMANN. Jawohl, Herr Oberst. So ist es. Ein bißchen leise. Ein bißchen weich. Und müde, Herr Oberst, müde, müde, müde! Ich kann nämlich nicht schlafen, Herr Oberst, keine Nacht, Herr Oberst. Und deswegen komme ich her, darum komme ich zu Ihnen, Herr Oberst, denn ich weiß, Sie können mir helfen. Ich will endlich mal wieder pennen! Mehr will ich ja gar nicht. Nur pennen. Tief, tief, pennen. (152)

In the face of this new reality that he has conjured up solely through his words, Beckmann communicates a strong desire to go deeply into the realm of sleep. He later explains his wish to the 'Andere': 'Ein Herz hat man, das will pennen, tief in der Elbe, verstehst du' (176). The word 'müde' gains progressively more significance as Beckmann repeats it four times. He then ends the fragmentary sentence with an exclamation point. Afterwards he lets himself slip back into a dream-like state when he ends with the words 'Tief, tief pennen'. 'Pennen' and other colloquial terms are regularly used instead of their more formal counterparts to provide constant reminders of the reality of the situation. Yet the adverbs 'tief' and 'endlich' give the strictly collo-quial verb 'pennen' a depth and dimensionality it did not possess before.

In the second scene, Beckmann comments on the oversized jacket of the girl's missing husband. Although this may seem to have no purpose other than merely pointing to the symbolism of death by drowning in the Elbe, words lose their *raison d'être* as signifiers once Beckmann begins his soliloquy, in which he does not use the more traditional military verb 'fallen', but rather the subjective 'liegen-bleiben':

> BECKMANN *starr*. In Stalingrad? In Stalingrad, ja. Ja, in Stalingrad, da ist mancher liegengeblieben. Aber einige kommen auch wieder. Und die ziehen dann das Zeug an von denen, die nicht wiederkommen. Der Mann, der Ihr Mann war, der der Riese war, dem dieses Zeug gehört, der ist liegengeblieben. Und ich, ich komme nun her und ziehe sein Zeug an. Das ist schön, nicht wahr? Ist das nicht schön? Und seine Jacke ist so riesig, daß ich fast darin ersaufe. (*hastig*) Ich muß sie wieder ausziehen. Doch ich muß wieder mein nasses Zeug anziehen. Ich komme um in dieser Jacke. Sie erwürgt mich, diese Jacke. Ich bin ja ein Witz in dieser Jacke. Ein grauenhafter, gemeiner Witz, den der Krieg gemacht hat. Ich will die Jacke nicht mehr anhaben. (145)

We see not a body gripped by tension but rather a developing tension within language that becomes a body. As the intensification of relative pronouns that describe the missing soldier increases, so does the anxiety: 'Der Mann, der Ihr Mann war, der der Riese war, dem dieses Zeug gehört, der ist liegengeblieben. Und ich, ich komme nun her und ziehe sein Zeug an.' The bad fit of the soldier's uniform emphasizes that Beckmann is not merely 'einer von denen'. Instead, this act stresses the converse fact that Beckmann himself is no less an indi-vidual and can neither replace another nor be replaced by him.

Beckmann's difficulty in coming to terms with his own identity determines his reactions to how other characters treat him. The 'Oberst' commands him: 'Werden Sie erstmal wieder ein Mensch!!!' (159). The 'Direktor' insists: 'Werden Sie jemand!' (165), that is, forget your time as a soldier without individuality. In the warm room of the girl, Beckmann tries for the moment not to identify with his old self; instead, he assumes the mannerisms of another. His fragmentary

90

sentences are now no longer saturated with the relative clauses that characterize the other man. Instead, he suddenly switches to the first person pronoun and proceeds to repeat the word 'ich' eight times in the following few lines. This moment of identification is the beginning of Beckmann's process of coming to terms with his position 'draußen vor der Tür'.

The limits of language are finally reached and the 'Sprachnot' of the characters creates a caesura. The girl cannot deal with the tension created by Beckmann's words:

> MÄDCHEN (*warm, verzweifelt*). Sei still, Fisch. Behalt sie an, bitte. Du gefällst mir so, Fisch. (145)

As she continues to talk, the silence that greets her words becomes intolerable for her:

> Du sagst gar nichts. Sag was, Fisch, bitte. Sag irgendwas. Es braucht keinen Sinn zu haben, aber sag was. Sag was, Fisch, es ist doch so entsetzlich still in der Welt. Sag was, dann ist man nicht so allein [...] Komm und sag was, damit etwas da ist. Fühlst du nicht, wie grauenhaft still es ist? (145)

In 'Was ist Metaphysik?' Heidegger (1976a, 105) asks: 'Wie steht es um das Nichts?' He then suggests that this question deprives itself of its own subject. In his view, in the state of 'Angst', our feelings are like those in an encounter with the nothing. 'Angst' reveals the nothing: 'Die Angst offenbart das Nichts' (112). Heidegger tries to explain this more fully:

> Das Nichts enthüllt sich in der Angst – aber nicht als Seiendes. Es wird ebensowenig als Gegenstand gegeben. Die Angst ist kein Erfassen des Nichts. Gleichwohl wird das Nichts durch sie und in ihr offenbar [...] Wir sagten vielmehr: das Nichts begegnet in der Angst in eins mit dem Seienden im Ganzen. (113)

Furthermore, Heidegger's words in *Sein und Zeit* (1949, 255), 'Nur solange Dasein ist, gibt es Sein,' seem at first sight to confirm his belief that human subjectivity is ultimate. But he also points out that there are inverted commas around the words 'es gibt' to draw attention to the fact that in German the expression 'es gibt' means literally 'it gives': the 'it' that here 'gives' is Being itself. On Borchert's stage, the 'es' appears within the constantly reforming chiasmus between the 'ich' and the 'du' as what can be characterized in the Christian *Weltanschauung* only as the divine. It is a mysterious, unknown quantity. For example, Beckman is unable to express what he feels. He responds to the girl's question instead with the visual act of 'ansehen':

> BECKMANN *verwirrt*. Ich sehe dich gerne an. Dich, ja. Aber ich habe bei jedem Schritt Angst, daß es rückwärts geht. Du, das hab ich. (146)

Consequently, the first- and the second-person personal pronouns reflect each other. 'Ich' looks ('ansehen') at 'dich' and then reflects back onto itself again: 'Ich ⟵⟶ dich'. Furthermore, a chiasmus develops:

> Ich sehe dich gerne an.
> Du, das habe ich.

This chiasmus confirms the self-reflection of the 'ich' and the 'du/dich'. However, in this process, the 'ich' cannot remain stationary. Instead, it exists in a constantly moving and shifting state. 'Aber' at the middle of this exchange forms a focal point, the center point of a circle around which the pronouns turn and return but never reach a beginning, an end, or a fixed state. Furthermore, Beckmann's fear that the 'es' will go backwards is the 'Angst' necessary to disclose the nothingness. What remains within the individual, that is, the feelings and perceptions that can never be expressed, reaches a climax at this turning point as the movement of the inversion continues to increase in energy and direction towards a projected nothingness.

The spectator begins to perceive that the alliterations and the rhythm provide a tempo that seems to pulsate with life. These musical elements form a basis for understanding Beckmann's experience. The characters hear and feel this with a keen and sensitive ear and pass it on from the stage. Meyer-Marwitz, in the epilogue to Borchert's *Gesamtwerk*, describes this process:

> Die für Borchert charakteristischen Wiederholungen, Worthäufungen und Satzvariationen […] enthüllen ihre letzten eigenwilligen Feinheiten, Feinheiten

92

einer stark rhythmischen Musikalität, erst dann, wenn sie wieder Ton werden, also zur ursprünglichen Bestimmung der Sprache zurückkehren. Ein unbewußter Kontrapunkt steckt in diesen Worthäufungen und Wiederholungen. Man täte Borchert Unrecht, wollte man sie als Manier bezeichnen, die um jeden Preis originell zu sein beabsichtigt. Borchert schrieb Klänge, Klangreihen, gebrochene Akkorde. Das ist das Geheimnis seiner flutenden Dynamik, seiner ungewöhnlichen Lebendigkeit. (287–88)

Besides the repeated leitmotiv of the creaking door that closes, the gurgle of the alcohol bottle, the labored breathing, and the repeated use of onomatopoetic words, sounds throughout the play are magnified or diminished. Every sentence pulsates with activity, rhythm, and movement.

Beckmann understands why he never became an officer during the war: 'Meine Stimme war zu leise, Herr Oberst, meine Stimme war zu leise' (152). Now, however, his soft voice is generating extraordinary energy:

> BECKMANN *schlaftrunken, traumhaft.* Hören Sie, Herr Oberst? Dann ist es gut. Wenn Sie hören, Herr Oberst. Ich will Ihnen nämlich meinen Traum erzählen, Herr Oberst. Den Traum träume ich jede Nacht. Dann wache ich auf, weil jemand so grauenhaft schreit. Und wissen Sie, wer das ist, der da schreit? Ich selbst, Herr Oberst, ich selbst. Ulkig, nicht, Herr Oberst? Und dann kann ich nicht wieder einschlafen. Keine Nacht, Herr Oberst. Denken Sie mal, Herr Oberst, jede Nacht wachliegen. Deswegen bin ich müde, Herr Oberst, ganz furchtbar müde.
> MUTTER. Vater, bleib bei uns. Mich friert.
> OBERST *interessiert.* Aber von Ihrem Traum wachen Sie auf, sagen Sie?
> BECKMANN. Nein, von meinem Schrei. Nicht von dem Traum. Von dem Schrei. (153)

The crescendo in the unrelenting grinding on the same motifs with their nerve-racking musical rhythm creates an uncontrollable temptation for the spectator to come closer to the transforming emotions occurring on the stage. Referring to one of his short stories, 'Die Hundeblume' (1949e), Borchert clearly expresses his intent to force the reader into a complete identification with the prisoner:

> Ich weiß, es ist schwer mir zuzuhören und mit mir zu fühlen. Du sollst auch nicht zuhören, als wenn einer dir etwas von Gottfried Keller oder Dickens vorliest. Du sollst mit mir gehen, mitgehen in dem kleinen Kreis zwischen den

unerbittlichen Mauern. Nicht in Gedanken neben mir – nein, körperlich hinter mir als mein Hintermann. Und dann wirst du sehen, wie schnell du mich hassen lernst. Denn wenn du mit uns (ich sage jetzt 'uns', weil wir dieses eine alle gemeinsam haben) in unserm lendenlahmen Kreise wankst, dann bist du so leer von Liebe, daß der Haß wie Sekt in dir aufschäumt. (43–44)

In *Draußen* the viewers are urged especially to hear the events as if no physical or mental boundaries exist between them and the stage. The more the audience relies on words and not merely on the visual, the less conscious it is of the distance between it and the stage. The listener is also encouraged to immerse himself in the climactic movement that the characters on the stage are experiencing. In the short story, the reader is driven to identify with the prisoner, to walk behind him as the soldiers do their daily march, and to begin to feel the experience of hatred that the narrator feels for his fellow inmates. Beckmann's situation is similar.

Experience has become so intense for Beckmann that he enters into a '*schlaftrunken, traumhaft*' state of being. Only in such a state is he able to remember the recurring grotesque dream. This adds even more force to the moment. The first thing we are told, however, is that a scream torments his deep sleep. 'Jemand' disturbs his 'tief, tief pennen' with a scream ('Schrei'). This unidentifiable interrupts the experience of death that Beckmann has allowed himself to enter into in much the same manner that the Elbe did not allow him to remain in the death-like state 'unter[m] Rock'.

The identification process, however, cannot and does not continue on the same level. 'Jemand' has authored a new voice that creates a sudden and necessary gap between the stage and the audience. The act of 'schreien' belongs to the act of writing the 'zwanzigtausend unsichtbaren Seiten' of the world. 'Schreien' is part of a new text that expresses orally more than any of the printed words on the two hundred pages of the already written book would ever be able to do. Timothy Bahti (1996, 226), analyzing the poem 'A la point acérée' by Paul Celan, describes such writing:

Here, a cut opens a poem, an addressee plunges within, and a quill writes, penultimately, of the reading I – named 'I' – can give the plunging 'you.' Only if the poem cuts, if you cry, go overboard and under – only if there is cry-writing (Schrei-schreiben) – can the flare be lit and the guiding fingers write their way to your being read.

A case in point occurs in Beckmann's nightmare. As the bones on the xylophone decrease in size, the tones they produce increase inversely in pitch. The very last and smallest bones, the bones in the mouth, produce the highest pitch:

> BECKMANN. [...] Es muß ein ganz fremdartiger Musiker sein, der General, denn die Hölzer seines riesigen Xylophons sind gar nicht aus Holz. Nein, glauben Sie mir, Herr Oberst, glauben Sie mir, sie sind aus Knochen! [...] Ja, nicht aus Holz, aus Knochen. Wunderbare weiße Knochen. Schädeldecken hat er da, Schulterblätter, Beckenknochen. Und für die höheren Töne Armknochen und Beinknochen [...] Und zum Schluß, ganz am Ende des Xylophons, wo die ganz hohen Töne liegen, da sind Fingerknöcheln, Zehen, Zähne. Ja, als Letztes kommen die Zähne. (154)

As we saw earlier, Beckmann's voice was always too 'leise'. Similarly, the bones of the mouth now correspond in tone to his voice. Albeit the smallest bones, they give voice to the dismembered and dead body. It consequently becomes essential that the fixed representation give way to a yielding imagination that flows ('mündet') into an articulated sound – a cry that expresses more than a word that is merely a signifier could ever do.

The musician-general of the dream discloses the rigid exterior framework of all signifiers. The grotesque description of the skeletal images that constitute the general's instrument evokes a visual as well as a corresponding audible image of the fixed and frame-like character of the words. Each word stands as an objectified signifier represented by a physical part of the body's structure. Inversely, each imagined sound played on the instrument acquires great importance as a flexible non-signifier that speaks louder than any word. Rainer Nägele, in *Theater, Theory, Speculation* (1991, 2), explains it this way:

> The dominant *Vorstellung* of theater since the eighteenth century has been theater as drama: (re-)presentations of human subjects who affirm themselves in antagonistic dialogues and self-reflective monologues [...] In the disappearance of the hero's body, the voice of the autonomous subject emerges: *mündig*, a mouth that speaks, is the German word for the mature, grown-up subject.

Nägele's 'voice' is to be understood for our purposes in the sense that the spectator must hear the sound and speech of each bone ('sich vorstellen'). The active effort of imagination must occur on the part of the spectator. Yet there is also the act of 'vorstellen', the German term meaning to put forward, present, or imagine (2). Theater can be a 'Vorstellung', in the sense of a performance or show. These bones are therefore an imagined image, a re-presentation of a visionary new voice. Through the act of 'vorstellen' and as physical relics of a former body, the bones in Beckmann's dream receive a mouth through which the 'autonomous' individual is finally able to express himself. Beckmann recognizes the possible emergence of such a creator-subject when he identifies the author of 'schrei(b)en' with 'ich selbst'.

The musician-general has undergone a dismemberment of a different type:

> BECKMANN: [...] Da steht ein Mann und spielt Xylophon. Er spielt einen rasenden Rhythmus. Und dabei schwitzt er, der Mann, denn er ist außergewöhnlich fett […] Und dabei schwitzt er, denn er ist tatsächlich sehr fett. Aber er schwitzt gar keinen Schweiß, das ist das Sonderbare. Er schwitzt Blut, dampfendes, dunkles Blut. Und das Blut läuft in zwei breiten roten Streifen an seiner Hose runter, daß er von weitem aussieht wie ein General. Wie ein General! Ein fetter, blutiger General. Er muß ein schlachtenerprobter General sein, denn er hat beide Arme verloren. Ja, er spielt mit langen dünnen Prothesen, die wie Handgranatenstiele aussehen, hölzern und mit einem Metallring. (153–54)

Whereas the bones of the xylophone speak of the missing body, the general's body speaks of the absent bones. His fat body is missing arms, yet this does not prevent him from resolutely playing war tunes. The fat stumps of his arms have grown grotesque new arms: long, grenade-style wooden handles with a metal head. These artificial protrusions give the appearance of deformed outgrowths that, in their hideous disfigurement, resemble extremities that have the power to destroy whatever they come in contact with. At the same time, they are essential for the bones to receive a voice. Furthermore, the endless amount of blood that issues from his pores marks a physical representation of the absent bodies as well as the stream of new life that flows through them. The musician's presence and his gestures allow us to read the body of the voice that emerges.

As the dream continues, however, many bodies reappear 'aus den Wäldern [...] aus Ruinen und Mooren, schwarzgefroren, grün, verwest': 'Aus der Steppe stehen sie auf, einäugig, zahnlos, einarmig, beinlos, mit zerfetzten Gedärmen, ohne Schädeldecken, ohne Hände, durchlöchert, stinkend, blind' (155). The body must undergo this re-lived and repeatedly re-membered and dis-membered state in order to be able to discard its physical significance and arrive finally at a non-signifying embodiment of an identity. Paradoxically, then, the material presence of these dismembered corpses becomes a suggestive 'Vorstellung' of what is not physically represented.

Borchert often uses the term 'Welt' in his works as a comprehensive designation for elevated experiences and moods. A few lines earlier, the girl declared her fear of the silence in the world: 'es ist doch so entsetzlich still in der Welt.' In the short story 'Der Kaffee ist undefinierbar' (1949g), the reader is presented with the resigned statement: 'eine Weltmüdigkeit, die nichts mehr erwartet' (241). In the 1946/47 story 'Im Mai, im Mai schrie der Kuckuck' (1949f, 278), we read of a 'Weltgeschrei' caused by the homeless cuckoo. In the same story, the author is writing a book about the world:

> Aber es wird nicht mehr drin stehen als ein paar Glossen, Anmerkungen, spärlich erläutert, niemals erklärt, denn die zweihundert bedruckten Seiten sind nur ein Kommentar zu den zwanzigtausend unsichtbaren Seiten [...] aus denen unser Leben besteht, für die wir Vokabeln, Grammatik und Zeichen nicht kennen. Aber auf diesen zwanzigtausen unsichtbaren Seiten unseres Buches steht die groteske Ode [...]: Unsere verrückte kugelige Welt, unser zuckendes Herz, unser Leben! (281)

The 'Weltkugel' acquires characteristics as it becomes a 'kugelige Welt'. Not only is this 'Welt' in movement, but its movements have now become 'verrückt', turning, progressing, or regressing and forming a 'kugelige', elliptical shape. It is no accident that Borchert returns to the familiar topos of the world as a book. He brings out the difficulty facing us all: the impossibility of expressing the world through words. Since the two hundred pages of 'Glossen' and 'Anmerkungen' cannot express life, other texts consequently begin to develop from the 'verrückte' turning movements.

The loss of meaning of words, the musicality of the form and the combination of the word constructs combine to create a constant movement, an 'Unterwegssein'. The statement 'Ich bin unterwegs' (297) begins the story 'Die lange lange Straße lang' (1949h), and it is also the situation of Beckmann's 'ich' in *Draußen*. Beckmann is afraid of the change in his state of being and direction. He remains constantly 'unterwegs', an outsider on the street who is searching for a safe haven. Beckmann is always on the move and searching in every direction for an open door through which he may enter and find his own place and identity. Paradoxically, the answer to his quest is found precisely *in* the painful search, in the 'Fluch' and 'Abendgebet'. The girl points this out in the next lines:

> MÄDCHEN. Ach du. Vorwärts, rückwärts. Oben, unten. Morgen liegen wir
> vielleicht schon weiß und dick im Wasser. Mausestill und kalt. Aber heute
> sind wir doch noch warm. Heute abend nochmal, du Fisch. Fisch, sag was,
> Fisch. Heute abend schwimmst du mir nicht mehr weg, du. Sei still. Ich
> glaube dir kein Wort. Aber die Tür, die Tür will ich doch lieber abschließen.
> BECKMANN. Laß das. Ich bin kein Fisch, und du brauchst die Tür nicht
> abzuschließen. Nein, du, ich bin weiß Gott kein Fisch. (146)

The two words, 'Vorwärts, rückwärts', suggest a pendulum oscillating between the two already mentioned poles. 'Oben' and 'unten' evoke a feeling for depth and width that not only increases the perceived dimensions of the stage, but also implies the reversibility of the greatest 'above' and the lowest 'below', heaven and earth. These four words are connected in the middle by a period that negates directions as leading to a specific goal and instead produces a never-ending revolution. For heaven and earth continually rotate on this period as an axis to maintain a 'kugelige' world. For this reason, Borchert is always outside of society while at the same time he can never leave it behind. In his 1945/46 short story 'Generation ohne Abschied' (1949d), Borchert explains it with the following image: 'Und die Winde der Welt, die unsere Füße und unsere Herzen zu Zigeunern auf ihren heißbrennenden und mannshoch verschneiten Straßen gemacht haben, machten uns zu einer Generation ohne

Abschied' (77). This, a feeling similar to the *Weltschmerz* felt in Büchner's *Dantons Tod*, reveals Beckmann's deepest concern – and hesitation – throughout the play to realize his authentic self. This becoming what you are reveals the circular structure of human existence.

The girl repeatedly refers to Beckmann as 'Fisch'. Although he constantly attempts to overcome this state of rejection both in the water and on land, he remains an inauthentic self. Donald F. Nelson (1975, 348) sees in the designation of Beckmann as a fish a symbolic reference to Christianity:

> The symbolism of the fish and its connections with Christ have been traced extensively. In this context there are two phenomena which are of special interest. The first is that in Matthew 4:19. Christ wants to make Peter and Andrew 'fishers of men', and the second is the circumstance that the baptismal bath was very early called *piscina* which also meant 'fishpond'. This implies that those who believe in Christ are like fishes. In the passage from Matthew, Jesus explicitly compares man with a fish. Being fished out of the water would then mean that man is rescued by the New Gospel, that he is led to a new existence; in short, man is reborn. Without faith in God and in the New Gospel, man is only half-man; he is still half fish, half creature. Man must be fished out of the water, he must be reborn, he must become a new man by accepting the new faith. The new faith that Beckmann must accept is that life is worth living.

Although he takes this comparison too far when he claims that man is half man and half fish, Nelson's perception that Beckmann must 'become a new man by accepting the new faith' and that this 'new faith [...] is that life is worth living' comes close to the Heideggerian understanding of overcoming the inauthentic 'Man' within ourselves. His feelings of rejection both in the water and on land leave Beckmann in a state of homelessness, like a fish out of water. Yet by his refusal to be called a fish, 'Ich bin weiß Gott kein Fisch' (146), he acknowledges that his place is not in the Elbe. Beckmann's realization that he is not a fish underlines his unwillingness to remain in a state of inauthenticity. As long as this struggle for acceptance continues, he is unwilling and unable to overcome his inauthentic state. We are next tempted to ask with Heidegger in *Sein und Zeit* (1949), who am 'I' when 'I' am not my authentic self? This happens when the 'I' is absorbed in everyday routine and wishes to distinguish itself as little as possible from everyone else: 'Das Man ist ein Existenzial und gehört als ursprüngliches Phänomen zur positiven Verfassung des Daseins [...] Das eigentliche Selbstsein beruht nicht auf einem vom Man abgelösten Ausnahmezustand des Subjekts, sondern ist eine existenzielle Modifikation des Man als eines wesenhaften Existenzials' (129–30). His experience in the nightmare speaks of a heavy encumbrance he tries in vain to rid himself of. This load is also part of his fear of authenticity that is heavy with responsibility:

> Das furchtbare unübersehbare Meer der Toten tritt über die Ufer seiner Gräber und wälzt sich breit, breiig, bresthaft und blutig über die Welt. Und dann sagt der General mit den Blutstreifen zu mir: Unteroffizier Beckmann, Sie übernehmen die Verantwortung. Lassen Sie abzählen [...] Aber die Brüder zählen nicht. Sie schlenkern furchtbar mit den Kiefern, aber sie zählen nicht. (124)

These rotted corpses with no identity are physical representations that emphasize and articulate absent bodies and identities. Paradoxically, however, they rot yet a second time into one another, thus forming one voice: 'Aber sie rotten sich zusammen, die Verrotteten, und bilden Sprechchöre [...] Und wissen Sie, was sie brüllen, Herr Oberst? [...] Beckmann, brüllen sie' (156). Such speaking in unison and naming continues throughout the play, and Beckmann reaches a point where he cannot bear to be identified with his name:

> EINBEINIGER. Komm mit deinem Gesicht unter die Lampe. Ganz nah. (*dumpf*) Beckmann!
> BECKMANN. Ja. Ich. Beckmann [...]
> EINBEINIGER *leise, aber mit ungeheurem Vorwurf.* Beckmann... Beckmann... Beckmann!!!
> BECKMANN *gefoltert.* Hör auf, du. Sag den Namen nicht! Ich will diesen Namen nicht mehr haben! Hör auf, du.
> EINBEINIGER *leiert.* Beckmann. Beckmann.
> BECKMANN *schreit auf.* Das bin ich nicht! Das will ich nicht mehr sein! Ich will nicht mehr Beckmann sein! (148)

In the same manner that Jedermann heard voices calling his name before his death, 'Jedermann! Jedermann! Jedermann!' so Beckmann hears thousands of dead soldiers calling out his name: 'Beckmann... Beckmann... Beckmann!!!' As Jedermann felt fear and dread at hearing his name, so Beckmann, overcome by pangs of conscience, compares his calling to a 'Grab' and 'Weltuntergang' (117). Heidegger's understanding of guilt and conscience sheds some light on Beckmann's situation at this point. 'Der Ruf der Sorge', as Heidegger (1949) refers to conscience in *Sein und Zeit*, calls man back from his absorption in 'das Man', his living from instant to instant, by referring him back to his true origin and then calls him forward to the realization of his authentic possibility, which is the true moment of fulfillment. This moment is the 'Augenblick': 'Die in der eigentlichen Zeitlichkeit gehalten, mithin *eigentliche Gegenwart* nennen wir den *Augenblick*. Das Dasein ist rufverstehend *hörig seiner eigensten Existenzmöglichkeit*. Es hat sich selbst gewählt' (267–89). Beckmann's basic guilt is to be himself the cause of not realizing his authentic possibilities. The human being, though guilty, should be so in an authentic way. The voice of conscience does not allow him to assume a central subject position opposite a world that he should understand as the object of his search and that he should use as the object of his needs. Such a manner of thinking is called by Heidegger 'Seinsvergessenheit', 'bekundet sich mittelbar darin, daß der Mensch immer nur das Seiende betrachtet und bearbeitet' (371). Beckmann's assertion that he no longer wants to be 'Beckmann', his guilty conscience, signals his desire to break free of the 'Seinsvergessenheit' of his society. It signifies his wish no longer to regard the closed doors around him as the object of his desire. It is also the beginning of a 'deinauthentification' process through which Beckmann will ultimately understand that he is free of the guilt of the world. The act of assuming the guilt of his society and the subsequent refusal to accept society's present condition are necessary parts of this process of authentication. Beckmann cannot deal with his guilt, yet he also proclaims a convincing 'Nein' to the passivity of the society around him. This is also a step for Beckmann toward the realization that he does not need to stand in front of the closed doors of society, since what is behind those doors is not an answer to his searching questions in the final lines of the play.

As we have seen from some of the examples given here, the spectator regularly experiences identification with the action or the characters throughout the play. This, however, is soon followed by a complete distancing effect, during which the spectator is completely detached and made aware of a gap between herself and the stage. Grotesque and surreal scenes merge with painfully realistic ones. Fragmented sentences, exaggerated repetitions, and regular and irregular rhythmical movements merge with concrete examples of the hero's suffering. This oscillation between a breach and a bridge is in harmony with the already familiar image of a rotating and reflecting 'kugel' in the spherical shape of the world. Just as Beckmann struggles between an 'ich' and a 'du', so the spectator also reflects his own identity as well as actions and characters on the stage, only to have the reflection returned once again onto himself in an ongoing process of identification and lack thereof.

For Beckmann as well as for us, the only way out of the hopeless situation of standing in the cold void in front of closed doors is to allow the vital yet often negative movement of the text and of the stage to bring us into the presence of the divine. If Beckmann is able to do this, the divine will lighten his heavily burdened conscience. As we have seen throughout the play, the ever-heightening effect of acoustic imagery, staccato, leitmotiv, repetition, alliteration, assonance, and enumeration have been providing an extraordinary effect. Moreover, not just the words propel the story; the rhythmic atmosphere these words create is also crucial.

Thus carried forward, the individual begins to feel like part of greater mankind already 'unterwegs', perhaps on the way to God. She seems to be on a constant search for an open door and a place of rest without ever knowing what she is looking for. Deprived of God and of an acceptable past, Beckmann is part of the new generation that is unable to deal with itself and the ethically barren society. Always on the move, without a home and unable to return to the past, he disdains any 'Ersatzreligion' and a future based on it.

The older generation behind the closed door remains static in its confinement. But the new generation, for which the constant motion and agitation initially seems to bring no hope, is not only always in the state of 'Unterwegssein', it is also the generation of arrival: 'Vielleicht sind wir voller Ankunft zu einem neuen Lieben, zu einem neuen Lachen, zu einem neuen Gott. Wir sind die Generation ohne Abschied, aber wir wissen, daß alle Ankunft uns gehört' (79). The individual struggles to find an identity, yet at the same time his 'Angst, daß es rückwärts geht' makes him fear that he will fall victim to society's shallowness beneath which lies a void:

> DER ANDERE. Die Menschen sind gut [...] Nur das Leben läßt es nicht zu, daß sie ihr Herz zeigen. Glaube doch, im Grunde sind sie alle gut.
> BECKMANN. Natürlich. Im Grunde. Aber der Grund ist meistens so tief, du. So unbegreiflich tief. (189)

Yet the spectator is now able to recognize that this remains 'unbegreiflich'. The theological task of enclosing God in concepts or figures is not possible since the motions in the text and the gestures of the characters on the stage create an opening beyond which we experience the divine. We realize that Beckmann must cross this threshold, even though he does not realize the implications of his words when he speaks in cynical irony and despair:

> BECKMANN. [...] Hier unten kein Menschenohr. Da oben kein Gottesohr [...] Ich glaube sogar, ich bin schon im Himmel. (176)

'Keiner', found in the question, 'Gibt denn keiner Antwort?' (200), whose name is inexpressible and who is not visible or material, is already everywhere within the ethical void of society. 'No-one', no representation or figure, replaces the negated image of the old man God. As a result, a new set of religious values replaces the gloomy situation of society and of the future. Such a break from and negation of religious traditions calls forth a new God who liberates mankind from adherence to a Christianity that merely accommodates the status quo. Instead, the new God offers an undesignated alternative to the resulting void.

Borchert's short story 'Die Hundeblume' (1949e) also speaks of the pervasive, ungraspable presence of God. A prisoner narrates the humiliation and isolation in a dark cell and at the hands of the authoritarian enemy: 'Und das ist das Entwürdigendste: Ganz ohne die Möglichkeit zu einer Tat zu sein.' Fear, the product of his isolating inability to act, becomes 'ein Ungeheuer, und die Nacht kann furchtbar werden wie ein Gespenst' (39). Under such circumstances, the narrator asks how man can even think of life or God. Yet ultimately the desperate man finds that even in the plainest and least significant flower of the field, as its diminutive 'Hundeblume' indicates, he can sense the divine:

> Angesicht in Angesicht mit seiner Blume [...] Er war so gelöst und glücklich, daß er alles abtat und abstreifte, was ihn belastete: die Gefangenschaft, das Alleinsein [...] die Gegenwart und die Zukunft, die Welt und das Christentum – ja, auch das! [...] So befreit war er, und nie war er so bereit zum Guten gewesen, als er der Blume zuflüsterte [...] werden wie du [...] (52)

In the lonely dark void of his cell, the prisoner disregards everything – yes, even the present, the future, and Christianity as *he* understands it – but regards this flower as sacred and life-inspiring. Face to face with it, he has indeed found himself face to face with a divine 'Other'.

In the fifth scene of *Draußen*, Beckmann, lying on the streets, reaches a dream-like state in which he is ready to cross over the threshold from a barren life into death. Although he still tries to believe in the essence of the present society, he fears that he will fall endlessly in the void of his world, in the 'Grund' that is 'unbegreiflich tief'. He no longer has the energy and courage to remain in motion:

> BECKMANN. Nein, ich bleibe liegen. Hier vor der Tür. Und die Tür steht offen – hat er gesagt. Hier bleib ich liegen. Aufstehen soll ich? Nein. (186)

Beckmann's refusal to resume his motion reminds us of how *Le mythe de Sisyphe* (1942, 99) by Albert Camus begins with the fundamental question whether life is or is not worth living: 'Il n'y a qu'un problème vraiment sérieux: c'est le suicide. Juger que la vie vaut ou ne vaut pas la peine d'etre vécue, c'est répondre a la question fondamentale de la philosophie.' This decision, of course, depends also upon the understanding one has of life. According to Camus's existentialist perspective, life can be reduced to the absurd and we must deal with it. Beckmann is confronted with what Camus calls the 'benign indifference' of the universe. The author of *Le mythe de Sisyphe* poses the question whether man can live without appeal to God and without hope. He defines the absurd as the confrontation of human need with the unreasonable silence of the world. The most important question for Camus is this: how can man, albeit recognizing the blatant absurdity of his predicament, come to grips with such an un-responding world? The answer is not suicide, for suicide in Camus's terms amounts to acceptance of the absurd. There remains only revolt against the absurd, for only revolt restores value to life. Beckmann finds himself in a similar situation when faced with the option to choose between death and an absurd life:

> BECKMANN. […] Du bist tot, Gott. Sei lebendig, sei mit uns lebendig, nachts, wenn es kalt ist, einsam und wenn der Magen knurrt in der Stille […] (182–83)

In the 'Stille' of the night, when words, labels, names, and concepts are meaningless because they cannot be confirmed, the lonely individual is not distracted from his own suffering. Yet the text and the representations on the stage make it clear that Beckmann's choice to live under such circumstances stems not from the existentialist acceptance of life as philosophically absurd, but rather from his conscious acknowledgement that there exists nothing for him to grasp in the midst of the void of nothingness surrounding him.

Although this may seem to echo a nihilist's or absurdist's description of the German situation after the war, Beckmann's choice of recognizing this nothingness gives way to action, to movement leading not to revolt but to restoration. The restoration, as we have seen, comes about through turning directions and perspectives that consequently bring about another presence to fill the void. As he lies passively in his motionless position on the street, Beckmann has two alternatives. On the one hand, he can cross over the threshold of the open gate of death. On the other, he can order himself to become part of the dark abyss that has been created on stage:

> BECKMANN. Alle Türen links und rechts der Straße sind zu. Alle Laternen sind ausgegangen, alle. Und man kommt nur vorwärts, weil man fällt! (192)

Beckmann prefers death to the unknown endless abyss:

> BECKMANN. Tod, Tod, laß mir die Tür offen. Tod, mach die Tür nicht zu. Tod –

> STRASSENFEGER. Meine Tür steht immer offen. Immer. Morgens. Nach-
> mittags. Nachts. Im Licht und im Nebel. Immer ist meine Tür offen. Immer.
> Überall. (185)

It seems that he has already made the decision to cross the threshold into death:

> BECKMANN. [...] Nur der Tod, der Tod hat zuletzt doch eine Tür für uns.
> Und dahin bin ich unterwegs. (186)

The decision to step into the 'Finsternis' of the world, however, is a more difficult one, for it requires faith, and he is afraid:

> DER ANDERE. [...] Deine Straße wartet [...] Bist du feige, daß du Angst hast
> vor der Finsternis zwischen zwei Lanternen? (177)

Yet Beckmann's fear and negativity have the potential of acquiring positive attributes:

> BECKMANN. [...] Nein! [Das Mädchen] hat mich nicht gesucht! *Kein* Mensch
> hat mich gesucht! [...] Mich sucht *kein* Mensch! (160)

No one, that is a non-being, offers communication within open and unspoken nothingness. Negation opens the door and allows entrance into a place of a new reading and a new stage where that is located which cannot be contained in material and visible signs and terms. In Heideggerian terms, at this place, the 'Nicht-Seiende' 'west als das Sein'.

Under the pressure of history, Borchert, and many other writers during the 'Stunde null', contributed to what Sartre (n.d., 250) calls the literature of 'situations extremes'. Although Beckmann's feeling of homelessness and exclusion reflects the despondent situation of the German individual in a culturally, ethically, politically, and socially dead nation, the character Beckmann does not realistically represent the situation of the returning soldier after the war. As Leslie Wilson (1972, 471) points out,

> Beckmann [ist] keineswegs der typische Heimkehrer, der aus dem Krieg nach
> Hause kommt und sich abgewiesen und isoliert sieht. Der typische Soldat
> schlug sich irgendwie durch, wenn er auch auf der Straße herumlungerte oder

zum vagabundierenden Alkoholiker wurde. Der typische Soldat war erfinderischer als Beckmann, der von Zurückweisungen zermalt wird und keine Zuflucht findet, Gott.

Beckmann speaks with the anguished voice of the individual who finds she lives in a chaotic moral and social vacuum.

Beckmann's spark of life surrenders to an imperious will for extinction as he screams his pessimistic 'Nein' to existence. In his 1947 essay 'Dann gibt es nur eins' (1949b), Borchert addresses us all and repeatedly urges us and the mothers of future generations to say 'NEIN' in the same way that Beckmann has reacted throughout the play. If not:

> Dann wird der letzte Mensch, mit zerfetzten Gedärmen und verpesteter Lunge, antwortlos und einsam unter der giftig glühenden Sonne und unter wankenden Gestirnen umherirren, einsam zwischen den unübersehbaren Massengräbern und den kalten Götzen der gigantischen betonklotzigen verödeten Städte, der letzte Mensch, dürr, wahnsinning, lästern, klagend – und seine furchtbare Klage: WARUM? Wird ungehört in der Steppen verrinnen, durch die geborstenen Ruinen wehen, versickern im Schutt der Kirchen, gegen Hochbunker klatschen, in Blutlachen fallen, ungehört, antwortlos, letzter Tierschrei des letzten Tieres Mensch – all dieses wird eintreffen, morgen, morgen vielleicht, vielleicht heute nacht schon, vielleicht heute nacht, wenn – wenn – wenn ihr nicht NEIN sagt. (384)

There is 'life' in this play, and it comes from an inward energy that manifests itself as the individual's act of denial.

The 'Jasager' also brings to light this form of negativity. He is always present or not present at all; he is faceless and has a thousand faces. He possesses no specifically human traits, yet he understands Beckmann's needs. He is an externalization or personification of an inner force. He is 'die Stimme, die jeder kennt'. At the beginning, he shows his presence as Beckmann's conscience, by saying Yes when Beckmann says No and giving answers when Beckmann needs them:

> DER ANDERE. Ich bin auch der vom Dreck. Ich bin immer. Du wirst mich nicht los.
> BECKMANN. Du hast kein Gesicht. Geh weg.
> DER ANDERE. Ich bin der Andere, der immer da ist. Der andere Mensch, der Antworter [...] Ich bin der Optimist, der an den Bösen das Gute sieht und

die Lampen in der finstersten Finsternis [...] Und der Ja sagt, wenn du Nein sagst, der Jasager bin ich. (139)

Nevertheless, the affirmation of the 'Jasager' is not the complete answer to the basic negativity underlying the play. From the very beginning, he is indeed an inner voice that escapes the power of consciousness and accepts the present order. With his cunning instinct for survival, he advises Beckmann to transfer his guilt feelings, to forget and believe in the present world and figures.

The nihilistic atmosphere of the play is so embracive that it seems to swallow up both the 'Ja' of the Other and the 'Nein' of Beckmann. The 'Jasager' has shown Beckmann, the guilt-ridden 'Neinsager', the definitively closed position of the doors and has brought him to an awareness of his need to make a choice for life. The Other and Beckmann acquire a common identity when the positive and the negative become one. The saving 'yes' in *Draußen* is unique, for it is possible only if Beckmann chooses neither of the two options available to him – death or life. Instead, he must be willing to plunge into the depths of an in-betweenness.

Borchert emphasizes the great transformation that must occur within the individual:

Horch hinein in den Tumult deiner Abgründe. Erschrickst du nicht? Hörst du den Chaoschoral aus Mozartmelodien und Herms Niel-Kantaten? Hörst du Hölderlin noch? Kennst du ihn wieder, blutberauscht, kostümiert und Arm in Arm mit Baldur von Schirach? (372)

Mankind now seeks artificial means and noise to avoid facing the guilt and memories that it has heretofore denied. He continues in 'Das ist unser Manifest' (1949a, 372–73), 'ehe der Clown kräht, haben wir es dreimal verleugnet.' Yet once the meaningless tumult of society fades to silence, we are frightened by what we can now hear within our own selves. Listening, however, has the potential to change the nihilistic 'Nein' of those who cannot accept themselves and society to a 'Ja' of a new life: 'Unser Nein ist Protest. Und wir haben keine Ruhe beim Küssen, wir Nihilisten. Denn wir müssen in das Nichts hinein wieder ein Ja bauen. – Häuser bauen in die reingefegte Luft der Nihilisten' (374). Unless we first deny everything around us, the 'Tumult der

Abgründe' of our hearts will remain unheard while we cry 'Warum' into utter desolation. The coming together of the 'yes' and the 'no' that develops in *Draußen* is a potentiality within us, yet we have failed and feared to recognize it. The only way out of this situation has been to inject it with nihilism.

Lying near death on the ground in the last act, Beckmann asks questions, but receives no answer: 'Wo bist du jetzt, Jasager? Jetzt antworte mir!' (200). The 'Jasager' no longer has a voice as the silence allows a thousand suffering voices to speak united with one voice of a new writing. 'Warum schweigt ihr denn?' Beckmann asks them all. In the final, climactic moments on the street, Beckmann ultimately begins to realize that he will receive no answer:

> Gibt denn keiner Antwort?
> Gibt keiner Antwort?
> Gibt denn keiner, keiner Antwort??? (200)

His questions develop into a need to have faith in 'keiner'. The more Beckmann repeats 'keiner', the clearer it becomes that *no one* will in fact provide an answer and fill the emptiness. Consequently, no one replaces the stage God and writes with a new ink within the empty space that once was filled by 'der liebe Gott' with 'zuviel Theologentinte im Blut' (183). As a consequence of the unbearable emptiness and silence, Beckmann is urged to enter into this nothingness in which he must rely on a belief that in it, his 'Beck' will also be filled:

> BECKMANN. Und man kommt nur vorwärts, weil man fällt! Und du sagst ich soll weiter fallen! (195)

He must believe in what he cannot see or hear. He must have faith enough to allow himself to fall into the abyss of nothingness.

It can be reasoned that silence has meaning only as the absence of speech. The existence of language is therefore contingent on that of the spoken word. As we have seen, language cannot exist within a vacuum, yet at the same time, this vacuum cannot exist without another language. Finally faced with the decision of choosing between the open door of death or the constantly shifting life outside, Beckmann, left alone with unbearable emptiness and stillness, must search himself and finally decide whether he will fall into the 'Finsternis' that has opened up. This is not the end, however. This negation also stimulates *our* denial, *our* 'Nein' as well as our 'yes' and therewith our 'Vorstellungskraft'. We sense that we, too, will be filled if we do the same.

Yet, one may at this point ask how the spectator is able to actively use his 'Vorstellungskraft', his ability to imagine, to present as well as put forward the energy developing on the stage. Nägele (1991) understands 'vorstellen' as well as 'darstellen' as both theatrical and epistemological concepts. They are both compounds of the word 'stellen' that is translated by 'putting something in one of three positions: sitting, standing, lying'. Furthermore, 'they structure the world and our knowledge of it in terms of position, that is, in terms of relation rather than substance' (2). The wretchedness of Beckmann's situation and the hopelessness of his fate is cast in such horrifyingly and piteously nihilistic circumstances that it seems only natural that the spectator expectantly await either a great deus ex machina to bring Beckmann out of his nihilist state and save him from his guilt or a final decision on Beckmann's part to commit suicide in recognition of his heavy burden and as catharsis from it. In fact, as we have seen, neither of the two possibilities is chosen. The play *Draußen* does not have an ending. Instead, as the text progresses, it gathers energy through its form and style. The movements soon take the shape of inversions. Walking 'up' and 'down' the reality of our streets and over life's intersections through the spherical shapes of the circumstances of the world, we suddenly find ourselves face to face with a great 'Nichts'. At this point, we, like Beckmann, have a third option. We can let ourselves fall into the great silence that has developed:

> Man steht da, spinnt, friert, hungert und ist verdammt müde. Und dann auf einmal plumpst es, und die Wellen machen niedliche kleine kreisrunde Kreise, und dann rauscht der Vorhang [...] Ist das viel mehr als Nichts? [...] Mein Gähnen ist groß wie die weite Welt! (179)

This falling, however, in not the same falling that Beckmann experiences when he throws himself into the Elbe. Instead, while Beckmann even at the end still wishes to die by drowning, the inversions and circles occurring once he enters into the nothingness simultaneously flow ('münden') into and form a new world.

When the spectator sees the curtain fall, he feels immediately taken back to the beginning of the play:

> Ein Mann kommt nach Deutschland.
>      Und da erlebt er einen ganz tollen Film. Er muss sich während der Vorstellung mehrmals in den Arm kneifen, denn er weiss nicht, ob er wacht oder träumt. Aber dann sieht er, dass es rechts und links neben ihm noch mehr Leute gibt, die alle dasselbe erleben. Ja, und als er dann am Schluss mit leerem Magen und kalten Füssen wieder auf der Strasse steht, merkt er, dass es eigentlich nur ein ganz alltäglicher Film war. (132)

When the spectator first enters the theater, he, like anyone watching a film, expects to be entertained:

> BECKMANN. Das ist herrlich, wenn man satt und warm ist, vom Elend anderer Leute zu lesen und so recht mitleidig zu seufzen. (151)

This passive attitude becomes even clearer to Beckmann as he learns from the words of the theater director in *Draußen*:

> Aber das Ganze hat natürlich noch zu wenig Esprit, mein lieber junger Mann. Das schillert nicht genug. Der gewisse Glanz fehlt. Das ist natürlich noch keine Dichtung. Es fehlt noch das Timbre und die diskrete pikante Erotik, die gerade das Thema Ehebruch verlangt. Das Publikum will gekitzelt werden und nicht gekniffen. (167)

Yet, as we see in the reactions of Borchert's critics, our expectation to be 'gekitzelt' turns into disappointment as the play progresses into a mad ('toll') portrayal of one soldier's return to his country. Beckmann does not die. Nor is there a grand entrance by a deus ex machina who changes the situation with a stroke of his powerful hand. Experiencing the discomforting challenge of no longer being passive observers, we now watch the play with a new attitude. We now relate increasingly to Beckmann's situation. As observers of Beckmann's situation, we become more and more aware of the movement and development that takes place on the stage and within us. Finally, we too are faced with nothingness and silence.

As we observe Beckmann's 'Film', we recognize that Beckmann, too, not only represents something but is also himself a spectator of a presentation. This show is Beckmann's own as much as his show is ours. As the film begins again, Beckmann realizes he is now a spectator of his own life. The spectator of *Draußen* is Beckmann as well as the spectator in the audience, who finally, 'am Schluss', is able to see actors performing as well as observe herself observing. The presentation of the actor is now no longer a nihilistic portrayal of one returning soldier's struggle after World War II. Instead, Borchert is now able to re-experience his own 'ganz alltägliche[n] Film' (102), as are we, and to see his own self developing within the theatricality of the stage.

Beckmann's circumstances in front of the door are unbearable. Yet, like the prisoner face to face with his 'Hundeblume', Beckmann must close his eyes and have faith in the nothingness:

> Er ertrug den Raum nicht mehr und schloß die Augen und staunte: Aber du riechst nach Erde. Nach Sonne, Meer und Honig, liebes Lebendiges! Er empfand ihre keusche Kühle wie die Stimme des Vaters, den er nie sonderlich beachtet hatte und der nun soviel Trost war mit seiner Stille. (51–52)

Once he is able to do this, he experiences the silent voice of God: 'Vielleicht war es ein Gott aus dir – du warst es! Denn du bist auch Gott, alle, auch die Spinne und die Makrele sind Gott. Gott ist das Leben – das ist alles' (51). The decision is an active one. It requires his involvement and an affirmative first step. The prisoner places the exhausted flower, 'das erschöpfte kleine Wesen', into his water cup and dreams of a transformation, of 'werden wie du':

> Die ganze Nacht umspannten seine glücklichen Hände das vertraute Blech seines Trinkbechers, und er fühlte im Schlaf, wie sie Erde auf ihn häuften [...] und wie aus ihm Blumen brachen [...] -winzige, unscheinbare Sonnen. (52)

In the same manner, Beckmann's previously empty 'Beck' provides the ground for finding an identity and a new life. At a time in history when everyone yearns for quick and soothing answers, Beckmann and we, his audience, are confronted with a larger-than-life silence that delimits our subjective and human space against another space, an empty space that requires *us* to cross the threshold ourselves and to rely on faith that God will fill the 'Finsternis zwischen zwei Lanternen'. This place between is the 'Augenblick' that Heidegger calls in *Sein und Zeit* (1949, 264) the realization of an individual's authentic possibility, 'die Möglichkeit eines existenziellen Vorweg-nehemens des *ganzen* Daseins'. The 'Augenblick' is the moment of fulfillment. Beckmann is at length no longer driven by the need to escape from his situation. He now has the freedom to choose his authentic self and consequently to overcome guilt. There occurs here a shift from the human being to Being. As Heidegger writes: 'Sein – nicht Seiendes – "gibt es" nur, sofern Wahrheit ist. Und sie *ist* nur sofern und so lange Dasein ist. Sein und Wahrheit sind glei-chursprünglich' (212–30). This shifting from the human being to Being emphasizes the complete necessity to rely on the always-present Dasein. It subsequently leads to a 'Vorlaufen zum Tode', the possibility of an existential anticipation of one's entire existence, and finally, a 'Freiheit zum Tode' (266). While 'die andern ersaufen in Angst und Verzweiflung', Beckmann is able to build for himself 'aus seinem Traum eine Arche Noah und segeln saufend und singend über das Entsetzliche rüber in die ewige Finsternis' (130). Written on his deathbed, Borchert's final words to the world assert such a freedom to face even death despite the dread:

> Die Erde sinkt zurück
> die Fesseln und die Schmerzen:
> ich bin am Himmel Stern geworden
> und fühl im All den Schlag
> von Gottes weitem Herzen. (396)

The dying Borchert was convinced on the eve of the premiére of *Draußen* that he, like a star in heaven that feels God's heartbeat directly, would look down and see how a new narrative of Germany's present pulsates with the rhythm of God's heartbeat while the remnants of the past, language and representations, that is, the doors of society, fall away.

# Chapter Four
# Epic Theater

In the introductory chapter we addressed briefly the unique qualities of language on the stage: in the extreme, especially during the heyday of Naturalism, language belonged strictly to the characters on stage, and the insufficiencies and other aspects of this language served only to illuminate these insufficiencies and aspects in the individual characters. To the extent that subsequent dramas of the modern era tended away from such strict realism, the language on the stage again began to shift toward that of the playwright. Despite the impossibility of a successful active and intentional involvement, the poet is very present within his drama. Yet he remains part of the play while the creative and self-productive character of poetic language continues to inspire and motivate a revelation of the text. Thus, the verse and vocabulary, among other qualities, made it obvious in *Jedermann* that the limits of language itself were being put to the test. The same could be asserted regarding the ecstatic tone and 'telegram-style' of Wolfgang Borchert's *Draußen vor der Tür* as a throwback to Expressionism.

The anti-naturalistic attitude towards language implied in Hugo von Hofmannsthal's and Borchert's works is given a theoretical foundation by Bertolt Brecht with his concept of an 'epic theater'. For despite his protestations that 'epic' was a social category, not an esthetic one, we recognize that language, as a means to signify aspects of the non-artistic, real world, now acquires a degree of absolute accountability otherwise associated only with its use in non-dramatic genres. Brecht's epic theater must be viewed as an exception to the originality of certain aspects of modern theater over other genres in testing the limits of language. His theater contains elements of typical classical theater and a similarity to the epic style of narration while, at the same time, it insists on a break with the illusions of Aristotelian theater. Brecht refers to this process as an 'Akzentverschiebung', a shift in emphasis from 'traditional' theater to his own. One sees this most clearly in Brecht's 'Anmerkungen zur Oper *Aufstieg und Fall der Stadt Mahagonny'*. He writes in *Schriften zum Theater* (1993, 1008–09): 'Das moderne Theater is das epische Theater.' In a footnote to this comment, he states: 'Dieses Schema zeigt nicht absolute Gegensätze, sondern lediglich Akzentverschiebungen.' He proves his point by comparing the two forms, the 'dramatisches Theater' and 'episches Theater' side by side (1009). Brecht stresses the need to break free from the illusion of traditional theater by emphasizing what has always been in drama and allowing some of the traditional dramatic aspects to remain the same. It is therefore essential to examine Brecht's theory of epic theater, albeit briefly, to ascertain its relevance for the main thesis: where language, that ultimate traditional tool of a writer for ordering the world by its own rules, breaks down, a lacuna comes into being in which a person instinctively feels the possible presence of the supernatural or divine.

Modern drama, as we have seen, must deal with the dilemma of deciding when the limits of language are only reflective of the limits of the characters (e.g., lack of articulation, self-deception, or simple stupidity) and when they are indicative of all language. Brecht, by breaking the illusion of the stage, that is, by reducing characterization to a minimum, shifts the emphasis to the latter. This shift in emphasis allows the audience to perceive even more strongly the limits of language as a social product and force and to become more receptive of its metaphysical implications.

The most common term for Brecht's dramatic theory and practice has remained 'epic theater', the one that Brecht himself coined and promoted from the late 1920s onward. In subsequent years he attempted to vary and refine his characterizations of it. 'Dialectical' and 'scientific' were some of the terms he later introduced. Yet 'epic' does adequately embrace the major premises of Brecht's theater. It seeks, through careful use of theme and structure, to make the audience detached observers whose distance from the events portrayed on the stage allows analysis of problems and promotes their subsequent participation in finding solutions for these problems in real life. Epic theater wants to stimulate, not satisfy, the viewers, so that they will go out and change the world.

116

In a larger context, epic theater should be seen as symptomatic of the suppressed necessity and longing to break with not only a literary and social but also an outdated religious tradition. As Brecht sees it, the religion of society is a religion of the powerful theological institutions. Consequently, because we do not have God, we must concentrate on man, especially society. Contempt for bourgeois society with its morality, values, and respectability motivated Brecht's attempt to create a new artistic approach. Antipathy towards all products of the capitalist machinery of exploitation underlies Brecht's atheistic negation of the existing order of things. From his earliest years, he could not endure the ugliness and vulgarity of the respectable bourgeois society, and subsequently his moral sensitivity was shattered by the horrors of the war and the postwar era. This ultimately produced in him a vehement denial of all values or dogma. Brecht always saw injustice in the misuse and unequal distribution of wealth and resources. For the anarchist and atheist Brecht, as one can see very clearly in his early prose and plays, the discovery of Marxist doctrine brought a new esthetic and, consequently, a new social purpose. He wholeheartedly insisted that criticism, doubt, and free inquiry, the essential elements of the scientific attitude, must be the basis of Marxism, and asserted that society is dominated by the more powerful institutions that abuse the socially and economically weaker collectives. Furthermore, those in power are prepared to go to extremes in order to keep the masses suppressed and under control. The bourgeois-Christian society, despite its moral, cultural, and ideological façade, is but another product of a godless society in which the individual subject is destroyed in compliance with a doctrine of survival of the fittest. Brecht's Marxist epic theater aims at a change. His theater is a 'Theater einer neuen Welt' and an attempt to transform the passive mentality that traditional dramaturgy promoted into a politically active one.

What excited Brecht, as one can see in his theoretical writings as well as in productions of his works, was the dramatic quality inherent in the coexistence of opposites as thesis and antithesis. According to Friedrich Hegel, the resultant dialectic provides the best starting point from which to approach the concrete world as an entity constantly reshaping itself. Adapting Hegel's abstract principles to characterize

117

concrete social ones over which man has control, Karl Marx asserts that real human beings can dialectically advance towards the over-throw of capitalism. For Brecht, contradictions and the inherent ambiguity of language, as well as the idea that nothing is really what it seems, can provide the foundations for a truly 'modern' drama.

By presenting and calling into doubt traditional codes and representations, Brecht reveals the contradictory state of mankind and history. Brecht's epic theater clearly sets out to demolish traditional values, ideologies, and, consequently, all conventional signifiers. The task of the artist is now to denaturalize the rigidified world of signs by means of formal devices that focus the spectators' attention on contradictions. Brecht thematizes demystification and breaks the illusion of everyday life in order to give a proper reference to reality. This, in turn, may explain why the atheist Brecht – like Nietzsche – includes biblical topics and imagery to bring across his ideas.

Brecht's epic theater has the ability to destroy traditional language and to break the illusion of the stage. His theater creates contradictions, interruptions, and negations that, in turn, allow caesurae to develop on the stage that are the result of such a break with the conventional methods and language of society. The audience, in turn, is as a result receptive to the limits of language as a social product. Theodore Adorno, among others, criticizes Brecht's epic approach to the stage and refers to it as impotent, especially the manner in which he urges this spectators to become involved in finding a solution. In *Ästhetische Theorie* (1965a, 360) he writes:

Umgekehrt war das Werk Brechts, das spätestens seit der Johanna verändern wollte, wahrscheinlich gesellschaftlich ohnmächtig, und der Kluge hat darüber schwerlich sich getäuscht. Auf seine Wrikung trifft die angelsächsische Formel vom preaching to be saved zu. Sein Programm von Verfremdung war, den Zuschauer zum Denken zu veranlassen. Brechts Postulat denkenden Verhaltens konvergiert merkwürdig mit dem einer objektiv erkennenden Haltung, die bedeutende autonome Kunstwerke als die adäquate vom Betrachter, Hörer, Leser erwarten.

His major dissatisfaction with Brecht's theater is his use of 'Engagement' as a means of arriving at a solution. Adorno continues: 'Sein didaktischer Gestus jedoch ist intolerant gegen die Mehrdeutigkeit, an der Denken sich entzündet: er ist autoritär' (360). Yet he later adds:

> Aber die sententiöse Drastik, mit der er dergleichen keineswegs taufrische Einsichten in szenische Gesten übersetzte, verhalf seinen Werken zu ihrem Ton; Didaxe führte ihn zu seinen dramaturgischen Neuerungen, die das zermorschte psychologische und Intrigen-Theater stürzten. In seinen Stücken gewannen die Thesen eine ganz andere Funktion als die, welche sie inhaltlich meinten [...] Brecht's Engagement tut dem Kunstwerk nochmals gleichsam an, wohin es geschichtlich von sich aus gravitiert: zerrüttet es. (366)

A lacuna develops on the stage at the place where the break occurs. The space thus occurring, it appears, is 'der Spielraum Gottes'. Within this space God emerges. Despite the size and variety of Brecht's dramatic oeuvre, only one play, *Der gute Mensch von Sezuan*, allows a divine presence to appear on the stage.

*Der gute Mensch von Sezuan*, albeit taking place in China, portrays the contemporary situation of Germany, its politics seen from a Marxist perspective. Begun during Brecht's exile in Svendborg/ Denmark in 1938, this play was finished in Finland in 1941 and first performed on February 4, 1943, in the Schauspielhaus at Zürich under the direction of Leopold Lindtberg. It shares with many of his plays the designation 'Parabelstück', the aptness of which is more obvious in the original title, *Die Ware Liebe*, for in it, the province of Sezuan indeed serves as an example of 'alle Orte [...] an denen Menschen von Menschen ausgebeutet werden'. The pun in the original title later gives way to the ironic formal designation of *Der gute Mensch von Sezuan*, which reveals the deceptive relationship between language and signification.

Brecht questions continuity and successive discourse and accepts the right of the playwright to make speech and writing discontinuous, literally. As Roland Barthes states in 'Brecht and Discourse' (1989, 248), to 'dismember the erroneous text is a polemical act'. Barthes writes:

> *Poor B.B.*: this is the title of a poem by Bertolt Brecht [...] these two letters (and repetitive ones at that) frame a void, and this void is the apocalypse of Weimar Germany [...] Hence, there are two discourses in Brechts' oeuvre: first, an apocalyptic (anarchizing) discourse concerned to express and to produce

> destruction without trying to see what comes 'afterwards', for 'afterwards' is just as undesirable [...] then, an eschatological discourse: a critique constructed with a view to ending the fatality of social alienation (or the belief in this fatality): what does not go well with the world (war, exploitation) is remediable: a time of cure is conceivable. (245–53)

Previous discontinuity of discourse keeps the last meaning from being the final meaning. Marx was the first to claim that both the objective world of the product and the institutional relations that the market inevitably induced took on a given rigidified form that externally seemed real. He named the reification of the product 'commodity fetishism', because he regarded this aspect of reification as a delusion in which imaginary characteristics were being given a thing-like status. In Marxian terms, human beings also became fixed in the same type of relations, governing all their social interactions. Epic theater, Brecht asserts in *Aufstieg und Fall* (1955, 279–83), cuts the cohesion of such signification.

Brecht tries to deliver contradiction by a new manner of presentation that he calls 'Verfremdung', because it constantly interrupts the continuity necessary to maintaining the stage illusion. This allows for silences, gaps, and questions in the discontinuities that it presents. Instead of a unified work of art, with all its esthetic and ideological consequences, Brecht proposes for an epic theater one in which the language, acting, music, and design, conceived as a bundle of separate elements, would operate autonomously, but at the same time in a relation of commentary and contradiction with each other. As Brecht asserts in his *Kleines Organon für das Theater* (1960b), the purpose of 'Verfremdung' and the ultimate subject of his drama is to produce alienation between the rational and the irrational.

Yet 'Verfremdung' is not simply the breaking of illusion, and it does not mean alienating the spectator in the sense of making him hostile to the play. It is a matter of detachment and of reorientation. We also find this in the following assertion by Peter Szondi in *Theorie des Modernen Dramas* (1978b, 110):

> Durch diese Verfremdungen erhält der Subjekt-Objekt-Gegensatz, der am Ursprung des Epischen Theaters steht: die Selbstentfremdung des Menschen, dem das eigene gesellschaftliche Sein gegenständlich geworden ist, in allen

120

Schichten des Werks seinen formalen Niederschlag und wird so zu dessen allgemeinem Formprinzip.[1]

Brecht's reworking of language can best be understood against the background of naturalist thematics. Szondi (1978b) understands well that Brecht had his ideological reasons for finding its dramatic principles not completely satisfactory:

> Gleich Piscator ist Bert Brecht ein Erbe des Naturalismus. Denn auch seine Versuche setzen dort an, wo der Widerspruch zwischen sozialer Thematik und dramatischer Form in Erscheinung tritt: im 'sozialen Drama' der Naturalisten. Nicht der Naturalismus selbst, sondern sein innerer Widerpart, der unter der Herrschaft des dramatischen Formgestzes nur in thematischer Verhüllung auftreten durfte, wird von Piscator und Brecht in Schutz genommen und auf Kosten der dramatischen Form zum Durchbruch geführt [...] [Brecht] geht es um die Inthronisierung des wissenschaftlichen Prinzips, das zwar – wie Zolas Romane erweisen – wesenhaft zum Naturalismus gehört, im naturalistischen Drama aber nur akzidentell, etwa in der Gestalt einer dramatis persona (Loth in *Vor Sonnenaufgang*) zur Geltung kommen durfte. (105)

In a similar manner, Antonin Artaud (1964) argues that rational discourse minimizes the importance of the body and reduces the dynamic forces of life into ossified categories: 'Etre cultivé [...] c'est savoir que les livres mentent quand ils parlent de dieu, de la nature, de l'homme, de la mort et du destin.' The same, Szondi argues, applies to naturalistic dialogue: the more it is clear-cut and coherent, the more fraudulent the version of human reality that it gives, which is, according to Artaud, a 'fusion inextricable [...] de l'abstrait et du concret' (187–88). Brecht's objections are perhaps subtler: while verbal language can be implicated in an ideological suppression of truth, this is not the inevitable result of rational discourse per se. Rather, such suppression stems from the willful manipulation and abuse of language by the ruling classes. Language comes into being as the product and then serves as the tool of social forces and the circumstances they have created. Brecht writes in *Schriften zur Politik und Gesellschaft* (1974, 13):

> Haufen von Bildern machen die Dinge schicksalhaft und verschleiert, schnell Hinunterquirlendes wird wieder zu Muskelgefühlen. Viele Dinge sind erstarrt, die Haut hat sich ihnen verdickt, sie haben Schilde vor, das sind die Wörter [...]

121

Das Schlimmste, wenn die Dinge sich verkrusten in Wörtern, hart werden, weh tun beim Schmeißen, tot herumliegen [...] Im Anfang war nicht das Wort. Das Wort ist am Ende. Es ist die Leiche des Dinges.

Brecht did not experience the early 'Sprachkrise' that brought young Hofmannsthal's poetic years to an end. He never suffered from a struggling relationship with language so clearly expressed by Lord Chandos. Hans-Harald Müller (2003, 135) writes on this:

Eine 'Sprachkrise' gibt es beim frühen Brecht nicht, seine Lyrik liest sich weithin, wie Walther Killy vor 30 Jahren festellte, 'als ob Hofmannsthal den Schandos-Brief nie geschrieben hätte'.

Instead, from play to play throughout his career, Brecht controls language to meet the demands of characterization for diverse registers and styles. The potential variety seems endless as it unfolds from the concrete imagery of the 1919 play *Baal* to the sentimentalism of the operas; from the disciplined simplicity of the *Lehrstücke* written between 1929 and 1938 to a more naturalistic idiom in the 1931 play *Die Mutter*; and from the parodic verse of his 1959 play *Die heilige Johanna der Schlachthöfe* (1960a) to the combination of concrete metaphor with aphorism in the 1938/39 play *Galileo Galilei*. These different idioms are further enriched by linguistic influences ranging from Luther's Bible to Anglicisms. This multiplicity tends to stand out more in production than in the reading of a uniformly printed page.

*Der gute Mensch* criticizes any attempt at conformity to the parameters determined by linguistic rules and constrictive, conventional forms and representations. The play portrays force and destruction in order to make us aware of the inadequacy of the capitalist ideology of oppression vis-à-vis Marxism. Yet Brecht's 'profane' play does much more by attempting such a criticism of conformity.

Religious language in *Der gute Mensch* turns from divinely inspired language into an ideological instrument or clichés wielded by the religious hierarchy. These hackneyed words, in turn, expose how such restrictive linguistic rules and conventional representations fail to stand on their own. We find examples of such numerous religious clichés throughout the text:

DER ERSTE GOTT. Nimm das nächste Haus, mein Sohn! Versuch es zunächst mit dem allernächsten! (595)

DER ERSTE GOTT. Schwanken macht nichts, wenn man nur siegt! (598)

DER ERSTE GOTT. Freilich, freilich! Aber ein umsichtiger Gärtner tut auch mit einem winzigen Fleck wahre Wunder. (610)

DER ERSTE GOTT. Sie kann es! Sie ist eine kräftige Person und wohlgestaltet und kann viel aushalten. (640)

DER ERSTE GOTT. [...] Deiner, Shen Te, des guten Menschen, gern In kalter Finsternis die kleine Lampe trägst. (640)

These expressions appear familiar and appropriate, especially to Wang, the pious man who seems to have faith in every word of the gods. But an audience made critical through 'Verfremdung' recognizes that such religious language, taken out of its original context and placed into a new one intended to serve a political ideological purpose, loses its authoritative function within the society of Sezuan, so much so, that it appears not only conventionalized but also ridiculously banal.

The breakdown of linguistic rules is first seen in Wang, the religious representative. Wang appears to conform to the gods' demands yet, as we shall see, his words imply the opposite. Wang greets the gods with reverent words and pious acts:

WANG. [...] Seit drei Tagen warte ich hier am Eingang der Stadt, besonders gegen Abend, damit ich sie als erster begrüßen kann. Später hätte ich ja dazu wohl kaum mehr Gelegenheit, sie werden von Hochgestellten umgeben sein und überhaupt stark überlaufen werden [...] Da sind sie! Verfügt über mich, Erleuchtete! *Er wirft sich zu Boden.* (595)

His belief in the power and authenticity of the gods does not diminish. Yet the confidence that Wang has in the gods negates itself in the last scene, the 'Gerichtslokal'. Wang asserts:

WANG. Ja, nur die Götter könnten die Wahrheit ausfindig machen. (637)

Although one might be tempted to take this remark as proof of Wang's faith in the authority of religion, it can readily be understood as showing the contrary. It turns into the trite cliché: only the gods can help us now. In other words, the situation is hopeless. If one analyzes Wang's religiosity still further, the contradictory nature of his religion becomes even clearer. Compared with his reverence toward the gods, Wang's attitude toward the people leaves much to be desired in him as a theologian:

> WANG *schimpft ihm nach.* Du schieläugiger Schieber! Hast du keine Gottesfurcht? Ihr werdet in siedendem Pech braten für eure Gleichgültigkeit! Die Götter scheißen auf euch! Aber ihr werdet es noch bereuen! Bis ins vierte Glied werdet ihr daran abzuzahlen haben! Ihr habt ganz Sezuan mit Schmach bedeckt! *Pause.* Jetzt bleibt nur noch die Prostituierte Shen Te, die kann nicht nein sagen. (596)

At this point, the audience becomes aware of the abrasive contradiction inherent in society's established religious institution, the Church. Wang lies, steals, and lives in the gutter, yet he simultaneously worships and fears the gods. He is the only person in Sezuan who recognizes the omniscience and omnipotence of the gods and is aware of the significance of their presence. Wang falls at their feet, calls them 'Erleuchtete', fears displeasing them, and holds little esteem for the morals of his society. He actively judges his society for living in a moral vacuum. At the same time, however, Wang is blind to contradictions in his own attitudes.

Wang's words contain contradictory characteristics even when he addresses the gods themselves. For example, Wang quickly realizes that he will not be able to find lodging for the gods. He therefore treats them with all the more respect to gain their favor. He wishes to meliorate any unpleasant situation (such as not finding lodging) with sympathetic words:

> DER ERSTE GOTT. Nimm das nächste Haus, mein Sohn! Versuch es zunächst mit dem allernächsten!
> WANG. Ich habe nur etwas Sorge, daß ich mir die Feindschaft der Mächtigen zuziehe, wenn ich einen von Ihnen besonders bevorzüge. (595)

This attitude can then be compared to the one he displays a few lines later:

DER ERSTE GOTT. [...] Hoffst du noch, mein Sohn?
WANG. Wie kannst du so etwas fragen [...]? (596)

Despite his hypocrisy, the gods still choose Wang as their middleman since they achieve the highest state of religious authority through him:

DIE GÖTTER.
   O du schwacher
   Gut gesinnter, aber schwacher Mensch!
   Wo da Not ist, denkt er, gibt es keine Güte!
   ..........................................................................
   O Schwäche, die an nichts ein gutes Haar läßt!
   O schnelles Urteil! O leichtfertige Verzweiflung!
WANG. Ich schäme mich sehr, Erleuchtete! (603)

The authenticity and validity of their godly speech remains unquestioned by Wang, just as the gods do not question the honesty of Wang's religious convictions.

The gods themselves also contribute to the breakdown of religious communication. As we have seen, they attempt to use their words to appease the people about the state of their society and the existence of goodness:

DER ERSTE GOTT. Wir müssen *einen* finden! Seit zweitausend Jahren geht dieses Geschrei, es gehe nicht weiter mit der Welt, so wie sie ist. Niemand auf ihr könne gut leben. (265)

*One* representative of goodness suffices. The gods insist throughout the play on this 'pars pro toto'. If they succeed in finding just one good person, their mission on earth is accomplished, and they may return to their 'Nichts'. Even such limited success guarantees that neither their norms will be repudiated nor their representative role as sovereign benefactors and appeasers of misery endangered. They find consolation in proving to the people that established theology remains unchanged and uncontested as the deliverer of comfort and peace in the midst of adversity. As Brecht understands it, it is necessary for those in authority, that is the Church and the state, to sustain tradition in order to be able to oppress the masses. From the social standpoint, such theological reasoning damns society permanently to an unquestioning frame of thinking that benefits the authorities.

Yet, as we have seen, these gods by their very presence deny the claim that established religion remains stable and established. The first god habitually speaks in religious clichés, which, in turn, negates the authenticity of the message all three are bringing. The other two gods, in turn, also disclaim any authority through their speech:

> DER ZWEITE GOTT. Aber ein kleines Zimmer genügt uns. Sag, wir kommen.
> WANG. Auch wenn es nicht aufgeräumt ist? Vielleicht wimmelt es von Spinnen.
> DER ZWEITE GOTT. Das macht nichts. Wo Spinnen sind, gibt's wenig Fliegen.
> DER DRITTE GOTT *freundlich zu Wang*: [...] mein Sohn, ich ekle mich vor Spinnen doch ein wenig. (595)

> DER DRITTE GOTT. So wollen wir uns hierhersetzen und warten.
> WANG. Aber es ist viel zuviel Verkehr hier, fürchte ich. Vielleicht gehen wir dort hinüber.
> DER ZWEITE GOTT. Wir sehen uns gern Menschen an. Gerade dazu sind wir hier.
> WANG. Nur: es zieht.
> DER ZWEITE GOTT. Oh, wir sind abgehärtete Leute. (597)

They accept Wang's deceiving words as truthful in a way similar to Wang's acceptance of their false divinity. Wang's 'authenticity' negates the divine authority of the gods' words because he remains socially inferior as a liar and a 'Betrüger' (596). Inevitably, the religious language of the gods turns from a divine utterance into an ideological instrument wielded by the religious hierarchy. Moreover, as we have seen, such ideological uses of religious language are in themselves failed attempts at bringing about submission to, and observance of, conventional forms and representations. As a result, a break in the authority of language occurs and leaves a void in its place. Neither the characters on the stage nor the language they use can fill this void.

Repeatedly, Brecht rebels against the tradition-bound daily use of religion. As a result, he begins to use the Bible as an argument against the Church. In the Scriptures he finds the criteria to interpret the existing society and enumerate its weaknesses. Although Brecht is an avowed atheist, criticism has shown his consistent use of biblical allusions and motifs. Many critical studies have confirmed Ilja Fradkin's (1965, 156–75) findings:

> Fast jedes Stück von Brecht enthält zahlreiche Reminiszenzen, direkte und versteckte Anspielungen, parodistische und polemische Entlehnungen aus der Bibel [...] Brecht bedient sich seiner Bibelkenntnis, in der er es mit jedem Theologen hätte aufnehmen können, jeweils in unterschiedlicher Weise, mit unterschiedlichem Ziel.

Brecht's atheism is generally accepted as a self-evident fact: almost every presentation of Brecht's ideological stance mentions his atheism along with his Marxism. However, this should strike not only scholars but also casual viewers of Brecht's work as a one-sided interpretation of Brecht's poetic production: for the frequency of the word 'God', religious statements and the resemblance to Biblical language must impress anyone moderately familiar with Brecht's works. In turn, it is difficult to contest Wolfgang Beutin's (1961, 260) view: 'Bertolt Brecht's critique of Christianity is not an inessential component of his art.'

The Bible fascinated Brecht. Already at fifteen he wrote a drama called *Die Bibel*. In 1928, when asked by a Berlin reporter what – from a literary viewpoint – had made the 'greatest impression' on him, he – in light of this youthful effort – quite understandably answered, 'Sie werden lachen, die Bibel.' After the completion of *Baal* (1918/19), Brecht attempted several times to write a biblical theater project focusing on David and Bathsheeba (1919). He noted in his diary after attending a passion play in Augsburg's Metropol Theater:

> Abends in der 'Großen deutschen Passion' der Brüder Faßnacht. Elender Text, geschmacklose Aufmachung. Aber gewisse Bibelworte nicht totzukriegen. Sie gehen durch und durch. Man sitzt unter Schauern, die einem, unter der Haut, den Rücken lang herunterstreichen, wie bei der Liebe. (153)[2]

Brecht's critical approach towards Christianity developed progressively. It began as subjective lyrical nihilism. His early works convey a sense of a world and nature tinged with Nietzschean nihilism. The themes always revolve around death and nothingness, and as a reaction to this, an extreme will to live. In the collection 'Hauspostille' (1990), written between 1917 and 1927, Brecht praises the night, which is all embracing, because one looks to heaven in vain. He glorifies transitoriness and nothingness, for example, in the poem 'Gegen Verführung', which expresses a radical renunciation of transcendence. Originally entitled 'Luzifers Abendlied', it epitomizes the nihilism of the entire 'Hauspostille'. Each line pointedly articulates an avid negation of the Christian world view and hope for redemption: 'Laßt euch nicht verführen! / Es gibt keine Wiederkehr / [...] Es kommt kein Morgen mehr' (260). The world revealed in Brecht's first book of verse knows neither kindness nor comfort, but only brutality and danger. Along with the ballads, we find in the 'Hauspostille' many poems that dwell on nature's inability to escape rot and decay as a mirror or symbol of the transitoriness of all life. In the poem 'Vom ertrunkenen Mädchen', God has forgotten the girl and therefore let her slowly decompose in the river. Again and again, these poems express the young Brecht's bitter notions almost like bad memories of heaven. With sadness and bitterness and, most often, with defiance and cynicism, the poet sings of a world forgotten and forsaken by God. Yet his early cynical and blasphemous style, the habit of invoking the name of God as well as modeling individual poems after hymns, prayers, and psalms in a biting manner, preclude labeling Brecht as nonreligious or indifferent to religion.

A literal interpretation of the Bible and the religious way of life became two separate issues for Brecht. His lifelong criticism of Christianity grew out of his observation that Christianity was no longer serving mankind. Instead, it revealed itself to be nothing but idle devotion and futile consolation. If there had once been a Christian spirit capable of awakening the multitude to act, it has by now become a collection of mere signifiers, useful for the manipulation of society but without relevance for understanding reality. Brecht writes in *Schriften zur Politik und Gesellschaft* (1974, 11):

> Aber die Kirche ist ein Zirkus für die Masse, mit Plakaten außen, auf denen Dinge sind, die es innen nicht gibt [...] Es mußte etwas sein, das alle hören konnten, auch die Tauben, auch die weit weg, daß sie nicht fortliefen [...] Der

Katholizismus ist ein Ausbeutersystem, ein amerikanisches Unternehmen, mit Gleichheit für alle, mit Stufenleitern, mit Lohntarifen [...] Und in dieser Kirche sind unabsehbare Wände leergelassen, mit Absicht, für die Phantasten, in den Speichern hat alles Platz, alle Ideen sind in den Dogmen unterzubringen.

For his part, Brecht uses the Bible as a tool for acquiring reason through doubt, for his mere mention of it implies a critical question directed toward the false ideologies of the Church and society. Brecht's vehement attack on established religion offers a necessary complement to what has too often been seen as Brecht's overriding intention, namely, to legitimize the replacement of traditional ideologies with the values of Marxism. At the same time, however, Brecht's work accomplishes more through the use of the Bible than merely a convenient and effective propaganda furthering Marxist aims.

The word 'Gott' appears four times in the singular in *Der gute Mensch* and eleven times in the plural. It quickly becomes an empty word. Rational constrictions of form break down as sentences disintegrate and as each synthesis is revealed as an illusion. What appears at first to be the long-awaited arrival of the gods on earth, the final deliverance of society from oppression, and lack of morality breaks down into contradictions and fragments of power and divinity. Likewise, theology has accommodated its beliefs to the prevailing power structures and has become the means for institutional self-preservation. Religion has forfeited its significance in order to make the functioning of the market smoother.

Over the centuries, divine words have been deprived of all functionality as signifiers of the truly holy. They endured in the service of the Church for too many centuries as appeasers of the masses. This, it is clear, explains the arrival of the gods. Since society has reached an almost chaotic state of disarray, the three godly representatives acceptable to the Church arrive to quiet the cries of the masses through religion. Yet they are unable to attain their goal, as their words are rendered void. No one listens to them and the cries grow louder. Their 'divine' words, as we have seen, have degenerated into mere clichés that only social forces continue to treat as significant.

The character Shen Te further emphasizes the inability of words to bridge the chasm. She expresses her frustration at the social and economic situation that commits her to acts (and words) that she recognizes as incompatible with her conscience and what it admonishes her to do. She appeals to the gods for help:

> SHEN TE. Halt, Erleuchtete, ich bin gar nicht sicher, daß ich gut bin. Ich möchte es wohl sein, nur wie soll ich meine Miete bezahlen? (271)

She awaits a statement from the gods through which she will be able to synthesize the two contradictory worlds, but the gods respond with an assertion of their own impotence:

> DER ZWEITE GOTT. Da können wir leider nichts tun. In das Wirtschaftliche können wir uns nicht mischen. (271)

Albeit refusing to meddle in economic matters, the gods present Shen Te with a large monetary gift as gratitude for her providing them with a place to sleep. By this action they force Shen Te to enter even more directly into the workings of the market. Now Shen Te is faced with a further dilemma: the gods impose goodness on her, yet their token of appreciation, money, stresses even further the incompatibility of morality and capitalism. When she admits her guilt before the gods in the courtroom, the opposition between moral requirements and survival in the world is openly displayed:

> SHEN TE. Jedoch Mitleid
> Schmerzte mich so, daß ich gleich in wölfischen Zorn verfiel
> Angesichts des Elends […] Und doch
> Wollte ich gern ein Engel sein den Vorstädten […]
> Verdammt mich: alles, was ich verbrach
> Tat ich, meinen Nachbarn zu helfen […] (354)

Brecht's dialectical approach leads him to present a society in which good and evil both depend on their very incompatibility in order to survive. This, in turn, cancels both out:

> SHEN TE. Gut zu sein und doch zu leben
> Zeriß mich wie ein Blitz in zwei Hälften. Ich
> Weiß nicht, wie es kam: gut sein zu andern
> Und zu mir konnte ich nicht zugleich. (353)

Therefore, language based on the concepts of good and evil breaks down and causes gaps in the significance of religious discourse. The most important stage in reworking language, once it has been stripped of its supposed concreteness, is, as Brecht writes in *Schriften zum Theater* (1993, 21), the replacement of the illusionistic synthesis by 'die radikale Trennung der Elemente'.

Brecht's epic theater, which recognizes that an awareness of the illusion as such facilitates the 'study' of it, achieves its goal at this point. The spectator finally realizes that the active attempts at identifying meaning are futile because the events taking place on the stage and the religious representation are mere illusions of reality that, in turn, likewise break down. To the extent that it is a political work, *Der gute Mensch* presents the domination of society by the prevailing power structure. Yet as an autonomous work, this play does not serve any single political ideal. Signifiers have been reduced to a 'Scheinexistenz', and the events on the stage stand out as autonomous units. This, in turn, inevitably creates a chasm between our own experience, which is embedded in the continuity of reality, and the fragmented events in the society of Sezuan. The great gap between the audience and the events on the stage, as well as the developing spaces on the stage, deprive of effectiveness not only the religious language of the gods but also all other ideological rhetoric. In the ensuing vacuum, as we shall observe, there then emerges a divine presence that refuses all forms of signification, definition, or interpretation and, therefore, ideology. Paul de Man, in *The Resistance to Theory* (1971, 11), defines ideology in the following manner: 'What we call ideology is precisely the confusion of linguistic with natural reality, of reference with phenomenalism.' De Man defines the term ideology in a manner that perfectly elucidates the present situation on the stage of Brecht's play.

Brecht's play *Der gute Mensch* undermines the naturalistic limitations of linking language to the characters. In epic theater, as we have seen, realistic dialogue is certainly not banished, but it is now juxtaposed with a variety of other types. The dialogues, the songs, and the monologues of *Der gute Mensch* are a part of this process of what Brecht (1993, 29) calls in *Schriften zum Theater* a 'Literarisierung des Theaters' that focuses primarily on rhetoric and ultimately renders

131

void any previous (mis)conceptions about the function of language. As a form of communication, the dialogue employed on Brecht's stage regularly gives way to a lyricism, a recognition that is absolutely indispensable for the present context. Eric Bentley (1963, 91–92) writes about Brecht's lyric theater as a genre:

> Bertolt Brecht's Epic Theater has been described in so many abstruse and pretentious ways that I recently attempted a simplification in a formula: Epic Theater Is Lyric Theater [...] I am saying that if Brecht's own paradox is permissible – that theater can lose the name 'dramatic' and acquire the title 'epic' – then it is equally permissible to call his nondramatic theater 'lyric' – for three reasons: first, that Brecht started out as a lyric poet and later developed his lyrics into plays; second, that the lyrics in his plays occupy a central, not a peripheral, position; and third, that, since the word *lyric* connotes the voice of the poet himself [...] Brecht's works can be called, like Goethe's, 'fragments of one long confession'.

Songs, obviously used in the theater before Brecht, now undergo an 'Umfunktionierung', a conversion of their function and status within the whole spectacle: Brecht's songs intervene between the stage and the audience and make it impossible for the audience to forget that it is seeing the reality of a performance and not illusionary slices of true reality. Through song, the performance acquires another dimension. Brecht's songs bring to our attention the autonomous character of the individual events occurring on the stage and break the effect that the tradition of illusionary theater creates through its emphasis on 'realistic' continuity and homogeneity. Like the narrator of a novel, the singer of the song manipulates the stage at will. The Brechtian idea of incorporating song into the play suggests to the audience the divided character of the stage. The actors participate as characters on a level of their own that corresponds to the situation at that moment on the stage and at the same time as individual performers on a level that may be completely contradictory to it. Consequently, by denying the conformity of events to only one level or sphere, the words and overall effect of the song create openings.

One example of this is the song 'Das Lied vom Rauch'. Ironically, the poor and depraved people who exploit Shen Te's goodness sing of the evilness of the world in order to entertain Shen Te as she works:

> DIE FRAU. Könnt Ihr nicht etwas singen, damit die Gastgeberin etwas
> Unterhaltung hat?
> DER NEFFE. Der Großvater fängt an!
> *Sie singen 'Das Lied vom Rauch'.*
> DER GROSSVATER.
>
> ...................................
> Darum sagt ich: laß es!
> Sieh den grauen Rauch
> Der in immer kältre Kälten geht: so
> Gehst du auch. (602)

The grandfather's complaints about the hopelessness on earth reiterate society's pessimistic perspectives as well as the distressing state into which society has lapsed. The smoke symbolizes what Brecht sees as the completely desolate direction toward which society and language are heading. From the point of view of the audience, the seemingly inherent nihilism of the song reflects the author's opinion of hopelessness and resigned fear and doubt. However, although the song continues in the same tone, the spectator is able to detect a shift away from the first impression:

> Die da alt sind, hör ich, haben nichts zu hoffen
> Denn nur Zeit schafft's, und an Zeit gebricht's. (602)

We must now understand the doubt in the progress of mankind and in existence as only a reaction to the bourgeois society.

Not only do society's members thus prove themselves aware of their inevitable doom by merely sitting and waiting passively for a better world to make itself known; they also emphasize their collectively stagnant character. This reveals the authoritarian character of a system that depends on the hopelessness and resignation of the individual for its survival and development. Furthermore, the dramatic exit of the gods at the end of the play in a cloud of smoke underscores even further the rigidity, hypocrisy, and absurdity of the three representatives of religion. As a result, the symbol of the smoke, which appears – according to Brecht – to stand for the transitoriness of a society controlled by an ideological institution, is itself transitory and finally disperses. Nothing remains in its place but a clear space. The morality and character of the individual who lives under the dominating control of economic circumstances in 'Das Lied vom Rauch' disintegrate into nothingness. Within this vacuous space, the disappearance of all forms of identification of the spectator with the character and situations on the stage leaves him to experience the song as a discontinuous and therefore autonomous performance.

The transitoriness of society and the destruction of lasting signifiers are further accentuated as the song continues:

Sah den Redlichen, den Fleißigen geschunden
So versucht ich's mit dem krummen Pfad.
Doch auch der führt unsereinen nur nach unten
Und so weiß ich mir halt fürder keinen Rat. (602)

The individual must come to the conclusion that neither rhetoric nor deeds are capable of overcoming oppression. These means, as well as immorality, lead into the same 'Nichts' to which the gods belong:

Doch uns Jungen, hör ich, steht das Tor weit offen
Freilich, hör ich, steht es offen nur ins Nichts. (602)

Society is dependent on temporality and stability. It is unable to overcome the imprisoning frame of signifiers. For this reason, society needs the arrival of the three gods. They represent physical authority, control, and the supremacy of institutionalized religion. Yet, as we shall see, since they negate their own role and thus reveal themselves to be empty representation, the false illusion of stability is dispelled. The 'Nichts' of the gods is exposed in its vacuity, and we are left with awareness of the illusionary machinery of the culture industry. This was indeed Brecht's objective. Through the act of 'Verfremdung', we are no longer able to take art for life. At the same time, the play does not lapse into propaganda.

Shen Te appears in front of the curtain in the 'Zwischenspiel' between Act 5 and Act 6. She addresses the public directly when she sings 'Das Lied von der Wehrlosigkeit der Götter und Guten'. Her position *in front* of the stage, her addressing the audience directly, and her singing instead of speaking lift her out of the stage action: so we, too, are momentarily liberated from the confines of the illusionary realism on stage, and we become detached observers of Shen Te's act. Whether the melody is beautiful or repulsive, all of these aspects of the song keep us from experiencing sentimentality or otherwise being emotionally affected. Instead, Shen Te, now outside of her traditional role and place, presents us with the revolutionary character of epic theater and articulates the tension between morality and religious representations:

> In unserem Land
> Braucht der Nützliche Glück. Nur
> Wenn er starke Helfer findet
> Kann er sich nützlich erweisen.
> Die Guten
> Können sich nicht helfen, und die Götter sind machtlos.
>> Warum haben die Götter nicht Tanks und Kanonen
>> Schlachtschiffe und Bombenflugzeuge und Minen
> Die Bösen zu fällen, die Guten zu schonen?
> Es stünde wohl besser mit uns und mit ihnen […] (614)

The powerlessness of the gods in the society of Sezuan is juxtaposed with a possibility of a change through force and violence. As Brecht sees it, this text intends to awaken and inspire the audience towards exactly such a change through force and revolt. Yet the violence and destruction have already occurred within the text. The contradictions within the form and within the content present the actions on the stage as autonomous events. This autonomy shatters the control that illusion might have over the play or over the audience. As a consequence, spaces open up on the stage. These spaces cannot be attributed to any thing. In the place of 'Tanks und Kanonen' of the three gods and of the moral and religious vacuum of Sezuan, a presence, an 'es', appears on the stage. Such a presence would stand better, 'stünde besser', than the language and presence of three helpless representations that, as we have seen, stand only for 'Nichts'. This presence is indeed capable of inspiring the audience by revealing that God exists, not as an ideological representation, but rather at the place where conventions and linguistic rules shatter.

By successively forestalling the illusion that individual characters have spontaneously invented their own discourse, the use of the aside and other forms of addressing the audience breaks apart the world of on-stage illusions and shows its artificiality. The artifice of addressing the public from the stage in *Der gute Mensch* has a distancing effect on the spectator. The naturalists rejected asides and monologues by simply arguing that they never occurred in real life but were only theatrical conventions to assist the audience at the cost of the illusion of reality. Brecht, on the other hand, makes use of these conventions in order to destroy the illusion of reality on the stage.

The direct address to the audience presents the situation on stage in a manner that proves to be quite biased. This occurs already in the 'Vorspiel':

> *Es ist Abend. Wang, der Wasserverkäufer, stellt sich dem Publikum vor.*
> WANG. Ich bin Wasserverkäufer hier in der Hauptstadt von Sezuan [...] Der Himmel soll sehr beunruhigt sein wegen der vielen Klagen, die zu ihm aufsteigen. Seit drei Tagen warte ich hier am Eingang der Stadt [...] damit ich sie als erster begrüßen kann. Später hätte ich ja dazu wohl kaum mehr Gelegenheit, sie werden von Hochgestellten umgeben sein und überhaupt stark überlaufen werden [...] Mit denen sieht es schon ganz anders aus. Sie sind wohlgenährt, weisen kein Zeichen irgendeiner Beschäftigung auf und haben Staub auf den Schuhen, kommen also von weit her [...] (595)

Wang introduces us to the play and acquaints us with the unfortunate situation of the society of Sezuan. He appears to be the play's narrator, yet we soon realize that he is also one of the characters and that we have based our understanding of the situation on the statements of a character whose words are colored by his own role in events. Wang's biased introduction appears to have no immediate consequence beyond preparing us, through an illusion, to accept Wang as a religious person. Yet as soon as the spectator becomes acquainted with the situation, the introduction induces a strong distancing effect and the illusion is shattered. This approach creates an intended gap between the stage and reality and hinders the possibility that the spectator might in the end identify with the character. The address to the audience is therefore another way in which the stage becomes a 'Literarisierung des Theaters'.

Through Shen Te's progressive emphasis on the situation of society, the spectator is gradually driven to confront the evil of humanity, not through an emotion, but through a critical examination. Shen Te's first monologue already begins to bring to light the artifice of addressing the public:

> SHEN TE *zum Publikum*. Drei Tage ist es her, seit die Götter weggezogen sind […] Ich habe mir mit dem Geld einen Tabakladen gekauft. Gestern bin ich hier eingezogen, und ich hoffe, jetzt viel Gutes tun zu können. Da ist zum Beispiel die Frau Shin, die frühere Besitzerin des Ladens. Schon gestern kam sie und bat mich um Reis für ihre Kinder. Auch heute sehe ich sie wieder über den Platz kommen mit ihrem Topf. (598)

As she expresses to the audience the divisive character inherent in society and her frustration with it, the tension increases:

> SHEN TE *zum Publikum*.
> Sie sind schlecht.
> Sie sind niemandes Freund.
> Sie gönnen keinem einen Topf Reis.
> Sie brauchen alles selber.
> Wer könnte sie schelten? (600)

The first four lines reiterate what the audience and Shen Te saw and experienced, that is, the lack of morality of the people whom Shen Te tried to help. The fifth line, however, asks a question that puts us in the position of those we might otherwise have condemned. The depravity of society observed in the play threatens to turn Shen Te and us into judges, yet this fifth line cancels out the possibility of such a judgment. The question demands from the audience an answer, not a verdict. Brecht's purpose in bringing the spectator to such awareness is to drive him to action and to compel him to change the passive, ideology-infested, bourgeois world. However, the spectator now realizes that doing good in the world leads to further contradiction and opposition. The spectator is now conscious of the fact that as an individual belonging to this society, one cannot arrive at a transformation of one's own. Instead, the spectator, who simultaneously senses the nearness of the stage and the chasm between it and him, now feels compelled and stimulated to search for answers within the chasm.

Shen Te describes in the following lines the failings of the individual. Too many people grab hold of the boat that would otherwise have saved at least some. Instead of using it as a lifeboat for a few, the people cause the boat to sink. The spectator, confronted with the vivid imagery of this new depiction, becomes aware of a corresponding pulling and sinking around him:

> SHEN TE [...] *Zum Publikum:*
> Der Rettung kleiner Nachen
> Wird sofort in die Tiefe gezogen:
> Zu viele Versinkende
> Greifen gierig nach ihm. (602)

Perhaps the spectator experiences a similar force drawing him onto the stage. This process of identification, however, ceases before it can begin, due to Shen Te's direct appeal to the spectator, who recognizes his role as observer and recognizes the deceptive attraction of words. The process of alienation instantly tears down any form of emotional attachment. Consequently, we begin to discern, critically, in what manner the stage relates to our own reality and at the same time the width and depth of the distance that exists between the platform and us. Szondi is aware of this ability of epic theater. He writes in *Theorie des Modernen Dramas* (1978b, 107):

> Der Vorgang auf der Bühne füllt die Aufführung nicht mehr vollständig aus, wie einst der dramatische, bei dem das Moment der Aufführung deshalb untergehen mußte (historisch faßbar am Verschwinden des Prologs in der Renaissance). Der Vorgang ist jetzt Erzählgegenstand der Bühne, sie verhält sich zu ihm wie der Epiker zu seinem Gegenstand [...] Ebenso wird der Zuschauer nicht außerhalb des Spiels gelassen, ins Spiel aber auch nicht suggestiv hineingerissen ('illudiert'), so daß er aufhörte, Zuschauer zu sein, sondern er wird dem Vorgang als Zuschauer gegenüber gesetzt, der Vorgang wird ihm als Gegenstand seiner Betrachtung dargeboten.

As we are thus 'in die Tiefe gezogen' (602), we become aware of the vast depth of the vacuum of meaning. At this moment, the spectator finally realizes that all representation and signification has been broken down and all optimism for a better society through ideology has been invalidated. As Shen Te tells us:

*Zum Publikum:*
In unserem Lande
Dürfte es trübe Abende nicht geben
Selbst die Stunde zwischen Nacht und Morgen
Und die ganze Winterzeit dazu, das ist gefährlich.
Denn angesichts des Elends
Genügt ein Weniges
Und die Menschen werfen
Das unerträgliche Leben fort. (608)

All of Shen Te's attempts at goodness turn against her. On her wedding day, as the guests depart because there is no priest, Sun sings 'Das Lied vom Sankt Nimmerleinstag':

Und an diesem Tag zahlt die Güte sich aus
Und die Schlechtigkeit kostet den Hals
Und Verdienst und Verdienen, die machen gute Mienen
Und tauschen Brot und Salz.
    Am Sankt Nimmerleinstag
    Da tauschen sie Brot und Salz. (623)

The impossibility of such a day on earth – already evidenced by the title of the song: 'Sankt Nimmerleinstag' – will take place 'never in this life', as Langenscheidt defines the word. The oppressed will never see the day on which goodness will be rewarded and evil punished. Paradoxically, Sun sings hopelessly of that time on earth when the poor will prosper and have peace and harmony. At this moment we become aware of the incompatibility of morality and the masses' economic needs. Conflicting statements multiply in the first two verses. Sun sings the third verse:

Und das Gras sieht auf den Himmel hinab
Und den Fluß hinauf rollt der Kies
Und der Mensch ist nur gut. Ohne daß er mehr tut
Wird die Erde zum Paradies. (322)

Sun sings that paradise will arrive, not when measured time so dictates, but rather as soon as the new 'day' appears. 'Sankt Nimmerleinstag', a common expression of the impossibility of something, is a day that clearly cannot arrive in the world as it currently functions.

139

This, of course, is not much different from the traditional reasoning that states that 'der Mensch' will be good only when hell freezes over. This expression furthermore resembles the traditional Messianic thinking that asserts the need of a savior in order to bring the world out of its hopeless condition. Yet on that day of revelation the present world will be turned upside down. The grass and the sky will exchange positions and rivers will no longer submit to a pulling force. The revolution Brecht advocated takes on new dimensions. Similarly, Frederick Tollini (2003), writing on this particular song, expresses what he refers to as 'images of social reversal' (74) that ultimately become 'Christian'. He writes:

> It seems to me that Brecht's use of scripture is analogous to Marx's setting Hegel 'on his head', but in this case, the inversion of values brings about a greater appreciation of what is implied in the original, even as the 'Urtext' is mocked. If that is so, Brecht's message turns out to be eminently 'Christian'. (75)

In Tollini's 1998 production of the play, he specifically emphasized the 'ironic juxtaposition of traditional faith and injustice in the world, while giving it the voice of the "common man"' (75).

Further incongruities between what appears to be reality and what appears to be an illusion occur in the epilogue of the play:

> *Vor dem Vorhang tritt ein Spieler und wendet sich entschuldigend an das Publikum mit einem Epilog.*
> Verehrtes Publikum, jetzt kein Verdruß:
> Wir wissen wohl, das ist kein rechter Schluß.
> Vorschwebte uns: die goldene Legende.
> Unter der Hand nahm sie ein bitteres Ende [...] (641)

The gods have departed and nothing has changed. Since Shen Te's goodness did not secure her the title of 'saint', she cannot appear in the history books as a legendary saintly figure. Furthermore, the spectator, despite his awareness of it, still does not have an answer for the dialectical tension inherent in society. Instead, he gazes at the breaks and spaces opening on the stage. The actor expresses in the 'Epilog' the 'zerschmettert' state of reality ('nicht nur zum Scheine'). His prodding words incite a search for an ending to the play:

Wir sind bankrott, wenn Sie uns nicht empfehlen!
Vielleicht fiel uns aus lauter Furcht nichts ein.
Das kam schon vor. Was könnt die Lösung sein?
.................................................................
Soll es ein andrer Mensch sein? Oder eine andre Welt?
Vielleicht nur andere Götter? Oder keine?
Wir sind zerschmettert und nicht nur zum Scheine!
Der einzige Ausweg wär aus diesem Ungemach:
Sie selber dächten auf der Stelle nach […] (641)

Yet the deficiency and incongruity of religious language and representation does not allow for an ending. Instead, it brings forth the very need for an alternative to an ending. This total rupture in communication in the last act produces a space. A similar space can be experienced in the openness in the conclusion of the play:

Den Vorhang zu und alle Fragen offen […] Was könnt die Lösung sein?
Wir konnten keine finden, nicht einmal für Geld. (356)

Yet how can we find an answer when we are presented with only more questions? The possibility of an answer lies in the questions themselves and within the breaks and gaps that have arisen on the stage and between the stage and the audience. The increasing tendency of drama, the most social and communal of the arts, is to refuse to speak about man's relationship to himself, his world, and his God. These four questions in *Der gute Mensch* leave us, the viewers, with open endings. We are prompted to actively search for the answer. Szondi (1978b, 107) explains in *Theorie des Modernen Dramas*:

Die Bühne, die Welt, nun nicht mehr bedeutend, sondern nur abbildend, verliert mit ihrer Absolutheit die Rampe, dank der sie das Licht sich selber zu spenden schien. Sie wird mit Scheinwerfern aus dem Kreise der Zuschauer beleuchtet, zum deutlichen Zeichen, daß ihnen hier etwas gezeigt werden soll. Das Bühnenbild wird verfremdet, indem es keine wirkliche Örtlichkeit mehr vortäuscht, sondern als selbständiges Element des Epischen Theaters, zitiert, erzählt, vorbereitet und erinnert.

The realization that the representation of 'andere Götter' could not alter the situation incites the spectator to examine the former representations and the significance of negativity and open endings. In the

141

absence of gods, in the word 'keine' a divine presence that is not visible or tangible emerges.

Language, as we have seen, is a means of representation. As much as characters or stage props do, it too acts as a sign and functions as a representation of a pre-established and deceptive meaning. Brecht's concept of the 'Literarisierung', the addition of titles or short commentaries as well as the use of language to project an attitude or position, not only serves to punctuate and complement the action, but also functions as a necessary component of the concept of 'Gestus'. Brecht's theory of 'Gestus' revolves around the process of giving effective verbal expression to socially directed perspectives. Brecht himself cites a celebrated sentence from Luther's Bible as an illustration of the 'gestic' principle: 'Wenn dich dein Auge ärgert, reiß es aus.' This is a forceful piece of syntax built on the two connected notions: the reasons for a particular action followed by the action itself. The syntactical structure itself, therefore, is mimetic of the precise form of action to be taken. However, Brecht also has recourse to non-verbal forms of expression to supplement linguistic and syntactical devices.

Brecht's 'Gestus', consequently, is a method of literalization of the theater that strives to destroy the aura of aesthetic illusion, to divert the attention of the viewer, and thus to undermine the theater's capacity to absorb the viewer's concentration totally within the boundaries of the artificial reality it has created. Brecht points out in *Kleines Organon für das Theater* (1960b, 28–29):

> Wir brauchen ein Theater, das nicht nur Empfindungen, Einblicke und Impulse ermöglicht, die das jeweilige historische Feld der menschlichen Beziehungen erlaubt, auf dem die Handlungen jeweils stattfinden, sondern Gedanken und Gefühle verwendet, die bei der Veränderung des Feldes selbst eine Rolle spielen.

The technique of literalization seeks to abolish all traditional, culinary enjoyment of theater.

Brecht's non-Aristotelian theater – that is, one not devoted to evoking catharsis – is designed to promote a new reaction on the part of the spectator. His stage advocates a radical tension between fixed linguistic and theatrical traditions and his constructions in progress. In

'Was ist das epische Theater', Benjamin (1977e, 521) describes this quality of Brecht's epic theater as 'gestisch'. Benjamin illustrates his use of this term by enumerating the devices by which Brecht strips theater of all illusionary pretenses and thereby prevents the traditional empathetic relationship of the observer to the events and people on stage. Brecht's theater, he continues, points to its own artificiality, to the fact that it is distinct from reality, something merely constructed and in contrast with other forms of theater:

> Die naturalistische Bühne, nichts weniger als Podium, ist eine durchaus illusionistische. Ihr eigenes Bewußtsein, Theater zu sein, kann sie nicht fruchtbar machen, sie muß es, wie jede dynamische Bühne, verdrängen, um sich ihrem Ziele, das Wirkliche abzubilden, unabgelenkt widmen zu können. (521–22)

In the same essay, Benjamin considers the Brechtian principle of 'Montage', which became for him the modern, constructive, and active form of allegory, namely the ability to connect dissimilars in such a way as to 'shock' people into new recognitions. Benjamin came to regard 'montage' as the major fundamental principle of the artistic imagination in the age of technology. By referring to this term, Benjamin brings to our attention that Brecht's epic theater is concerned with the problem of esthetic reception and that it uses every possible modern technological device to break the 'spell' that the traditional theater of illusion exerts over the spectator. In an essay entitled 'Der Autor als Produzent', Benjamin (1973a) argues that a Brechtian 'Umfunktionierung' is the only way in which a politically committed art could engage with the class struggle. He writes:

> Für die Veränderung von Produktionsformen und Produktionsinstrumenten im Sinne einer fortschrittlichen – daher an der Befreiung der Produktionsmittel interessierten, daher im Klassenkampf dienlichen – Intelligenz hat Brecht den Begriff der Umfunktionierung geprägt. Er hat als erster an den Intellektuellen die weittragende Forderung erhoben: den Produktionsapparat nicht zu beliefern, ohne ihn zugleich, nach Maßgabe des Möglichen, im Sinne des Sozialismus zu verändern [...] Wir stehen nämlich der Tatsache gegenüber – für welche das vergangene Jahrzehnt in Deutschland Beweise in Fülle geliefert hat –, daß der bürgerliche Produktions- und Publikationsapparat erstaunliche Mengen von revoltionären Themen assimilieren, ja propagieren kann, ohne damit seinen

eigenen Bestand und den Bestand der ihn besitzenden Klasse ernstlich in Frage zu stellen. (691–92)

The term 'Wende' has considerable significance as a form of 'Gestus' in the play *Der gute Mensch*. As Rainer Nägele (1991) explains it, a pause or an interruption is a 'Wende' and the center from which a rotation originates. Just as it is possible to create breaks and spaces in the spoken or written word of Brecht's play, so too the physical representations can be torn down to allow for a divine presence that cannot be literally labeled or grasped. Shui Ta excuses his 're-presence' with the statement 'Es kommt alles von der Not.' As Rainer Nägele (1991) argues in *Theater, Theory, Speculation*, the word 'Not' exists in the term 'Notwendigkeit'. 'Notwendigkeit' is a necessity as well as a turning point or 'Wende' (135–66). He writes in detail of the terms 'Notwendigkeit' and 'Haltung' as it relates to Brecht's theory. It is offers a point of stability and a place of shift away from the need, 'Not', while at the same time it marks a necessary rupture and change in the repetition of need. Nägele describes this term as carrying a strong element of negativity, lack, or absence, from which force and resistance to repetition seem to arise (146). If everything in the present world of Sezuan originates from need, then a turn ('Wende') cuts into its continuous repetitive movement and interrupts its present flow of life and its illusory ideology of progress. A break with this narrowness, tightness ('Enge'), and friction produces a place of positive openness and space. The moment of this interruption and of the turn is the moment of the caesura. In the 'Vorspiel' of *Der gute Mensch*, the gods insist that they have finally found one good person. Shen Te could have simply agreed, yet she responds: '*Halt, Erleuchtete, ich bin gar nicht sicher, daß ich gut bin*' (271). With the gesture and word 'Halt', she calls upon the gods literally to stop walking. 'Halt' is a command to stand still as well as to stop talking. Epic theater seeks to disrupt the normal flow of events in life in order to isolate them and subject them to intensive critical scrutiny. Brecht's strategy of interruption was an attempt at distraction, an effect opposed to the immersion of the recipient in traditional esthetic or – to use the terminology developed by Benjamin (1963) later in *Das Kunstwerk im Zeitalter seiner technischen Reproduzierbarkeit* –

auratic works of art. At the end of the play, Shui Ta is standing before his judges, the gods. He refuses to answer any questions until a climactic point develops. Once this point is reached, the change occurs:

> ALLE. Wo ist sie?
> SHUI TA. Verreist.
> WANG. Wohin?
> SHUI TA. Ich sage es nicht!
> ALLE. Aber warum mußte sie verreisen?
> SHUI TA *schreiend.* Weil ihr sie sonst zerissen hättet!
> *Es tritt eine plötzliche Stille ein.*
> SHUI TA *ist auf seinen Stuhl gesunken.* Ich kann nicht mehr. Ich will alles aufklären [...] Ich kann nicht mehr schweigen. (639)

The moment in which the 'sudden' silence occurs is the same moment that a change, a 'Wende', must take place. Paradoxically, because of the 'plötzliche Stille', Shui Ta/Shen Te can no longer keep silent ('schweigen') and reveals her double identity through the gesture of taking off her theatrical mask. The mask and the clothes have comprised her persona up to this point. The act of revelation provides a recognition that transcends the information confirmed in any words she has spoken up to this point. Yet Shui Ta speaks before physically revealing Shen Te: 'Dann laßt mich euch die furchtbare Wahrheit gestehen: ich bin euer guter Mensch' (353). The caesura *produces* knowledge; it does not communicate it. Shen Te, before her revealing gesture, communicates a 'Wahrheit' that is meaningless. She is not 'der gute Mensch', since the good person cannot 'be' in the present world. However, in the act of taking off her mask and standing there, 'Shen Te steht da', she presents a paradoxical doubleness: on one hand, the demasked human being exposed in its contradictory nature to its society, and, on the other hand, the same demasked human being exposing the false morals of society.

The caesura of Brecht's epic theater is a point of departure that cuts through the representation and interrupts false ideology. According to Benjamin, 'Haltung' (posture) replaces interiority, the constitutive space of the bourgeois subject. Nägele, in *Theater, Theory, Speculation* (1991, 149), quotes Benjamin:

Ich glaube nicht, daß es zu kühn ist, zu sagen, daß wir auf Haltung stoßen, wo die essentielle Einsamkeit eines Menschen in unser Blickfeld rückt. Die Einsamkeit, die sehr wohl, weit entfernt Ort seiner individuellen Fülle zu sein, der Ort seiner geschichtlich bedingten Leere, der persona als seines Miß-geschicks sein könnte.

At the lonely place of the divided self of Shen Te, the personal 'Leere' gives way to a new posture. Shen Te creates discontinuity through her '*Halt*ung'. As Nägele (1991, 142) asserts,

'Halt' opens the re-presentation of the constitution of a 'Haltung' by interrupting the smooth narrative of the revolutionary process. It condenses the intricate economy of movement and rigidity that 'Haltung' articulates in Benjamin and Brecht. It is both a *Halt* that gives a certain stability in the midst of change ('daß im Finstern für uns einiges Haltbare sei') and a destabilizing interruption, a 'stop!' in a smooth flow of orders.

Through the use of 'Gestus' as the product of 'plumpes Denken', Brecht's theater lays bare the devices at work on the stage and in the audience in order to make these devices reveal inherent contradictions in traditional codes and representations and, consequently, to reveal the contradictory state of history. The Brechtian 'plumpes Denken' refers to a need for thought to simplify itself and to crystallize out into essentials before it can be made practice: 'Die Hauptsache ist, plump denken lernen. Plumpes Denken, das ist das Denken der Großen.' Benjamin retains Brecht's term when he writes in a review of the 'Dreigroschenroman' in *Versuche über Brecht* (1979, 90):

Es gibt viele Leute, die unter einem Dialektiker einen Liebhaber von Subtilitäten verstehen [...] Plumpe Gedanken gehören gerade in den Haushalt des dialektischen Denken, weil sie gar nichts anders darstellen als die Anweisung der Theorie auf die Praxis.

'Plumpes Denken' requires 'Vorstellung' as much as 'Vorstellung' re-quires 'plumpes Denken'. 'Vorstellung' is possible only after the spectator has been made aware that representations are merely vacu-ous elements. The spectators must become critically active and banish the representations on the stage from their thinking and awaken to the possible implication of the resulting emptiness.

Verehrtes Publikum, los, such dir selbst den Schluß!
Es muß ein guter da sein, muß, muß, muß! (641)

Since no end is given, the audience must employ its 'Vorstellungs-kraft' to look beyond what is tangible and limited. The illusion of the stage has progressively given way to gaps and breaks. The open space and open end become a place in which representations and signification cannot exist. Since signification is impossible here and since the space cannot remain in such a vacuum, it becomes filled with what cannot be represented: 'der Spielraum Gottes'.

The relation of art to the prevailing power structure is central to the notion of crisis in modernity. The breakdown of classical theological systems and increasing social power of ecclesiastical institutions undermine traditional outward forms of religion in the eyes of the esthete who then may experience a feeling of despair in a desolate world thus deprived of a visible or at least signifiable God.

To rebuff rumors that it is impossible to be good in the world as it is, the three gods begin their search for morality with the assertion:

Die Welt kann bleiben, wie sie ist, wenn genügend gute Menschen gefunden werden, die ein menschenwürdiges Dasein leben können. (596)

Yet they must soon amend their formulation, and the search evolves from a search for 'genügend gute Menschen', to one for 'ein guter Mensch'. The three divinities represent the human conceptions of the highest authorities, for these omnipotent beings decide on meaning, morality, and value throughout the world in a manner that makes them identical with the traditional beliefs of the bourgeoisie. This is, of course, possible for Brecht, who, as a Marxist, sees class as an international phenomenon.

Society in Sezuan has reached a state of complete disorder that cannot continue. The masses are calling out in desperation:

WANG. Der Himmel soll sehr beunruhigt sein wegen der vielen Klagen, die zu ihm aufsteigen. (265)

The arrival of the gods in Sezuan is eagerly anticipated because, according to society, only divine intervention can alter the situation:

147

WANG. Aber in unserer Provinz herrscht überhaupt große Armut. Es heißt allgemein, daß uns nur noch die Götter helfen können. (265)

Through Wang's comment 'Es heißt allgemein' the spectator instantly understands the situation of the poor as a unified mass that will act only from a general consensus. Since no one from among them seems able to achieve such a consensus, it must be left to the gods to intervene and change their impoverished situation.

On the one hand, we instantly recognize that the gods who come to Sezuan represent merely the Church – in other words, an institution that serves the traditional cultural and political structure and with it the status quo. On the other hand, however, because they observe and judge their surroundings according to 'other-worldly' norms, they cannot relate to the actual economic and moral situation of society. They measure the world with norms that do not take into account its present status as a product of historical materialism. Consequently, they cannot comprehend mankind's situation, and merely reaffirm and legitimize their own authority over the masses.

Despite their commitment to sociopolitical aspects of life, it cannot be denied that the gods of *Der gute Mensch* still manifest several characteristics that bring to mind significant aspects of the Christian religion. In turn, the audience is from the beginning tempted to compare these three institutionalized gods to the Christian God, who likewise came in human form to save mankind. The initial entrance of the gods is simple and quiet. Their arrival as ordinary human beings instantly recalls the Bible's account of the arrival of Christ as a mortal and his birth outside in the stable. Only a few recognized Him. Now only one person awaits Brecht's three gods, and only a single person is willing to give them a place to sleep. More significant parallels can be drawn regularly from the text. For example, the gods, tired and disturbed by the cries of the masses, cannot help but recall the very beginning:

DER ERSTE GOTT. [...] Seit zweitausend Jahren geht dieses Geschrei, es gehe nicht weiter mit der Welt, so wie sie ist. (265)

Not only does this comment suggest certain reservations about the outcome of God's previous work on earth, but it also prompts the spectator to see the gods' arrival in Sezuan as a parallel event. Furthermore, this speaks directly of the morals of society, which are shown as not having changed since Christ's birth. The comment by the first god also brings to mind the biblical promise that God will return again soon. Wang, the water seller, points to this: 'das Himmelreich ist nahe herbeigekommen.' Yet what appears on stage is not what it seems to be, and one misses the presence of God all the more because it has been promised. Through Wang's presentation of the situation, Brecht prepares the audience for God's coming only to then consciously and visibly withhold it.

Wang perceives that these three travelers have human characteristics. First, these gods have physical qualities similar to those of humans. We become aware of this when Wang likens their appearance to that of other human beings and then describes them as such. Furthermore, they display emotions such as fear of spiders, loss of patience with one another, embarrassment, and surprise. Only Wang's comment at the beginning of the play makes it possible for the spectator to accept these three as the promised gods:

> WANG. [...] Nicht einmal diese Herren dort – *zwei Herren gehen vorüber* – kommen mir wie Götter vor, sie haben einen brutalen Ausdruck wie Leute, die viel prügeln, und das haben die Götter nicht nötig. Aber dort, diese drei! Mit denen sieht es schon ganz anders aus [...] Das sind sie! Verfügt über mich, Erleuchtete! (595)

The spectator directly understands that he is being presented with Wang's and, accordingly, society's conception of divine appearance.

Moreover, as the play progresses, we also realize that the three gods have individualized personalities. Their specific characteristics and personalities can distinguish them. Paradoxically, however, their individual identities find no more recognition than identification by ordinal numbers: 'der erste Gott', 'der zweite Gott', and 'der dritte Gott'. The first god speaks the most, regularly emphasizes the dogmatic need to fulfill their fixed program, and holds fast to the idea that goodness exists in the world. The second god is more skeptical and sets more realistic goals for the three. At the same time, he holds rigorously to a belief in mankind's goodness; thus he worries when Shen Te does not appear to live up to their expectations. The third god

149

tries to be more sensible and considerate towards the needs of mankind (he is the only one who thinks of money as a gift for Shen Te). He alone draws from experience the conclusion that the world is unfit to be inhabited and that their moral and ethical expectations of mankind are too high. The apparent contradictions among these personality types and their resultant views create an unresolvable threefold tension, not the familiar Trinity of Father, Son, and Holy Ghost. In any case, the spectator now understands that the three gods might, at least by earthly traditions and expectations, be considered divine.

But, perhaps more importantly, Wang also recognizes the gods as such by their distinctively wealthy attributes:

> Aber dort, diese drei! Mit denen sieht es schon ganz anders aus. Sie sind wohlgenährt, weisen kein Zeichen irgendeiner Beschäftigung auf und haben Staub auf den Schuhen, kommen also von weit her. Das sind sie! (595)

Wang's excitement at seeing the gods reflects his expectations of what a god would look like. His immediate recognition of the gods occurs because they present themselves in the very manner that Wang expected. Consequently, this brings to the spectator's attention the idea that, as Brecht would argue, in the eyes of the conditioned poor the rich are the representatives of authority and, hence, of religion. The masses, it seems, will be collectively ('allgemein') appeased by believing in the divinity of their creator(s) and by faith in their power. For the very purpose of appeasing society, the gods themselves need to be reassured that, despite the many complaints by the proletariat that the situation on earth is unbearable, the present world order should remain unchanged. The presence of these gods is necessary in order to quieten the people. Everything must remain as it has traditionally been.

Two reasons exist for the gods' desire to keep everything as is. First, as we have seen, they represent the highest authority on earth and enjoy having people praying to them and raising their voices in their desperation and need for help. The masses depend on the gods for peace and security. Second, because of their role as sovereign beings, the gods are able to act as conciliators in a world that would otherwise fall into turmoil. They expect to continue to function without changing the world. As it turns out, they *must* retain power since the masses depend on their omnipotence for their emotional well-being. Yet they are nothing more than false representations. They have no real authority and repeatedly remind the characters and the audience that they are 'nur Betrachtende'. As it turns out, these three gods cannot claim responsibility for anything.

On the surface, the three gods seem to satisfy the audience's traditional expectations of God as the almighty judge and benefactor and as the ally of the weak and the poor. Yet behind their masks, they are nothing – 'Nichts'. Together, the three gods of *Der gute Mensch* outwardly carry out the function of a deus ex machina. They come down mysteriously from heaven at the beginning of the play and return to heaven in a grandiose style that is meant to provide lasting confirmation of their omnipotence, omniscience, and benevolence, because as judges in the *Gerichtslokal*, the three gods appear to maintain their ultimate authority to decide the fate of Shen Te/Shui Ta. Having passed judgment and settled the issue of goodness on earth, they return to heaven in a manner befitting only gods:

> DER ERSTE GOTT *heftig:* Verwirrtes, sehr Verwirrtes! Unglaubliches, sehr Unglaubliches! Sollen wir eingestehen, daß unsere Gebote tödlich sind? Sollen wir verzichten auf unsere Gebote? *Verbissen:* Niemals! Soll die Welt geändert werden? Wie? Von wem? Nein, es ist alles in Ordnung! *Er schlägt schnell mit dem Hammer auf den Tisch.*
> Und nun – *auf ein Zeichen von ihm ertönt Musik.*
> Eine rosige Helle entsteht –
> Laßt uns zurückkehren […] Jedoch
> Gedenken wir dort über den Gestirnen
> Deiner, Shen Te, des guten Menschen, gern
> Die du von unserm Geist hier unten zeugst
> In kalter Finsternis die kleine Lampe trägst.
> Leb wohl, mach's gut!
> *Auf ein Zeichen von ihm öffnet sich die Decke.*
> *Eine rosa Wolke läßt sich hernieder. Auf ihr*
> *Fahren die Götter sehr langsam nach oben.* (640)

Without question, this 'Himmelfahrtsmoment' as the finale exaggerates the traditional uses of a deus ex machina to the point that it becomes not merely ludicrous but downright absurd. In other words, the deus-ex-machina function of the three gods has been allowed to degenerate into an absurd gesture symptomatic of an artificially sovereign and all-powerful divinity. Their artificiality negates the existence of these gods. Their physical appearance on the stage shows them for what they really are. Dietrich Bonhoeffer, in *Widerstand und Ergebung* (1932, 307–08), describes this aspect very clearly:

> Die Religiösen sprechen von Gott, wenn menschliche Erkenntnis (manchmal schon aus Denkfaulheit) zu Ende ist oder wenn menschliche Kräfte versagen— es ist eigentlich immer der Deus ex machina, den sie aufmarschieren lassen, entweder zur Scheinlösung unlösbarer Probleme oder als Kraft bei mensch- lichem Versagen, immer also in Ausnutzung menschlicher Schwäche bzw. an den menschlichen Grenzen; das hält zwangsläufig immer nur solange vor, bis die Menschen aus eigener Kraft die Grenzen etwas weiter hinausschieben und Gott als Deus ex machina überflüssig wird.

The gods are helpless and stand for the outdated values of the bourgeoisie. The audience, constantly presented with this negation, must finally acknowledge the artificiality of the gods as they make their final exit heavenward:

> DER ERSTE GOTT. Sie ist nicht umgekommen, sie war nur verborgen. Sie wird unter euch bleiben, ein guter Mensch!
> SHEN TE. Aber ich brauche den Vetter!
> DER ERSTE GOTT. Nicht zu oft!
> SHEN TE. Jede Woche zumindest!
> DER ERSTE GOTT. Jeden Monat, das genügt!
> SHEN TE. Oh, entfernt euch nicht, Erleuchtete! Ich habe noch nicht alles gesagt! Ich brauche euch dringend!
> *Die Götter singen das 'Terzett der entschwindenden Götter auf der Wolke':*
>
> Leider können wir nicht bleiben
> Mehr als eine flüchtige Stund:
> Lang besehn, ihn zu beschreiben
> Schwände hin der schöne Fund.
>
> Eure Körper werfen Schatten
> In der Flut des goldnen Lichts
> Drum müßt ihr uns schon gestatten
> Heimzugehn in unser Nichts.
> […]

*Während Shen Te verzweifelt die Arme nach ihnen ausbreitet, verschwinden sie oben, lächelnd und winkend.* (641)

The grandiose but ridiculous final exit of the gods does not even allow for a true deus ex machina: besides upsetting the order of things, the gods accomplish nothing, change no one, and leave on a paper cloud, operetta-style, smiling and waving to those below. The gods' return to their original dwelling – 'Nichts' – creates, as the ultimate gesture, a never-ending circle of repetition: the world is the same when they leave as when they arrived, and vice versa; heaven, we may therefore assume, will continue to receive many complaints and lamentations, and the gods will necessarily have to appear in person once more to prove that one virtuous person still exists in order to appease the people. Referring to the insufficiency of the open form, Theodor Adorno in *Ästhetische Theorie* (1965a, 327) writes of Brecht's endings:

> In der Insuffizienz der offenen Formen – ein schlagendes Exempel sind die Schwierigkeiten Brechts beim Schreiben überzeugender Schlüsse seiner Theaterstücke – kulminiert die geschichtliche Aporie des Nominalismus der Kunst.

This seems to be true as well in *Der gute Mensch*: by implying such a repetition of events, the play leads the viewer directly back to the beginning. Then, another Wang will wait for their coming and another Shen Te will struggle to be good, in what promises to remain an endless arrival and departure of gods, who are the only ones capable of initiating change but are still captives of outmoded ideas inimical to change, and promise no hope for an end to the meaningless repetition of history.

According to Brecht, the Church and its members – the representatives of religion – have made God impotent and relegated His promise of salvation to a useful tool in the hands of the exploiters. These exploiters are the theologians and other representatives of religion. In addition to the sharp criticism of the Church's role in society, Brecht's work is likewise saturated with allusions to or direct attacks on the various individual religious representatives of Christianity. Perhaps the most poignant example is the poem 'Bericht vom Zeck' located in the 'Hauspostille' collection. It is not difficult to conclude that this poem about a man in violet who sucks blood like a tick, is a priest, of whom it is said:

1
Durch unsere Kinderträume
In dem milchweißen Bett
Spukte um Apfelbäume
Der Mann in Violett [...]

3
Er schätzt die kleinste Gabe
Sauft Blut als wie ein Zeck.
Und daß man nur ihn habe
Nimmt er sonst alles weg. (187–88)

The religious person in contemporary society will, until it is changed, be personified by Wang, who considers the gods as merchandise and advertises them as commodities to be sold to the public:

WANG. [...] drei der höchsten Götter, von deren bevorstehender Ankunft ganz Sezuan schon seit Jahren spricht, sind nun wirklich eingetroffen und benötigen ein Quartier. Gehen Sie nicht weiter! Überzeugen Sie sich selbst! Ein Blick genügt! Greifen Sie um Gottes Willen zu! Es ist eine einmalige Gelegenheit! Bitten Sie die Götter zuerst unter Ihr Dach, bevor sie Ihnen Jemand wegschnappt, sie werden zusagen. (596)

The market and monetary necessities still dominate life in this society. Lacking insight and compassion, the gods are satisfied with their passive role as mere observers and content to accept that they too are commodities on which society depends. It soon becomes clear, however, that such gods are not the masters on earth. The supernatural omnipotence and divine authority necessary for such mastery disappear in contemporary society with its historically specific reality. As 'Erleuchtete', they are relegated to superficial brilliance, yet even in this seemingly vacuous role they fulfill a higher purpose, for they illuminate the way to another presence that without them would have remained hidden ('verstellt').

Through the character Shen Te, the concept of guilt, the inner 'Grund der Schuld', is no longer limited to the self but is broadened to cover all of the society in which the characters function. In *Mein Wort über das Drama*, Friedrich Hebbel (1965, 568) writes about the concept of guilt: 'Die Schuld ist eine uranfängliche, von dem Begriff des Menschen nicht zu trennende und kaum in sein Bewußtsein fallende, sie ist mit dem Leben selbst gesetzt.' Hebbel's concept of dramatic guilt centers around the nexus between the individual and the whole, whereby individuality – regardless of one's intentions – conditions guilt. Furthermore, Hebbel 'läßt daher nicht die Schuld unaufgehoben, wohl aber den innern Grund der Schuld unenthüllt', in order that the drama 'mit dem Weltmysterium in eine und dieselbe Nacht verliert' (569).

Shen Te can draw but one conclusion from her confrontation with the gods: 'Etwas muß falsch sein an eurer Welt'. Regarding the position of the gods in *Der gute Mensch* that not only finds one good person on earth enough but even considers this sufficient, Christiaan Hart Nibbrig (1974, 158) asserts in *Ja und Nein*: 'Solcher Gesinnungsethik aber widersetzt sich das Stück. Das Gute als bloße Einstellungssache erscheint in einer Welt, die trotzdem schlecht bleibt, wertlos.' It is not Shen Te who is 'falsch'. As the 'Welt' that belongs to and accepts false gods, the present world with its false morality and values negates itself. Because they can be negated, the false values of what is 'good' in the real world outside the theater can finally be demolished. Through Shen Te, the spectator experiences a break with the 'Gesinnungsethik' of Emmanuel Kant, according to which a person is good if there is good will within that person.[3] One discovers instead an insistence on a 'social' ethic. Such a social morality is not content with a *pars pro toto*, a single representative in society, but rather strives to create a collective of all members of society. The bourgeois 'ethical' individual has become incompatible with modern society, for his outdated values and morality force the self to divide and resort to capitalism in order to appear good. On this issue of the role of the individual in society, Hart Nibbrig (1974, 157) writes in *Ja und Nein*:

Das Identifikationsverbot, das Brecht den Spielern und den Zuschauern auferlegt, hängt mit dem Bestreben zusammen, den Konflikt der Handlung zu entindividualisieren. Weil er den einzelnen zum Repräsentanten geschichtlich-gesellschaftlicher Verhältnisse erklärt, kann er den Untergang nicht dulden, der auf Unkenntnis der objektiven Situation, in der der Held handelt, zurückgeht und deshalb subjektiv entschuldbar ist.

The gods finally leave and reassure Shen Te that she is in fact 'der gute Mensch' for whom they have been searching:

> DER ERSTE GOTT. Der gute Mensch, von dem alle nur Gutes berichtet haben!
> SHEN TE. Nein, auch der böse!
> DER ERSTE GOTT. Ein Mißverständnis! Einige unglückliche Vorkommnisse! (354)

Their misunderstanding is based on two contradictory factors: the intention of Shen Te (what she is trying to explain) and the (mis)-understanding of that intention by the god. The resultant clash of Shen Te's divided character with the misconception of the gods cancels both out by showing that they can neither exist together nor produce a higher synthesis. Since Shen Te attempts to explain what the god refuses to comprehend, the two will never arrive at an agreement. This rupture in communication in the last act produces a break in continuity and order. The gods nevertheless refuse to admit any incongruities in the structure of the world:

> DER ERSTE GOTT. Sollen wir eingestehen, daß unsere Gebote tödlich sind? Sollen wir verzichten auf unsere Gebote? *Verbissen*: Niemals! Soll die Welt geändert werden? Wie? Von wem? Nein, es ist alles in Ordnung! (354)

Since, however, they cannot give answers to the questions they ask, 'von wem', the gods only deny their own existence even further. With 'Nein' they disaffirm 'es ist alles in Ordnung.'

The 'Epilog' is the end that returns to the beginning and turns the spectator into an active participant who must search for an end:

> Verehrtes Publikum, los, such dir selbst den Schluß!
> Es muß ein guter da sein, muß, muß, muß! (356)

For in the theatricality of Brecht's theater, the spectator is himself being theatricalized: he too plays a role – that of being seen seeing – while he is engaged in seeing and reacting to what he sees. Roland

Barthes, in *The Rustle of Language* (1986, 219), explains it in this manner:

> We must always remember that the originality of the Brechtian sign ('Zeigen') is that it is *to be read twice*: what Brecht gives us to read is, by a kind of disengagement, the reader's gaze, not directly the object of his reading; for this object reaches us only by the act of intellection (an alienated act) of a reader who is already on the stage.

The gaze of the spectator turns toward itself. As a result, the spectator, too, is forced to acknowledge his own theatricality and, consequently, his 'split' subjecthood. *Der gute Mensch* ends at the point where the spectator is urged to find out for himself 'auf welche Weis dem Menschen man / Zu einem guten Ende helfen kann.'

Another play, *Die heilige Johanna der Schlachthöfe*, written between 1929 and 1931 but not premiered until 1959, already provides the answer by picking up on the dilemma of Shen Te:

> O folgenlose Güte! Unmerkliche Gesinnung!
> Ich habe nichts geändert.
> Schnell verschwinden aus dieser Welt ohne Frucht
> Sage ich euch:
> Sorgt doch, daß ihr die Welt verlassend
> Nicht gut wart, sondern verlaßt
> Eine gute Welt! (314)

A good world is possible only when one no longer attempts to express it and attain it through language. As Shen Te stated already, 'ein gutes Wort entschlüpft wie ein wohliger Seufzer' (627). The spectator must *search* for it. To arrive at the 'end' is to lose the energy of striving for a change. We are to become critical ('muß, muß, muß') observers of the incongruities, gaps, and caesurae inherent in the language and other modes of representation of the Brechtian stage. As such observers, we realize that the space between the stage and the audience is a negation of the stage gods and an affirmation of God's 'Spielraum'.

The basic problem of modern drama, therefore, has been one of determining when the limits of language are reflective only of the limits of the characters' lack of articulation or self-deception and when they are indicative of all language. As we have seen through the

157

analysis of the play *Der gute Mensch*, the 'Verfremdungseffekt' of Brecht's epic theater shifts the emphasis of drama from the limits of language as only reflective of the limits of the characters to the limits of language in general. It criticizes any attempt at conformity to the parameters determined by linguistic rules and conventional forms. The epic theater, through the use of language and 'Gestus', breaks the illusion of the stage and prevents the spectator from becoming emotionally absorbed by the play. It allows the audience to perceive the limits of language as a social product and to become more receptive to its metaphysical implications. Epic theater creates caesurae in the language and the representations of modern society. The ensuing abyss, a space where the limits of language as products of modern society are reached, becomes 'der Spielraum Gottes'.

# Chapter Five
## Dürrenmatt's *Ein Engel kommt nach Babylon*

The course of nineteenth- and twentieth-century history and society –
Friedrich Nietzsche's proclamation of the death of God, world wars
and their atrocities, atomic weaponry – led Friedrich Dürrenmatt to an
*ahistorical* perception of reality, to accept the modern world at face
value and to refer to the world in *Theater-Schriften und Reden* (1966d,
123) as 'ein Ungeheures […] ein Rätsel an Unheil'. History, according
to Dürrenmatt, must be seen as a series of senseless occurrences
through which 'alles wird mitgerissen und bleibt in irgendeinem
Rechen hängen.' History, Dürrenmatt further insists, will inevitably
repeat itself. Corrupt institutional authorities and exploitative theological and political power structures have taken the place of God. The
status quo remains, and nothing has been learned. As a 'Schriftsteller
in Rebellion gegen Ideologien und Gläubige aller Art' (122), and as a
dramatist who presents the chaotic and labyrinth-like structure of the
world in a grotesquely distorted manner, Dürrenmatt confronts his
audience with the repulsive reality of modernity as a 'gespielte Wirklichkeit'. Denying allegiance to any abstract philosophy, Dürrenmatt
maintains that modern drama can therefore only be an attempt to
replicate a senseless world, in which religion and morality no longer
play consequential roles (118). Since our world is 'sinnlos', accidents
and chance dominate its course in a repetitive process while, as he
writes in *Das Versprechen* (1958, 20): 'der Einzelne steht außerhalb
der Berechnung.'

   In this context, the isolation of self is the most powerful force
shaping Dürrenmatt's dramaturgy. The modern individual, moved
through time like a 'Spielball der Mächte' (60), submissively fulfills
his function and performs the role that fate has allotted him. Dürrenmatt writes in *Es steht geschrieben* (1947a, 95):

> Nicht unsere Person zügelt die Geschichte, sie ist es, die uns durch die Zeiten schleppt. Wir versuchen, gewisse Strecken abzumessen und uns nach dem zu halten, was wir vorauszusehen hoffen. Doch erhöhen unsere Taten die Verwirrung. Wir können die Köpfe nicht bessern und wir dürfen Experimenten nicht nachgehen, um das bißchen festen Boden nicht zu verlieren, welches wir noch unter den Füßen haben.

Modern society has produced an individual who no longer understands his world, yet is completely controlled by ideological doctrines. Dürrenmatt writes in *Theater-Schriften und Reden* (1966d, 19):

> Aus Hitler und Stalin lassen sich keine Wallensteine mehr machen. Ihre Macht ist so riesenhaft, daß sie selber nur noch zufällige, äußere Ausdrucksformen dieser Macht sind, beliebig zu ersetzen, und das Unglück, das man besonders mit dem ersten und ziemlich mit dem zweiten verbindet, ist weitverzweigt, zu verworren, zu grausam, zu mechanisch geworden und oft einfach auch allzu sinnlos.[1]

In contradiction to the mode of thought portrayed on his stage, Dürrenmatt sometimes constructs 'Nicht-Mitmacher', individuals who fight against the power structures of society and against the evolution of the modern condition. However, due to the senselessness of the modern predicament, all attempts of the heroes (such as Romulus, Herkules, Cop, etc.) to stand against the progress of history by proclaiming different values are unsuccessful, even ridiculous. The individual's situation appears hopeless in a godless and chaotic world in which religious institutional authorities and state powers subject the individual to their ideological dogmas.

As a result of portrayals of senselessness, a grotesque style, and contradictions and paradoxes with distinct, religiously elusive and enigmatic overtones, Dürrenmatt's theater has the *potential* to bring forth a divine presence. 'Das Groteske', he writes in *König Johann* (1968, 122), 'ist nur ein sinnlicher Ausdruck, ein sinnliches Paradox, die Gestalt nämlich einer Ungestalt'. The Naturalists, who had followed Emile Zola's dictum on the death of God, 'loaded the stage with specific objects', enclosed their characters within four walls and therefore 'shut the play into a museum showcase', writes Wilder.[2] Dürrenmatt's play written in 1954, *Ein Engel kommt nach Babylon*, on the other hand, abandons specificity related to the real, scientifically verifiable world and leaves us with no source of closure. Dürrenmatt's stage is closer to that of Thornton Wilder (1957, xi), who writes in a preface to his plays that everything that happened might happen anywhere and will happen again:

> Every person who has ever lived has lived an unbroken succession of unique occasions. Yet the more one is aware of individuality in experience (innumerable! innumerable!) the more one becomes attentive to what these disparate moments have in common, to repetitive patterns [...] which 'truth' do you prefer – that of the isolated occasion, or that which includes or resumes the innumerable?

On the stage Dürrenmatt replicates chaos and godlessness, the dominant characteristics of the world, through the use of the grotesque and paradox. His concept of history as a series of senseless catastrophes expresses itself in a form of grotesque comedy that is a game, the rules of which have meaning only on the stage.

For the isolated individual in an isolated theater there should be, in Dürrenmatt's view, no dependence on reality: rather, the stage, he maintains in *Theater-Schriften und Reden II*, presents only 'ein Spiel mit der Wirklichkeit, deren Verwandlung im Theater' (1972, 101). Theater is, he continues in an interview with Horst Bienek (1965, 73), 'nicht die Welt, nicht einmal deren Abbild, sondern eine vom Menschen in seiner Freiheit erstellte, erdichtete, erfabulierte Welt'. Dürrenmatt attempts in his later theoretical writings to establish the autonomy of the dramatic and to give the dramaturgical 'Einfall' the function of isolating reality from the stage.[3] Hence, during the sixties and seventies, Dürrenmatt repeatedly refers to the play as 'eine Fiktion' (1972, 185). It is, he writes (1972), a world that is 'eine in sich geschlossene Welt' (185) and as such 'vom Diktat der Wirklichkeit erlöst' (97). He begins to speak of a 'Dramaturgie vom Stoffe her' (228), in which the play's social function does not acquire importance, but rather the 'Einfall' itself that occurs within the play. Anton Krättli (2003) elucidates this and quotes Dürrenmatt in 'Dürrenmatts Abschied vom Theater'. He writes:

> Aber es gebe auch Autoren, die bezweifeln, dass sich die Bühne überhaupt beherrschen lasse. Sie begnügten sich damit, Theater zu ermöglichen 'oft

erstaunt und amüsiert, was sie alles anrichten, sei es bloß durch ein Missverständnis'. Aus all diesen Notizen spricht eine ironische Distanz zum Theater. Der Schriftsteller wird als Mitarbeiter in einem Geschehen verstanden, das er bei weitem nicht zu lenken vermag. Er macht zwar mit, ist aber gleichzeitig ein aufmerksamer Beobachter [...] (224)

Dürrenmatt's terms 'Zufall', 'Einfall', and 'schlimmstmögliche Wendung' are the building blocks for his theory and the theatrical tools that ultimately make possible a divine presence on the stage. Jiri Stromsik (1981, 53), in 'Apokalypse Komisch', describes most accurately Dürrenmatt's 'Zufall' as completely different from fate:

> der Zufall vereitelt jedes Zukunftsstreben der Figuren, alle ihre Berechnungen und Pläne. Es handelt sich keineswegs um eine bloß parodistische Umkehrung des Schicksalsbegriffs: in dem Umstand, daß der Zufall die Guten wie die Schlechten trifft, ist kein Schicksal, das heißt kein letztes Gleichgewicht von Gut und Böse, zu sehen [...]

As a playwright who refuses to tie his dramaturgy to a specific philosophy, Dürrenmatt argues in *Theater-Schriften und Reden* (1966d, 102) for a 'Dramaturgie von Fall zu Fall'. Chance, with its painfully grotesque repetitiveness and portrayal of senselessness, seems to be an end in itself as the text develops its own writing. Dürrenmatt confesses in an essay in *Theater-Schriften und Reden II* (1972) that he writes his plays 'ins Blaue' and is thus unable to predict what direction the text will take: 'Damit wird der Stoff entscheidend, der Einfall, der den Stoff entdeckt oder erschafft, die Technik, Stoffe zu erfinden [...] Schreiben wird zu einer Gehorsamkeit dem Stoffe gegenüber' (231). He contrasts his 'Dramaturgie vom Stoffe her' with a Schillerian-Brechtian 'Dramaturgie vom Zwecke her' (209) that proceeds not from 'Einfall' or 'Stoffe' but from a preconceived problem, idea, or 'Aussage' (215).

An 'Einfall' is an idea that occurs to a person. Accordingly, the source of a drama is an idea, not an observation of the 'real' world. Dürrenmatt, in an essay in *Theater-Schriften und Reden* (1966d, 63–64), indicates the autonomous relationship between the real world and the individual: 'Eine logische Eigenwelt kann gar nicht aus unserer Welt fallen [...] Das ist ein Geheimnis: die Übereinstimmung der Kunst mit der Welt. Wir haben allein am Stoffe zu arbeiten. Das genügt.' In response to Heinz Ludwig Arnold's (1976) questions in 1975 concerning the relationship between 'diese Welt der eigenen Gedanken' and the 'Welt der anderen', he responds:

> Das ist doch völlig egal, da brauchen Sie sich gar nicht drum zu kümmern. *Die Beziehungen zu Ihrer Welt schaffen die Leser.* Man kann nichts anderes tun, als in diese Welt die eigenen Gedanken hineinschießen wie Kanonen, Kugeln, wie Raketen. (71)

In another essay in *Theater-Schriften und Reden* (1966d, 185), Dürrenmatt describes the drama as a representation of the possible: of 'mögliche Welten' and 'mögliche menschliche Beziehungen'. The relationship of a 'Dramatik der Möglichkeit' (13) to reality is problematic, he maintains in 'Sätze über das Theater', because it contains 'ein subjektives Element [...] Der Mensch hält nur das für möglich, von dem er glaubt, daß es geschehen könnte; die Möglichkeit, an die der Mensch glaubt, hängt mit seiner Interpretation der Wirklichkeit zusammen' (5). In order to overcome this interpretive subjectivity, the drama 'muß [...] sich auf die Logik stützen', and as a result it becomes 'deterministisch' (12). The only possible way of eliminating this deterministic effect on the stage is to prevent the drama from arriving at a logical conclusion. This lack of logic, a result of the portrayals of senselessness, contradictions, and paradoxes in Dürrenmatt's theater, allows a divine presence to emerge.

Questions regarding God or His death recur as themes more often in Dürrenmatt's works than in most modern dramatists', but such concerns obviously grew out of Dürrenmatt's personal background and academic training. Dürrenmatt, the son of a Calvinist minister, rejects the historical dialectic of Friedrich Hegel and, as we read in *Die Ehe des Herrn Mississippi* (1966a), the existential and self-creative capacity of men in order to examine the question 'ob der Geist – in irgendeiner Form – imstande sei, eine Welt zu ändern, die nur existiert, die keine Idee besitzt, ob die Welt als Stoff unverbesserlich sei' (41). Dürrenmatt's dissertation, with the working title 'Kierkegaard und das Tragische', was never completed, but studies of the Danish philosopher's work had a lasting influence on Dürrenmatt's thinking and works. From Sören Kierkegaard's point of view in

'Furcht und Zittern' (1953a), faith is represented as the last and greatest of a series of movements, for one can acquire it only after renouncing all that one holds dear in the world:

> Die unendliche Resignation ist das letzte Stadium, das dem Glauben vorausgeht, dergestalt, daß keiner den Glauben hat, der diese Bewegung nicht gemacht hat; denn erst in der unendlichen Resignation werde ich mir selbst klar in meiner ewigen Gültigkeit, und erst dann kann die Rede davon sein, in kraft des Glaubens das Dasein zu ergreifen. (47)

Dürrenmatt's speech 'Über Toleranz' (1977) contains many allusions and direct references to Sören Kierkegaard's influence on him. In his paradoxically entitled 'Nachträgliche Vorbemerkung' to this speech, Dürrenmatt writes: 'Als Dissertation war "Kierkegaard und das Tragische" vorgesehen. Es kam nicht dazu. Doch beunruhigte mich Kierkegaard weiter' (117). Karl Barth was yet another theologian whom Dürrenmatt would later come to know personally and in whose commentary on the 'Epistle to the Romans' Dürrenmatt was immersing himself simultaneously with his philosophical studies. In 'Vinter' in *Turmbau: Stoffe IV–IX* (1990b), Dürrenmatt devotes several pages to a discussion of Barth's theology. According to Barth in *Protestant Thought* (1959), God is unapproachable. The qualitative gulf between God and humanity is a chasm that can be crossed only in one direction: from above. Always beyond human comprehension, the 'divine incognito' can be apprehended only with faith. Referring to Luther, Barth affirms that faith directs itself toward the things that are invisible. Moreover, those things are most deeply hidden which most clearly contradict experience. Consequently, according to Barth, religion is guilty of 'criminal arrogance' when it tries to comprehend the world in relation to God. This is the same dilemma with which Dürrenmatt struggles. He laments in *Turmbau* that it is impossible to know or understand God, for, if God exists, He is so remote as to be a nonentity. As a conclusion to his analysis of Barth, Dürrenmatt (1990a, 209) states: 'Barth erzog mich zum Atheisten.'

Much of Dürrenmatt's early work appears to be an indictment of God. In 'Weihnacht' (1952d), for example, a nihilistic anecdote in an expressionistic, fragmented style, the narrator encounters the Christ child frozen in the snow, eats his stale halo, bites off his head, which tastes like old marzipan, and walks on. Similarly, the short story 'Der Folterknecht' (1952a) is Dürrenmatt's most compact, expressionistic work. Although written in 1943, the same ideas found here often recur, not only in the early works but also in later narratives and dramas: God is a torturer who demands justice. Other prose works and plays revolve around this idea, as well as more vehemently anti-God, or even seemingly nihilistic, ideas. There is no God, only hell. 'Die Falle', a tale of desolation, bloody corpses, winter landscapes, and nightmarish realities, depicts humanity racing headlong into the fires of hell. The protagonist turns and fights his way back upstairs against the crowd, but as the red glow fades behind him, only darkness and increasing coldness lie ahead. There is nothing to go back to and only hell to go forward into. Screaming for grace, he throws himself headlong back down the stairs toward hell and the humanity from which he had separated himself. Dürrenmatt's short story 'Pilatus' (1986b) acquires a different perspective. Any sign from Christ that he is God, and Pilate would have fallen on his knees and worshiped him. Yet Pilate realizes that only he recognizes the deity in the man, and this realization increases his paranoia: 'da er allein die Wahrheit kannte. So war er gezwungen, eine Grausamkeit um die andere an Gott zu begehen, weil er die Wahrheit wußte, ohne sie zu verstehen' (112). Pilate is finally, like the majority of Dürrenmatt's characters, a doomed figure, for he not only remains as distanced from God as any other character, but he also experiences a chasm between sensing the truth and truly understanding it. Philipp Burkard, in *Dürrenmatts Stoffe* (2004, 4), correctly explains Dürrenmatt's own philosophical position in this stage of his writing:

> Fast von Beginn seiner Schriftstellerei an hat philosophisches und im Speziellen erkenntnistheoretisches Denken für Dürrenmatt eine zentrale Rolle gespielt, einerseits – paradoxerweise – als ein Grund für die Absetzung von der Philosophie, andererseits als Inspirationsquelle und Motor des eigenen literarischen Schaffens [...] Und die Erzählung 'Pilatus' sowie die Theaterstücke *Es steht geschrieben* von 1946 und *Der Blinde* von 1947 zeigen, wie die erkenntnistheoretische Problematik für den jungen Pfarrersohn aufs Engste verknüpft ist mit Fragen des religiösen Glaubens, die ihn in Auseinandersetzung mit den relgiösen Denkern Sören Kierkegaard und Karl Barth beschäftigen.

At this point in Dürrenmatt's work, the religious overtones gradually begin to give way to a new philosophical association between God and the individual. Man perceives a gap between himself and God, yet he is unable to understand it. Instead, he attempts to gain control of the circumstances and fails miserably.

In the 1950s and 1960s, Dürrenmatt replaced the 'religious' emphasis with a more humanistic one. Romulus, in 'Romulus der Grosse' (1957b), strives to give meaning to an 'absurd' life by accepting his 'Pensionierung' in the name of justice as atonement for the many deaths caused by his attempt to influence the course of history. Then Ill, in 'Der Besuch der alten Dame' (1957a), freely submits to the external 'Gewalt' of 'Gerechtigkeit' in order to overcome the injustice of the world and mankind. Even in this stage of his writing career, Dürrenmatt remains as critical as ever of society, yet now, through the mid-1950s, his perception of the individual and his views on religion are dominated by a new idea: the individual's orientation toward a higher dimension that he cannot understand. 'Der Tunnel' (1952c), for example, portrays the inexplicable: a tunnel that does not end. Science and logic fail. Yet the protagonist, whose fears have changed to fascination, is the only one on the train who can accept the full implications. To the conductor's anguished question 'Was sollen wir nun tun?' the protagonist answers, 'Nichts. Gott ließ uns fallen und so stürzen wir denn auf ihn zu' (157). In his revision of this narrative for a new edition of 1978, Dürrenmatt removes this final theological reference and allows the protagonist to respond to the conductor's question with only 'Nichts'. This deletion demonstrates the philosophical development that had taken place in the author's mode of thought. There is now an apparent refusal to allow any room for an explicitly theological interpretation. 'God' as a word means nothing. The only alternative to despair in a senseless world of 'Nichts' appears to be a Kierkegaardian 'credo quia absurdum' in a universe in which God is incomprehensible and humans are abandoned by Him to a senseless existence, plunging through a dark tunnel to death.

In his earlier plays, Dürrenmatt attempts to portray the senselessness of the world by means of distinct religious overtones. Characters hope to find meaning and understanding for the circumstances around them through absolute dependence on God. Such dependence turns out to be not only senseless, but also ridiculous. In *Der Blinde* (1960), for example, the blind duke holds a strong faith in 'Gott und seine Gerechtigkeit', which seems to enable him to transcend the chaos around him, when in fact he remains blind to everything. Übelhöle, in *Die Ehe des Herrn Mississippi* (1966a), does not perceive his defeat as an occasion for despair, but rather, ridiculously, as a further revelation of the insignificance of man and the grotesque humor of God.

In his later stage works, Dürrenmatt rails against the religious establishment instead of God. He denounces the representatives of religion because of their well-structured definitions of God and argues for a different kind of belief. In an interview with Heinz Ludwig Arnold (1976), Dürrenmatt argues: 'richtige Gläubige sind Verrückte, sind Don Quichottes, sind Gullivers' (17). He now tends to focus on a more personal and individual relationship to the question of existence and seems to accept Christianity as an essentially existential question.[4] Christianity as a bourgeois institution, in his view, affirms the status quo and holds a hypocritical, narrowly defined morality. In 1976 Dürrenmatt expressed his views on organized religion to Arnold, views that were already well established ten years earlier when *Der Meteor* premiered:

> Ich bin total gegen die Kirche. Für mich ist die Kirche etwas vom eben Schlimmsten, was es geben kann, weil die Kirche einen Zwang auferlegt, weil sie einen Scheinglauben, eine Scheinreligion, eine Scheinchristenheit, nur eine Staffage von Glauben hat. (80)

Dürrenmatt concludes that Christ's teachings have over the ages become mere religious dogma. In *Turmbau* (1990a, 195) he considers the question of God's existence irrelevant. Any mention of God necessarily becomes a subjective statement that, as such, cannot be transformed into objective knowledge and structural thought. In the same manner, referring to the death camps at Auschwitz and Birkenau, Dürrenmatt writes:

Er ist undenkbar, und was undenkbar ist, kann auch nicht möglich sein, weil es keinen Sinn hat. Es ist, als ob der Ort sich selber erdacht hätte. Er ist nur. Sinnlos wie die Wirklichkeit und unbegreiflich wie sie und ohne Grund. (266)

Dürrenmatt's early excursions into what appears to be nihilism were in fact a mask behind which he wrestled with the question of existence and chaos. He continued to grapple with the problem of humanity's separation from God and the possibility of divine grace for most of his life, yet as he entered his later stage, his preoccupation with the paradoxical, controversial, and enigmatic became more intense. Answering whether Dürrenmatt ever truly became the atheist that he claimed to be in 1990 demands more evidence than comments in 'Vinter' (1990b, 201) such as, 'Ich halte die Frage, ob Gott existiere, für sinnlos.' Furthermore, his strong conviction that everything occurs by chance in our world must now be viewed side by side with the belief in predestination he had as the son of a Calvinist minister. Dürrenmatt believes neither that humanity has any promise of a future on earth nor that a supreme being holds our future in His hand, and he uses scenario after scenario to think through these convictions on the stage before us. Yet, as will become clear, he is also too much of a satirist to hold the mirror up to humanity in vain.

According to Dürrenmatt, writing cannot depict or explain existence. It can only propose the true necessity of analyzing its inherent characteristics and possibilities. The more one attempts to interpret or define existence, the more one falsifies it. In 1981 in *Stoffe I–III* Dürrenmatt writes:

Je älter man wird, desto stärker wird der Wunsch, Bilanz zu ziehen. Der Tod rückt näher, das Leben verflüchtigt sich. Indem es sich verflüchtigt, will man es gestalten; indem man es gestaltet, verfälscht man es. So kommen die falschen Bilanzen zustande, die wir Lebensbeschreibungen nennen. (11)

Unlike many famous playwrights, but perhaps because he gained almost equal praise as a novelist, Dürrenmatt takes pains to articulate his views on language. Dürrenmatt places great importance on the individual's difficulty in comprehending and communicating in his world. In his 'Nachwort' to *Der Mitmacher* (1976a, 166), he writes:

Daß wir über unseren Planeten auf dem laufenden seien, ist noch jetzt ein Wunschtraum, nicht trotz, sondern wegen der modernen Kommunikationsmittel. Die Fakten, die uns erreichen, sind schon entstellt, formuliert und damit stilisiert, bald auf diese, bald auf jene Weltanschauung hin, fotografiert, gefilmt, ausgelesen und zusammengeschnitten.

In real life, the world is a labyrinth-like structure that cannot be comprehended as an objective totality but only as subjectively created fragments of one. On the stage, such objectivity can be encountered as fiction from a distance. He writes in *Stoffe I–III* (1981, 77):

Indem ich die Welt, in die ich mich ausgesetzt sehe, als Labyrinth darstelle, versuche ich, Distanz zu ihr zu gewinnen, von ihr zurückzutreten, sie ins Auge zu fassen wie ein Dompteur ein wildes Tier. Die Welt, wie ich sie erlebe, konfrontiere ich mit einer Gegenwelt, die ich erdenke.

Through writing, Dürrenmatt undertakes the task of acquiring an overview of the labyrinth of reality. In an interview with Bienek (1965, 103) in 1962 Dürrenmatt asserts: 'Schreiben ist das Bewältigen der Welt durch die Sprache.' It is a matter of going to language, not starting from language, continues Dürrenmatt (1981, 12) later in *Stoffe I–III*: 'Ich zähle [...] zu jenen Schriftstellern, die nicht von der Sprache her kommen, die sich vielmehr mühsam zur Sprache bringen müssen.'

In his interview with Arnold (1976), Dürrenmatt explains his fascination with the theater as an attempt to come closer to an understanding of the relationship between the word and that which it represents:

Ich wollte die Bilder weg haben. Und die Bilder gingen nicht weg, sie kamen immer wieder, und so kam ich eigentlich zum Schreiben, und dann fast als Befreiung wie eine Explosion die Entdeckung des Dramas: eine Form als Verbindung zwischen Malerei und Schreiben. (17)

The rhetorical representation, the word, and that which rhetoric attempts to represent, have in fact a false relationship.[5] In *Zusammenhänge* (1976c, 156) he argues: 'Erst mit der Erkenntnis, daß, was zur Sprache gebracht wird, auch bloß Sprache ist, wird das Ästhetische hinfällig, mehr noch, wenn die Sprache nur noch Sprache sein kann, wird alles hinfällig, wird jede Aussage unmöglich.' Everything that an individual experiences vanishes once it is rigidified into language.

*Ein Engel kommt nach Babylon* (1954) entails complex strategies of technical rationality that eventually give way to something that is decidedly not the senselessness it at first seems to suggest, although it is also not the metaphysical something toward which figural rational language traditionally points. In his theater, Dürrenmatt dwells on contradictions and paradoxes that appear meaningless and absurd. Such incongruencies in conceptions and ideas, paradoxically, bring forth a divine presence.

According to Dürrenmatt, society, having reached a communicative dead end, has two options for dealing with complete senselessness. The first consists of rejecting any one fixed idea within words and using instead verbal conflict to arrive at a relationship between any two opposing statements. In considering this first possibility, Dürrenmatt places a great emphasis on mathematics and physics and often draws parallels between the word and mathematics. He writes in his essay 'Vinter' (1990b, 201):

> Wenn es heißt, am Anfang sei das Wort, so ist es entscheidend, was ich unter dem 'Wort' verstehe, ob ich das Wort meine, das strukturelles, oder jenes, das sympathetisches Wissen vermittelt (Eddington). Unser strukturelles Wissen gilt den Strukturen, es ist ein mathematisch ausdrückbares Wissen, das nicht das Wesen meint, sondern die Struktur, so daß wir etwa nicht das Wesen, sondern die Struktur der Atome zu erforschen suchen, während das sympathische Wissen ein Verstehen ist, aber nicht ein 'Wissen'.

Dürrenmatt refers to Albert Einstein's physics as clarification for his understanding of the role of language as well as an example of the deceptive relationship between word and thing. Modern physics has become 'bilderfeindlich' and can no longer exist under the category of 'Anschaulichkeit'. Dürrenmatt, in *Albert Einstein. Ein Vortrag* (1979), refers to radio waves, quarks, and black holes as examples of imageless, figureless, and unrepresentable bodies that can exist only in the 'mathematical language' of physics and remain untranslatable into a common communicative language. Such hypothetical, self-contained constructions cannot be displayed in reality. As long as the individual strives to comprehend his own 'Wirklichkeit', he remains restricted to form and structure. Language consequently takes on the role of imprisoning the individual. Dürrenmat writes in an essay in *Theater-Schriften und Reden* (1966d, 248): 'Die Sprache rächt sich an Hitler, das Zitat verhaftet ihn, die Grammatik wird zur Guillotine [...] Die Dinge werden absurd, indem sie das Medium der Sprache passieren.'

Dürrenmatt emphasizes the importance of verbal conflict and the paradox. In 1990 in *Über die Grenzen* he (1990c, 89) asserts: 'Darum das Paradoxe: Was er jetzt weiß, von dem glaubt er, es könne auch anders sein.' Verbal conflict, he argues, gives way to a paradoxical relationship between two opposing statements. In his 'Nachwort' to 'Porträt eines Planeten', Dürrenmatt (1980, 197) explains this tendency to present conflicts:

> Ich versuche dramaturgisch immer einfacher zu zeigen, immer sparsamer zu werden, immer mehr auszulassen, nur noch anzudeuten. Die Spannung zwischen den Sätzen ist mir wichtiger geworden als die Sätze selbst. Meine Dramatik spielt sich zwischen den Sätzen, nicht in den Sätzen ab, vom Schauspieler her gesehen.

The only other alternative is, as Dürrenmatt calls it, a 'Kapitulation vor der Sprache' (197). This suggestion calls to mind Samuel Beckett's assertion 'schweigen wir zusammen', since, if there is anything to be said, it is unsayable. Unlike the Absurdists, who reduced language's role to that of showing the complete senselessness of life, Dürrenmatt does not use his theater as an extended exercise in *reductio ad absurdum*. He writes:

> Nur der kapituliert nicht, der den Glauben an die Sprache als Aberglauben durchschaut. Die unerbittliche Grenze des Menschen kerkert ihn nicht ein, sondern weist ihn nur zurecht, nicht das Unmögliche zu wollen, indem man das Mögliche unterläßt: sich einen Sinn zu geben, einen Sinn außerhalb der Sprache zu konzipieren. (197)

While Eugène Ionesco and Beckett deride language for its insufficiency as a medium of communication, Dürrenmatt observes the hidden possibilities of letting an unrepresentable image arise from language through internal contradictions. Doing this inevitably leads to paradoxical conclusions.[6] Dürrenmatt contends, as we see in an interview with Peter André Bloch (1980), that the role of the author is to present the text and to allow the text to develop on its own. He states: 'Ich stehe einfach vor einer Situation, vor der ich weiß, daß sie immer in Paradoxen mündet. Und ich wehre mich nicht dagegen. Ja, ich stelle die Bilder in ihrer Paradoxie dar.' He continues:

> Sehen Sie, jeder Mensch, jeder Künstler, arbeitet aus einer Einheit des Erlebens, des Durchdenkens und des Gestaltens heraus. Man is geprägt von gewissen Grunderfahrungen, Ureinfällen. Meine Phantasie ist wie ein See, in den bestimmte Erlebnisse hinabsinken und aus dem dann ganz neue Bilder auftauchen, die vielleicht auf den ernsten Blick mit dem ursprünglichen Erlebnis gar nichts mehr zu tun haben, aber doch aufgrund der Bildhaftigkeit irgendwie zusammenhängen. (29)

Ultimately, this tension between the dependence on language and the inadequacy of language leads to a 'Koppelung des Unvereinbaren'. Once a 'Methode des Denkens' is reached that is 'unabhängig von der Erfahrung' and once the validity of the assertion, 'jede Wirklichkeit [ist] eine Konzeption' is accepted, certain 'Zusammenhänge' become apparent in the thread created by the words and incongruencies of the text. Dürrenmatt states: 'so werden in und hinter den Worten Zusammenhänge deutlich. Ihnen zuliebe ging ich mehr von den religiösen Vorstellungen aus als von politischen' (156).

Obviously, Dürrenmatt's original plan for the drama was more political than religious. *Der Turmbau zu Babel* was the working title for a play Dürrenmatt had been writing and sending in installments to Kurt Horwitz in 1948. The theme of this play was the building of a tower that was to rise higher with every act, until only a few characters in oxygen masks would be left. King Nebukadnezar reaches heaven as the only survivor of the race he had enslaved to build the tower. In heaven he challenges God to a duel, but God is nowhere to be found. Only an ancient figure lives up there who is sweeping up a few stray atoms with a broom. *Der Turmbau zu Babel*, in which the inherent bitterness to be sensed in a direct confrontation with God reminds one of Dürrenmatt's youthful works, such as the poem 'Weihnacht', later developed into *Ein Engel kommt nach Babylon* (1954).

*Ein Engel kommt nach Babylon* was performed on April 6, 1957 at the Münchner Kammerspiele under the direction of Hans Schweikart.[7] While Dürrenmatt had by now developed a strong interest in the theater and its unique demands, his maturing dramaturgy seemed to be an extension of techniques learned for his early narratives and short stories. He writes in 'Theaterprobleme' in *Theater-Schriften und Reden* (1966c, 23): 'Das Bühnenbild will andeuten, bedeuten, verdichten, nicht schildern.' His continued emphasis on the written word in theater is clear from statements such as: 'Die Probleme jedoch, denen ich als Dramatiker gegenüberstehe, sind arbeitspraktische Probleme [...] Gewiss, auf dem Theater ist vor allem das Wort wichtig' (8–28). Word and presentation are intricately connected in a way that shows the mutual dependence of one on the other:

> Der Mensch des Dramas ist ein redender Mensch, das ist seine Einschränkung, und die Handlung ist dazu da, den Menschen zu einer besonderen Rede zu zwingen. Die Handlung ist der Tiegel, in welchem der Mensch Wort wird, Wort werden muß. (111ff.)

Yet to contradict the same image, Dürrenmatt writes in *Theater-Schriften und Reden II* (1972, 283): 'Leerer Worte wegen kamen bisweilen viele Menschen um.' The paradoxical reciprocity between the inadequacy of language to portray life and drama's dependence on language becomes most apparent in Dürrenmatt's play *Ein Engel*.

Initially Dürrenmatt's *Ein Engel* seems to be a play about the attempt to establish the perfect and permanent state once and for all time. Nebukadnezar, the present king, attempts to create a Babylon that will stand for ever. This attempt, however, as will become clear, stands in stark contradiction to the language of the play in its unique function as signifier. As it turns out, however, everything in the city of Babylon proves to be impermanent. *Ein Engel* is the portrayal of man's futile attempt to create any thing of permanence. The city of Babylon and its seemingly well-established state fall victims to the very language on which they are based.

One finds this already in the words of King Nebukadnezar, who constantly seeks to communicate fixed ideas fundamental to the ideology underlying his absolute rule:

NEBUKADNEZAR UND NIMROD *gleichzeitig:* Haut das Volk zusammen.
ERZMINISTER. Ein spontaner Aufstand braucht nicht niedergeschlagen zu
   werden, der zu einem Ziel gelenkt werden kann, das einem selber nützt.
*Nebukadnezar nimmt eine Denkerposition an, ebenso Nimrod.*
NEBUKADNEZAR UND NIMROD *gleichzeitig:* Ich höre.
NEBUKADNEZAR *verwundert:* Was redest du auf einmal meine Worte nach,
   Schemel? (70)

Nevertheless, his assertions lapse into mundane repetitive phrases
often shared with the former king, Nimrod. Just as the present and
former king simultaneously speak the same words, so Nebukadnezar
could also be replaced at any moment by Nimrod:

NIMROD. Jetzt bin ich unten, doch werde ich wieder nach oben steigen, jetzt
   ist Nebukadnezar oben, doch wird er wieder nach unten fallen (183).
NEBUKADNEZAR. Wir sind aneinandergekettet, ich und du.
NIMROD. Immerzu, immerzu.
NEBUKADNEZAR. Seit all den Tausenden von Jahren, die waren.
BEIDE. Oben ich, unten du, unten ich, oben du, immerzu, immerzu.
*Schweigen.* (225)

The king's authority diminishes at the same rate as the value of
the words the two men speak. Their words then acquire an orderly yet
chaotic motion as they exchange subjects and positions several times.
Down and up are inverted as 'du' and 'ich' conversely reverse positions with one another. Nebukadnezar and Nimrod are interchangeable
subjects as well as rulers. The point of axis between the ceaselessly
('immerzu') turning and spiraling of subjects leads ultimately to
silence. The multiplicity of possible meanings found in one assertion
has increased to the point where the assertion itself becomes meaningless.

The ultimate impotence of words becomes apparent in the extent
that the characters expect the signifier and the signified to be identical.
Several times the person and office are equated: 'Das Gesetz ist das
Gesetz […] Judico ergo sum.' After supporting the idea of judicial
power, the guard finds it necessary to back it up with a familiar but
altered Cartesian formula. Yet by doing this, he simultaneously undermines the originality of what he has stated and relies on hackneyed
historical assertions to bring meaning to his words and position. The

audience is surely aware that a guard's words, due to his lowly position, have relatively less importance in this argument than those of a member of a state would. Yet this assertion particularly emphasizes the banality of the resulting vacuous phrases. This effortless transferability to a different identity results in a similar mechanical interchangeability between words and their meanings. Peter André Bloch (1980, 30) asks Dürrenmatt in an interview:

> Gibt es nun bei Ihnen keine Spannung zwischen dem Bild und der Bedeutung – wie beispielsweise in der Allegorie? Ein allegorisches Bild steht ganz in der Spannung zwischen seiner Körperlichkeit und seiner abstrakten Bedeutung [...]

Dürrenmatt's answer explains his refusal to fix a meaning to a representation:

> Eine Allegorie hat für mich etwas Eingefrorenes an sich. Ich mag Allegorien nicht [...] Jedes Geschehen ist an sich zweideutig, mehrdeutig, die Allegorie hingegen eindeutig. Ideologie ist immer eindeutig. Und ich bin gegen das Eindeutige. Für mich ist immer das Zwei-, Drei-, Vierdeutige entscheidend. Eine Metapher ist nie eindeutig, im Bild treffen Sie eben immer das Nicht-Eindeutige, auch in den Naturwissenschaften. (30)

In the same manner, a few lines later the 'Erzminister' attempts to portray the extent of his and the king's power as Nebukadnezar orders Nimrod to be placed in a dungeon:

> ERZMINISTER. Ich bin Gesetzgeber. Ich habe den König damit definiert, daß sein Fuß auf den Schultern seines Vorgängers zu ruhen habe. Fällt die Definition dahin, fällt der König dahin.
> NEBUKADNEZAR. Dann ändere diese Definition. (225)

When two authorities dispute over a definition, the signification will fall apart if its definition is not altered. Any unwillingness on the part of the authorities to change a meaning is due to the knowledge of what that would cause:

> ERZMINISTER. Unmöglich. Sonst stürzen die fünfhunderttausend Paragraphen des babylonischen Gesetzes zusammen, die sich logischerweise aus der Definition des Königs ergeben, und wir haben das reine Chaos. (225)

175

The Erzminister has been able to avoid the problem of modifying a definition by adding to it. With the passing of time, the law has reached a ridiculous level of infinite definitions:

> NIMROD. Das sagte er mir auch immer.
> NEBUKADNEZAR. Und jedesmal war die Zahl der Paragraphen gewachsen. Ins Unermeßliche. (225)

This uncontrolled growth stands in stark contrast to Akki's stylistic economy in reciting his stories. As makames, an antiquated Persian form of poetry, Akki's narratives create an effect that conflicts with the language and general mood of other characters: 'Wie der Reiche verdarb und der Fromme starb, und auch der Starke den Tod erwarb, sagte sich meiner Mutter Sohn: Der Mensch sei wie Sand, Sand allein hält Stand' (197). This economy and precision intensifies language and elevates it to a level beyond its ordinary mundaneness in the play. Akki's makames lift language out of its representative role and emphasize, as Dürrenmatt describes it in *Theater-Schriften und Reden* (1966d, 114), 'die Freude am Fabulieren, am Wortgefecht, am Wortspiel'. Akki's use of tales, allegories, and anecdotes reveals his ability to manipulate language to his advantage and allows something other than a rigid structure to appear. Akki, through the use of this form of speech, becomes language himself, or, as Dürrenmatt writes: 'Die Makamen des Akki sind nichts anderes als die äußerste Möglichkeit seiner Sprache und somit eine Verdichtung seiner Gestalt. Akki wird in ihnen ganz Sprache, ist in ihnen Sprache geworden' (114). Akki does not try to possess or control language. Just the opposite, he uses the characteristics of language to go beyond it.

The Church, like the state, has not been able to overcome this lack of permanency inherent in abstract language. Religion and the state in Babylon have become almost indistinguishable from one another. Utnapischtim, for example, proudly asserts: 'Religion und Staatsraison fügen sich aufs schönste zusammen' (231). The 'Erzminister' agrees, to his own advantage, with the theologian's assertion: 'Wir haben die Möglichkeit, metaphysisch zu verankern, was politisch auf allzu schwachen Beinen stand' (231). Nevertheless, when a representative of the Church and also one of the state attempts to

176

interpret together the disturbing presence of an angel on the banks of the Euphrates River, they are unable to communicate in a constructive manner:

> UTNAPISCHTIN. Ein für Theologen verwirrendes Ereignis. Ich habe mich dagegen gesträubt, an Engel zu glauben, und habe verschiedene Schriften gegen diesen Glauben verfaßt, ja zwei Theologieprofessoren verbrennen müssen, die an ihm festhielten. Gott schien mir keine Werkzeuge zu benötigen. Er ist allmächtig. Nun bin ich fast gezwungen, meine Dogmatik in Hinsicht der Engel zu revidieren, ein schwierigeres Unternehmen, als ein Laie wohl glauben möchte, da die Allmacht Gottes natürlich nicht angetastet werden darf.
> NEBUKADNEZAR. Ich verstehe dich nicht.
> UTNAPISCHTIN. Macht nichts, Majestät. Auch wir Theologen verstehen einander beinahe nie. (227)

The viewer is presented over and over again with the idea that fixed definitions are not suitable. As a result, once definitions are no longer suitable, the futility of any attempt to create linguistic permanency becomes evident. The language in *Ein Engel*, therefore, has been shown to contain numerous inconsistencies, contradictions and paradoxes that negate the permanency of the powerful state established by king Nebukadnezar. Ultimately, *Ein Engel* is the portrayal of mankind's vain attempt to create anything of permanence, in this case the city of Babylon and its seemingly permanent state.

The assumed relationship between word and thing, between the linguistic representation and that which is being represented, is only imagined. Einstein's physics is the clearest example of this for Dürrenmatt. In his interview with Peter André Bloch (1980, 30), Dürrenmatt states:

> Ich setze mich mit Mathematik und Physik – statt mit Theologie – auseinander, das nennt man Verschreibung. Nur hat die Physik vielleicht eine andere Zukunft als die Theologie. Ich selber bin ja nicht Mathematiker, ich bin Schriftsteller. Das Weltall, die Mathematik, die Physik sind meine Träume. Wir sind ebenso real wie das Ganze und gleichermassen hypothetisch. Ich bin für Sie ein Andromedanebel wie Sie für mich. Ich weiß, daß wir in einer Welt der Hypothesen leben. Und dieses Bewußtsein ist für mich entscheidend.

In *Albert Einstein. Ein Vortrag* (1979), Dürrenmatt attributes to Einstein the ability to penetrate best into the modern world, 'in das wir hineingezeichnet sind, gerade noch als lächerliches Gekritzel in irgendeiner Weltecke erkennbar, dieses ungeheuerliche Labyrinth, in welchem wir immer hilfloser und hoffnungloser herumtappen' (42–43). Every expression about something fails to represent the expression that it wishes to represent. At the place where language ceases to function, 'Wirklichkeit', as we attempt to understand it, ceases to exist, and we are left with emptiness. As Dürrenmatt states in 'Die Stadt' (1952b), once words cannot accurately correspond to 'Wirklichkeit',[8] all we are able to do once we have had this realization is to accept language as 'das einzige halbwegs brauchbare Verständingungsmittel' (147).

Words, therefore, can be used as weapons to fight a 'Kampf'. In the first act, the king and Akki wager on language. Words must be suitable in such a manner that the king and Akki be able to extract as much money as possible from different characters. Akki understands the necessity of adjusting language to situation better than the disguised king does. He understands that language alone is the most powerful tool mankind has in order to function in today's society and therefore lets Nebukadnezar, who is not aware of this, go first:

> AKKI. Da trotten zwei Arbeiter quer durch Babylon, von einem Stadtteil zum andern, ohne Essen im Magen,einen Weg von drei Stunden, um ihre Frühschicht in der Zeigelbrennerei Mascherasch anzutreten. Ich lasse dich beginnen, Bettler aus Ninive (178).
> *Zwei Arbeiter kommen von links.*
> NEBUKADNEZAR *jammervoll:* Ein Almosen, ehrsame Arbeiter, ein Almosen einem Kameraden der Erzbergwerke Nebo, der invalid geworden ist. (178)

Whereas Nebukadnezar uses emotive platitudes on the workers and fails miserably, Akki fits language to the respective situation. He succeeds by accommodating his words to the situation at hand:

> AKKI. Jeder eine Kupfermünze, ihr Schufte. Da versuchen Sie ihre Bäuche für einen Silberling die Woche zu mästen, und ich, der ich die Ehre der Arbeiterschaft hochhalte und mich nicht zu dieser Ausbeutung hergebe, sondern bettle, hungere! Jagt den Besitzer der Ziegelbrennerei zum Teufel oder jeder eine Kupfermünze. (178)

Again, a few lines later, he chooses his words to accommodate a new situation:

AKKI. Ich bin glücklich, wenn du mir ein Lächeln deines roten Mundes schenkst. Das genügt mir.
TABTUM *verwundert*: Du willst mein Geld nicht?
AKKI. [...] Ich bin ein vornehmer Bettler, der bei [...] Damen der großen Gesellschaft bettelt und nur von einem Goldstück an aufwärts nimmt [...]
TABTUM *neugierig:* Wieviel geben denn die Damen der großen Gesellschaft?
AKKI. Zwei Goldstücke.
TABTUM. Ich kann dir drei Goldstücke geben.
AKKI. Dann gehörst du zur ganz großen Gesellschaft, schöne Dame. (180)

Akki manages to survive as an individual in the Babylonian society by not trusting language and by adjusting to other people's conceptions of him (i.e., the disguises and masks). Dürrenmatt refers to this sensible suspicion of language as a comprehension of words as 'Konzeptionen'. Dürrenmatt explains in 'Die Stadt' how 'der menschliche Geist verhält sich konzipierend, nicht "wahr", er dringt in die "Wahrheit" vermittels Konzeptionen, er ist nicht identisch mit der Wahrheit' (153). Akki is able to win the bet with the king because the latter cannot abandon his own and other people's conception of himself. Referring to Akki, Nebukadnezar states that what takes place between Akki and the king is a 'Kampf zwischen Konzeptionen, geführt in der Sprache, mit blutigen Folgen leider' (156). The king loses at this language game (which has indeed bloody consequences) when he attempts to speak outside of conceptions:

NEBUKDNEZAR. He!
ERSTER SOLDAT. Was will der Kerl? [...]
NEBUKDNEZAR. Beugt euch zu mir nieder, ich habe euch etwas zu sagen [...] Wißt ihr, wer ich bin?
DIE SOLDATEN. Nö.
NEBUKADNEZAR. Ich bin euer oberster Kriegsherr Nebukadnezar.
DIE SOLDATEN. Hehe.
*Sie schlagen Nebukadnezar mit den Schwertknäufen nieder.* (184)

When Akki explains to Nebukadnezar his mistake, he affirms yet again the shifting nature of words:

AKKI. Siehst du, das war der Fehler. Du mußt nie von dir behaupten, du seiest
der König, das wirkt unglaubhaft, sondern immer von einem andern. (187)

In everything we say we must deal with the relativity of conceptions, for timeless, absolute, objective truth does not exist in our 'Wirklichkeit'. Recognizing the adaptability and changeable nature of his seemingly powerful words as well as the insufficiency of his authoritarian position, the king's final statements in the play reflect disappointment with the state's impotence and ineffectiveness when it tries to establish order and totality in society through rationalism:

NEBUKADNEZAR *traurig*. Ich trachtete nach Vollkommenheit. Ich schuf eine
neue Ordnung der Dinge. Ich suchte die Armut zu tilgen. Ich wünschte die
Vernunft einzuführen [...] (249)

Nebukadnezar has no more success as a ruler than previously as a beggar in attaining his goals within rigid terminology. Since conceptions cannot be verified by our perceptions of reality, the more the modern individual tries to control his destiny through rational and scientific reasoning, the greater become the mathematical chances that the civilization created by him will crumble.

Through 'Abweichung' from any represented reality of God, a divine presence that exposes the futility of a purely limited and restricted God appears on the stage of Dürrenmatt's *Ein Engel*. A complete distrust of the ironies and paradoxes of signifiers holds the potential to bring forth such a divine manifestation.

Whereas in many of Dürrenmatt's plays God leaves those affected by his justice either to die a horrible death or to suffer a great loss, the God of this play is not interested in mankind and remains completely aloof from the earth. The God of the stage in *Ein Engel* does not make the final judicial decision, nor is his impotence as God brought to light. Though Nebukadnezar speaks of God's 'Gerechtigkeit', God in *Ein Engel* shows no sign of being interested in justice or burdening man with a 'fate'. The king's angry cries toward heaven in the final act return unanswered, for the God of the stage, if he exists, does not care. As a secular author and playwright writing for a secular modern audience, Dürrenmatt was aware of the fact that his portrayals of a God of justice reveal a paradoxical manner of thinking.

The short story 'Der Folterknecht' (1952a) portrays the world as a torture chamber and God as torturer: the 'Folterknecht ist Gott. Der foltert' (43). God as torturer of mankind appears often in Dürrenmatt's work as a product of a certain need to put a doctrine of justice and judgment into practice. In the same manner, one is able, through this grotesque portrayal of a just torturer God, to draw a parallel to the role of language in *Ein Engel*. Society has reached the point where nothing is fixed and all definitions are stretched or reduced to fit a necessary and just status quo.

Not unlike Brecht's three Gods in *Der gute Mensch* (1973b), Dürrenmatt's God seems only an invention of the institutions committed to keeping society under control. The existence of God is implied through certain characters, such as the theologian and the angel, but only as images and representations of their own fabrication. The king, dependent on this definition of God for control over Babylon and angry at God for not assisting him in perfecting his kingdom, dreams of building a tower to overcome his enemy. However, according to the early version of this play, *Der Turm*, King Nebukadnezar finds no God in heaven, only an old man sweeping stray atoms. Similarly, according to the biblical account, God does not, in his anger, destroy Babylon. Instead, he only creates a new diversity of languages to cause confusion and make the continued building of the Tower impossible.

The king's 'Gerechtigkeit' and the last remnants of hard physics are swept away. Dürrenmatt explains in his interview with Peter André Bloch (1980, 2):

> Die Zeit der geschlossenen Weltbilder ist vorbei. Ich wäre in dieser Beziehung vielleicht am besten Lessing vergleichbar, der nicht Wahrheiten darstellt, sondern die Suche nach Wahrheit. Im Grunde stellen wir heute auch in den Naturwissenschaften nur noch Scheinbilder dar, wie der grosse Physiker Hertz feststellt. Jedes Bild, jedes Werk, steht schon von seiner Entstehung an grundsätzlich im Spiegel seiner Mehrdeutigkeit.

No morally indignant God destroys the 'blasphemous' city of Babylon in the end, and no one dies. Instead, language's deceptive nature has led to the impossibility of creating anything of permanence. 'Wird aber einmal', Dürrenmatt concludes in *Theater-Schriften und Reden II*

(1972, 283), 'die schmerzliche Erkenntnis akzeptiert, alles (–alles? Das menschliche Leben, die Geschichte die Menschheit?–) sei ein Kampf zwischen Konzeptionen'. Dürrenmatt's essay 'Durcheinandertal' (1989, 58) describes modern society's understanding of God and emphasizes the irony of contradictions:

> Gegen das Ufer zu, durchnässt, Pornohefte, 'Stielers Handatlas über die Theile der Erde und über das Weltgebäude', erschienen bei Justus Perthes 1890, 'Meyers Konversationslexikon in 18 Bänden 1893–1898', 'Die Philosophie im Boudoir' des Marquis de Sade, Unmengen von Telefonbüchern, von Karl Barths 'Kirchlicher Dogmatik' der dritte Band: 'Die Lehre von der Schöpfung: Über das göttliche Regieren', Stösse von Börsenberichten, 'Der Spiegel', die Biblia Hebraica ad optimas editiones imprimis Everardi Van der Hooght', weitere Hefte und Schwarten, dazu Berge von ungeöffneten Briefen, sie bedecken den ganzen Strand.

The same must be said of *Ein Engel*, where countless paradoxes and contradictions mirror the unresolvable tensions of a godless modernity.

Dürrenmatt assumes the position of an author who, in the later stages of his works, reaches beyond the ironies and paradoxes of signifiers. As he allows writing to develop its own narrative, he soon realizes what was clear from the beginning, as he states in an interview with Arnold (1976, 65):

> Das Entsetzliche ist, ich komme zu keinem Trost, ich komme nur zu Fragen, und ich kann keinen Trost geben, ich kann es einfach nicht. Was mich anspornt: etwas zu formulieren, etwas zu machen, auch wenn das ganz unsinnig ist, auch wenn ich das Gefühl habe, daß, was ich tue, nicht stimmt.

The fact that the author is not in full control of his text allows 'eines aus dem anderen und durch das andere [zu] entwickel[n]'. This leads to the creation of an intense potential energy that permits God to appear outside the constraints of reality. Such designations as 'Gott' and 'Nichts' soon become invalid when conceptions allow 'der menschliche Geist' to reach a level that is no longer dependent on experience in the empirical sense. How Wittgenstein plays an important role in Dürrenmatt's distrust of words and simultaneous faith in their power is documented by Dürrenmatt's own statement in his essay 'Vinter' (1990b, 193):

> Aber dann muß die Fiktion fallen gelassen werden oder mit Wittgenstein: 'Meine Sätze erläutern dadurch, daß sie der, welcher mich versteht, am Ende als unsinning versteht, wenn er durch sie – auf ihnen – über sie hinausgestiegen ist. (Er muß sozusagen die Leiter wegwerfen, nachdem er auf ihr hinaufgestigen ist.) Er muß diese Sätze überwinden, dann sieht er die Welt richtig'. Ich warf die Leiter weg.

Logically speaking, a God outside of representations and descriptions is so inconceivable and improbable,

> daß wir an ihn glauben können, ohne Hoffnung, die geringste Stütze für unseren Glauben zu finden, es sei denn die, ihn unwahrscheinlicherweise erfahren zu haben, wobei diese Erfahrung einem anderen gegenüber durch nichts bewiesen werden kann,

Dürrenmatt insists in *Zusammenhänge* (1976c, 153). Such a belief, of course, requires a complete trust in something that cannot be signified externally in 'Wirklichkeit'.

Through 'Abweichung' from an experienced reality that is composed of tension and contradictions, the spectator is able to envision a divine presence that exposes the futility of a purely rationalistic search for knowledge. This is a paradoxical belief consisting of a 'Sprung' that Dürrenmatt writes of in *Turmbau* (1990, 204). Such faith in due course recognizes that 'Gott sich nur im Glauben offenbart' and, paradoxically, that a faith of this level is necessarily 'unabhängig vom Glauben an Gott' (124). Heinz Ludwig Arnold, in his essay 'Frieden und Krieg – Dürrenmatts Passion' (2003b, 130), explains this:

> Wer der Welt als Labyrinth gegenübertritt, vermag zwar ihre labyrinthische Struktur zu erkennen, aber er wird sie nicht durchschauen, er wird aus dem Gewirr keine Eindeutigkeit ablesen können […] Der Blick des Menschen aufs Labyrinth ist wie sein Blick in den Kosmos: Was er zu erkennen vermeint, sind Annahmen, Hypothesen, die man so lange glauben kann, bis sie widerlegt sind; aber es sind Hypothesen, die auf Glauben beruhen, sich nicht auf Erkenntnis und Wissen berufen können.

Kierkegaard's metaphysical speculations guided Dürrenmatt's thinking toward the presupposition that God is an unthinkable idea. History, wrote Karl Marx, repeats itself first as tragedy, then as farce. Although Dürrenmatt systematically attacked the Marxist ideology as a 'Wahrheitskonzeption', his dramaturgy of 'Arbeitshypothesen', prominently displayed in *Ein Engel*, suggests such a second repetition, no longer tragic, but instead into the world of tragicomedy.

The unique visual potential of the theater is of paramount importance in the emergence of a divine presence outside of signifiers and comes very close to the crucial role that language plays in *Ein Engel*. Dürrenmatt writes in 'Theaterprobleme' in *Theater-Schriften und Reden* (1966c, 28): 'Gewiss, auf dem Theater ist vor allem das Wort wichtig, aber eben: vor allem. Nach dem Wort kommnt noch vieles, was auch zum Theater gehört'. He quotes Max Frisch to emphasize a fundamental quality of modern dramaturgy: 'Entscheid end dabei ist, daß *mit* der Bühne gedichtet wird' (25).

Earlier, I discussed Brecht's reliance on 'Gestus'. A similar phenomenon can be discerned in the Swiss playwright. Dürrenmatt, who spent a good part of his youth drawing and painting, is acutely aware of the visual potentialities of the stage, and he uses them to communicate both verbal and non-verbal relations that are fundamental to his way of thinking. Dürrenmatt acknowledges the world as a tragi-comedy, and he replicates it on stage to the extent that drama as a genre and all of its characters and actions seek in vain to give such a world meaning. He asks in his 'Anmerkung' of *Es steht geschrieben* (1947b, 9): 'Was ist nun der Sinn des Schauspiels? Ich weiß es nicht, so wenig ich den Sinn dieser Welt weiß, die nicht sinnlos ist, nur daß es den Menschen nicht zukommt, diesen Sinn zu wissen.' Instead of offering the spectator clear guiding signs and perceptible representations, Dürrenmatt offers us 'Schreckbilder' that agitate us into recognizing the situation of our godless modern society. Adolf Klarmann characterizes this illusionary quality of history that sets the stage for Dürrenmatt's theater as 'the reality of illusion' (1952, 78).

Where Brecht, however, uses 'Gestus' to stimulate attention to the logical and comprehensible, quite the opposite is true with Dürrenmatt. From Dürrenmatt's point of view, history, by imposing limits, has assumed the role previously played by an unyielding tragic fate: 'wir haben nichts mehr zu bestimmen, die Geschichte hat uns widerlegt.' Consequently, 'so droht kein Gott mehr, keine Gerechtigkeit, kein Fatum wie in der fünften Symphonie' (1947b, 10). Dürrenmatt explains a certain necessity in modernity to move away from tragedy towards the 'Komödie' and even denies the possibility of tragedy in our age: 'Die Tragödie, als die gestrengste Kunstgattung setzt eine gestaltete Welt voraus. Die Komödie [...] eine ungestaltete, im Werden, im Umsturz begriffene, eine Welt, die am Zusammenpacken ist wie die unsrige' (9).

Great heroes are no longer conceivable on the modern stage. The individual must today be seen at his worst in his senseless attempts to change a senseless world. Such a presentation of the situation does not, however, lead into the dramaturgy of the absurd. In point 10 of the *21 Punkte zu den Physikern* in 'Theaterprobleme' (1966c, 12), he writes how such a story is 'zwar grotesk, aber nicht absurd (sinnwidrig)', and in point 11 he adds: 'Sie ist paradox.' Since the tragic hero is not longer representable on the modern stage, Dürrenmatt portrays individuals whose seemingly great actions are instead senseless acts of courage. In later years, as this depiction of the individual has become more pronounced, many of Dürrenmatt's later dramatic characters become increasingly introspective and self-oriented. Moreover, this preoccupation with self, with the isolated, existential individual, is accompanied in the later plays and theoretical writings by a preoccupation with the abstract and unrepresentable. He continues in 'Theaterprobleme' (1966c, 45):

Ich lehne es ab, das Allgemeine in einer Doktrin zu finden, ich nehme es als Chaos hin. Die Welt (die Bühne somit, die diese Welt bedeutet) steht für mich als ein Ungeheures da, als ein Rätsel an Unheil, das hingenommen werden muß.

By coming to terms with 'das Tragische', which marks modern life, in the place of 'die Tragödie', we come to understand the possibility of an abyss on Dürrenmatt's stage:

Doch ist das Tragische immer noch möglich, auch wenn die reine Tragödie nicht mehr möglich ist. Wir können das Tragische aus der Komödie heraus

185

erzielen, hervorbringen als einen schrecklichen Moment, als einen sich öffnenden Abgrund. (45)

In the same manner that the paradoxes, inconsistencies, and contradictions in the language of *Ein Engel* negate the permanence of the city of Babylon, the stage of *Ein Engel* shatters the very illusions of permanence it creates. As we have seen, King Nebukadnezar wants to create the perfect state and society:

> NEBUKADNEZAR. Indem meine Heere im Norden den Libanon erreicht haben, im Süden das Meer, im Westen eine Wüste und im Osten ein Gebirge, das so hoch ist, daß es nicht mehr aufhört, ist die Welt von mir erorbert worden. (170)

The audience is made to understand at the beginning that the king has established the Babylonian state within impregnable borders. Nebukadnezar has conquered the whole world and wants now to perfect his empire from within. Babylon appears as permanent as the king's position:

> ERZMINISTER. Im Namen der Minister –
> UTNAPISCHTIM. Der Kirche –
> GENERAL. Des Heeres –
> HENKER. Der Justiz –
> ALLE. Gratulieren wir Seiner Majestät dem König Nebukadnezar zur Neuordung der Welt. (170)

Although it appears impossible to deviate from such permanence, incongruities within this ordered community quickly become apparent. The first is that of regal power itself. Nebukadnezar's rule replaces King Nimrod's several times during the play, and vice versa, for thousands of years. Not only do the two kings speak simultaneously; before our very eyes they also continue to substitute for one another on the throne and as footstools and thereby visually destroy the idea of a single all-powerful authority. The more sinister implications of these farcical scenes suggest that the comic light is but a foreground to a deep darkness, a tragic irony. The idiot son, whose questionable paternity cements all the more firmly the identity of the two kings with one another, dances grotesquely across the stage:

186

NIMROD. Unser Sohn. Der Erbe unserer Macht. Keiner weiß, wer ihn zeugte. Wir schlichen beide betrunken zu seiner Mutter. (225)

Such a grotesque suggestion of the figurative impotence of an authoritarian ruler further underlines man's futile attempts to create something of permanence.

The more traditional device of disguise represents the impossibility of definitive representations. Nebukadnezar wants to eliminate the last beggar as the only remaining flaw in a society created in accord with his strict dogmas: Nebukadnezar's masking himself as a beggar in order to confront Akki symbolizes the ambiguous nature of the king's identity. Appearing on stage disguised in a beggar's costume taken from his court theater places the king's identity in question precisely because the king does not doubt his own identity. Nebukadnezar does not see himself as a beggar when he wears the mask, but rather as the king of Babylon. Seeing himself as the most powerful and richest man on earth, King Nebukadnezar refuses Kurrubi and cannot comprehend a God who would want to award a beggar, the lowest of all people on earth, beauty and purity:

NEBUKADNEZAR. [...] Deine Augen, dein Gesicht und dein Leib offenbaren die Schönheit des Himmels, doch was nützt die himmlische Vollkommenheit dem ärmsten der Menschen auf dieser unvollkommenen Erde? Wann lernt der Himmel, jedem zu geben, was er braucht? Die Armen und Machtlosen drängen sich aneinander wie Schafe und hungern, der Mächtige ist satt, doch einsam. Der Bettler hungert nach Brot [...] Nebukadnezar hungert nach einem Menschen. [...] *schlägt Kurrubi zu Boden, als sie ihn geküßt hat, und tritt sie mit Füßen*: [...] Der Himmel soll sehen, wie ein Bettler sein Geschenk behandelt, wie der geringste der Menschen mit dem verfährt, was König Nebukadnezar mit seiner Liebe und mit dem Golde Babylons überhäuft hätte! (192–93)

The greatest irony in this play revolves around the characters' (mis)understanding of the word 'gering' to mean materially poor. Instead, this word must be understood in the same way that it is used in the New Testament in Matthew 25:40: 'Was ihr getan habt einem unter dessen meinen geringsten Brüdern, das habt ihr mir getan.' Though he holds a high status, the king is indeed the figuratively lowest person on earth. Nebukadnezar does not realize this or the fact

187

that Kurrubi is a gift to him, the 'geringste der Menschen'. When he performs the role of a beggar, he still mistakenly acts within his limited role as ruler. He consequently puts all the blame on God for disproportionately distributing gifts to individuals:

> NEBUKADNEZAR. Entsetze dich nicht vor den Menschen, entsetze dich vor Gott: Er schuf uns nach seinem Bilde. Alles ist seine Tat. (192)

In his continual need to perfect his empire, Nebukadnezar is unable to break away from the rigid representations within which he is trapped. Ironically, he is indeed the lowest person on earth whether he is 'verstellt' or not. It seems true that, for Dürrenmatt, since man does not understand grace, he not only tries to put it in human terms, but even more, he cannot accept it and sees it as being deceived, as a crude joke or trick. Thus, viewing the circumstances from a socialist perspective, because the king cannot understand why a beggar should receive the grace of God instead of food when the most powerful person on earth is starving for human affection, he beats and steps on Kurrubi.

The visual potential of the theater is also realized when Nebukadnezar's attempt at perfection and the inflexibility with which he and Nimrod perform their comical roles find further embodiment in the gold masks they wear. These masks only emphasize the complete exteriority and materiality of the two kings and thus again categorize them as empty representation. Furthermore, the massive statues in the royal palace described in the stage directions of the third act create a similarly powerful first impression: 'Der Raum wird durch ein Riesengitter in einen Vorder- und Hintergrund geteilt, der sich un-ermeßlich irgendwohin erstreckt, mit zu ahnenden Riesenstatuen irgendwo, steinern, erstorben' (223).

Yet even this symbolic display of power and inflexibility proves impermanent. The heads of these statues replace one another when Nebukadnezar and Nimrod exchange their 'fixed' roles as king and footstool. Furthermore, solid and binding words such as 'Riesengitter' and 'steinern' stand in direct contradiction to vague ones like 'uner-meßlich' and 'irgendwohin'. Such inherent contradictions negate the extrinsic staging devices and open spaces in their place that are not fixed or representable on the stage. Nebukadnezar is left alone with his idiot successor. The stage directions read: 'Da seiltanzt der Idiot grinsend über die Bühne. Nebukadnezar bedeckt sein Antlitz in ohnmächtiger Wut, in ohnmächtiger Trauer' (250).

With his final despairing words 'Nein. Nein' (250), Nebukadnezar annuls everything he and Nimrod have tried to represent as kings of Babylon: the gesture of covering his face with his hands demonstrates his nakedness: he is the lowliest human being in Babylon. Nebukadnezar, however, never recognizes his true maskless position. If he had, he would not have begun the Tower of Babel. The Tower of Babel, as we well know, results in a plethora of languages, thus further contributing to the repeating nature of history and situation of society.

Such dramaturgical suggestions and ideas approach those of the Theater of the Absurd, as in the works of Beckett and Camus. However, the idea of an absurd theater is, according to Dürrenmatt, an absurdity. In an interview with Kenneth Whitton (1974, 19), Dürrenmatt asserts:

> Wissen Sie, erstens, das ist ein falscher literarischer Begriff, der aufgestellt wurde. Es gibt absurdes Theater nicht, absurd heißt sinnlos; es gibt paradoxes Theater [...] für mich ist das ein absurder, ein leichtferiger Begriff [...] Es ist ein leichtfertiges Schlagwort geworden.

*Godot*, he continues, is not absurd but grotesque. It is

> eine Gleichnisdichtung. Wenn man exakt sein sollte, würde ich das symbolisches Theater nennen. Sie wollen aber nicht Symboliker sein, sie meinen aber alles symbolisch – sie wollen das aber nicht sein und nennen sich absurd. Das ist ein Bürgerschreckbegriff. (19)

In the theater of Beckett, the individual asks in vain, whereas Dürrenmatt's theater seeks to bring to our awareness the conflicts and incongruencies of life, to urge us to ask questions even if an answer is not available. Those who see nothing portrayed on Dürrenmatt's stage but nihilism and meaninglessness are in fact merely reflecting their personal and rigid reading of the world. Dürrenmatt writes in his 'Dramaturgische Überlegungen zu den Wiedertäufern' (1967b, 107):

'Darin, daß viele der heutigen Zuschauer in meinen Stücken nichts als Nihilismus sehen, spiegelt sich nur ihr eigener Nihilismus wider. Sie haben keine andere Deutungsmöglichkeit.' Paradoxically, however, as Akki reminds us, the king is the highest in the kingdom of God as just such an empty representation:

> AKKI. [...] Gerade die schäbigen, verachteten, verabscheuten Berufe muß man heben, damit sie erlöst werden aus ihrer Niedrigkeit und etwas darstellen; sonst sind sie verloren. (219)

Consequently, the visual potential of the theater allows the stage of *Ein Engel* to shatter its own illusions of permanence in the same manner that the paradoxes and contradictions of the language of *Ein Engel* negate the permanence of the city of Babylon.

Contrary to the plays discussed in our previous chapters, in which the physical appearance of God is implied, if not seen, God remains absent from the stage of *Ein Engel*, both as a representation and through intervention. God is not interested in mankind and remains completely aloof from the earth. In the place of a physically present God, one finds only corrupt institutional authorities and exploitative political and theological power structures. These representations of religion are equivalent to those of the state and ultimately suffer a similar fate.

The sovereignty of the Church and the power of the state in Babylon are mutually dependent, so that the two, though outwardly separate, have become almost indistinguishable. We have already heard the 'Obertheologe Utnapischtim', who represents organized religion in the Babylonian society, assert 'Religion und Staatsraison fügen sich aufs schönste zusammen', and the Erzminister reply 'Wir haben die Möglichkeit, metaphysisch zu verankern, was politisch auf allzu schwachen Beinen stand' (231). Unexplainable deviations from the fixed order that are foreign to the pre-established religious meanings and therefore likely to lead to chaos must consequently be eliminated. A predetermined belief in established representations is necessary in order to keep the individual under control. In *Zusammen-hänge* Dürrenmatt (1976c, 188) writes on this subject:

Die Kirche ist durch ihre Dogmen nicht nur gerechtfertigt, sie ist auch mit ihren Dogmen identisch, sie stellt gleichsam ihre Gesetze selbst dar, die im Papst verkörpert sind. Zwischen der Kirche und dem Einzelnen gibt es keine Instanz. Im Gegenteil, die kirchlichen Dogmen binden den Einzelnen nicht nur an eine Lehre, die ihn erlöst und die ewige Glückseligkeit verspricht, sie binden ihn auch an die Kirche, weil diese die einzige sichere Instanz ist, die ihm die richtige Lehre vermittelt, das, was er glauben darf.

In such a rigidly constructed environment, any form of intrusion into the established definitions will upset the fragile and ordered society.

The pre-established order in Babylon is threatened by the arrival of a divine being, whose mere presence is a complete contradiction to the 'heaven on earth' that the state and the Church have been instituting. This unexplainable presence calls into question the very essence, significance, and value of rigid signifiers. By concealing his character upon arrival in Babylon and by taking on human form, the angel draws little attention to himself. However, because he can see only beauty wherever he looks,[9] and because of his intellectual curiosity, he becomes preoccupied with analyzing geographical and geological formations of the earth that he cannot understand. Consequently, his unmasked presence and angelic image roaming the area ultimately cause chaos in the 'Neuordnung der Welt'. The Erzminister explains this:

> ERZMINISTER. Allein das Erscheinen des Engels untergräbt die Autorität des Staates. (239)

The state recognizes the angel's appearance as an expression of unwanted divine intervention in the ordered religious realm. The Erzminister objects to the fact that the angel is putting in an appearance where he is not welcome:

> ERZMINISTER. Meine Kritik richtet sich nicht gegen den Engel, sondern dessen Erscheinen. Es ist reines Gift. Jetzt eben, zum Beispiel, schwebt er über den hängenden Gärten [...] Ich frage: Ist dies ein Benehmen? Ein Staat, eine gesunde Autorität ist nur möglich, indem die Erde Erde und der Himmel Himmel bleibt, indem die Erde eine Wirklichkeit darstellt, die von den Politikern zu gestalten ist, und der Himmel eine holde Theorie der Theologen, über die sonst niemand klug zu werden braucht. (239)

The Erzminister treats the divine image with little respect, and by asking: 'Ist dies ein Benehmen?' perhaps even with an annoyance similar to that of a parent toward an unruly child. The angel disturbs the seemingly ordered tranquility of a society that already believes in a God, albeit with certain aspects and definitions of its own making. Furthermore, the Erzminister's assertion emphasizes that the angel merely represents divinity. The angel does not understand the figurative meaning of his mission to earth and does not recognize in Nebukadnezar the least of Christ's brethren on earth. He thereby becomes a parody of the natural scientists and others who see only physical reality and beauty. Furthermore, the angel's fascination with earth is reinforced by his language. Dürrenmatt explains this in *Theater-Schriften und Reden* (1966d, 107):

> Der Engel etwa, der nach Babylon kommt, wird von Akt zu Akt über die Schönheit der Erde begeisterter, seine Sprache muß diese steigernde Begeisterung ausdrücken und sich bis zum Hymnus steigern.

In *Ein Engel* we read:

> ENGEL. So entschwebe ich denn, so entschwinde ich nun,
> Beladen mit bunten Steinen [...]
> Mit Seestern, Moos und Tintenfische,
> umsummt von Kolibris,
> in den Händen
> Sonnenblumen, Malven und die Ähren des Korns,
> Eiszapfenklirrne [...]
> So gehe ich ein in meinen Sonnen,
> in das milchige Weiß des Andromedanebels in dämmerhafte Ferne [...]
> (249)

Paradoxically, the physical appearance of the angel, as well as his interference with the physical reality around him, disrupts the accepted permance of the representations.

Akki, in contrast to the state and church, does not have a predetermined role and is therefore able to overcome the restrictive boundaries imposed by society. Because he has 'kein Geld und keinen Namen' (174), he is not bound to any restrictive terminology:

AKKI. Ich bin, was mir gefällt. Ich bin alles gewesen, und jetzt bin ich Akki der Bettler geworden. Doch wenn du willst, kann ich auch Nebukadnezar der König sein. (174)

Akki chooses what he wants to be and carries out the roles he selects with great creativity. With his own many reigns as a king, he emphasizes the eventual disintegration of every structure:

AKKI. Nichts ist leichter als ein König zu werden. Dies ist eines der einfachsten Kunststücke, das man gleich zu Beginn seiner bettlerischen Laufbahn lernen muß. Ich bin in meinem Leben schon siebenmal König gewesen. (174)

Akki's certainty of how ephemeral any form of authority is keeps him free of any doctrine or dogma. He asserts:

AKKI. Wir gehen in Fetzen, der Erbärmlichkeit des Menschen zuliebe, gehorchen keinem Gesetz, die Freiheit zu verherrlichen. (178)

He is in all senses of the word a 'Lebenskünstler' who survives as an individual precisely because of his non-occupation. Even the king unconsciously recognizes this fact when he paradoxically tells Akki, who is now clothed as the hangman, that he is the only person in the kingdom 'der sich nicht verstellt, der ist, der er ist' (233).

Akki continually reenters the world of representations only in order to defeat them and to contribute to the 'heimlichen Weltgerüst, in welchem sich die Dinge aufbauen und abbauen' (220). His contribution to the world stage ('Weltgerüst') is one of deconstructing fixed things. He 'artfully' begs professions, so that he can 'elevate' them by their destruction. His new role will be that of hangman in order to undo the former function of the executioner as contributor to the building of traditional institutions. By putting on the executioner's coat and mask, he, in accordance with his philosophy of life, attacks from within: 'Von innen greife an. Sei in der Festung schon am Tage des Gerichts. Schleiche dich ein, demütigen Gesichts, als Saufkumpan, als Sklave, Dichter, Schuldenbauer, erniedrige dich, und du brichst jede Mauer' (221–22). Akki is able to take the 'schlimmstmögliche Wendung' and use it as an exit from the present reality of ideologies and representations.[10] Ultimately, not belief in another ideology, but rather only 'Zweifel' in all ideology enables man to tear down fixed doctrines.

*Ein Engel* allows God to make an appearance on the stage as an entity that cannot be signified externally, but rather comes into being within the paradoxical and contradictory, and is contrary to all dramaturgical principles. Although Dürrenmatt admits that he does not believe in the miracles of Christ, the Incarnation, the Resurrection, or the Ascension, the play *Ein Engel* nonetheless suggests the possibility of the unrepresentable. Regardless of whether Dürrenmatt was aware of this, he writes of such a paradox in *Zusammenhänge* (1976c, 16):

> Nun glaube ich weder an seine Wunder noch daran, daß Gott ihn auf eine unnatürliche Weise zeugte [...] wird doch Gott, gibt es ihn, weil er ist, jedes theatralische Ablehnen, aus dem einfachen Grund, weil, wer ist, keinen Schein braucht, um sein Sein zu beweisen.

Although Kurrubi appears at first to be merely a theatrical representation, her presence is an attestation of an unrepresentable God. Visually as well as verbally, we are repeatedly reminded of the origins of Kurrubi: 'während [Kurrubi] von Gott aus dem Nichts gemacht worden bist' (168). The 'Nichts' of her birthplace remains part of the stage props hovering above and constituting the background for the entire play:

> *Um gleich mit dem wichtigsten Ort zu beginnen, der zwar nicht den Schauplatz abgibt, sondern nur den Hintergrund dieser Komödie, so hängt ein unermeßlicher Himmel über allem, in dessen Mitte der Andromedanebel schwebt, etwa so, wie wir ihn in den Spiegeln des Mount Wilson oder des Mount Palomar sehen.* (167)

This place accentuates the artificial, theatrical, and rigid qualities of heaven and portrays, in the words of Knipperdollinck in *Die Wiedertäufer* (1967, 163), 'Nichts als eine leere Bühne'. Dürrenmatt explains in *Theater-Schriften* (1966d, 107) how this heaven is in fact nothing more than theatricality:

> Nun, den Himmel könnte man einfach mit einem dunklen Hintergrund wiedergeben, als eine Ahnung seiner Unendlichkeit, doch da es mir in meiner Komödie darum geht, den Himmel nicht so sehr als einen Ort des Unendlichen,

> sondern des Unbegreiflichen, des ganz anderen einzusetzen, schreibe ich vor, daß den Hintergrund der Bühne, den Himmel über der Stadt Babylon, ein Riesenbild des Andromedanebels einnehmen müsse […] Damit versuch ich zu erreichen, daß der Himmel, da Unbegreifliche, Unerforschliche, auf der Bühne Gestalt annimmt, Theatergestalt.

The autonomy of the dramatic reigns supreme, by exhibiting the impossibility of any higher dimension. The fact that Kurrubi was created from this 'unermeßlicher Himmel' seems to affirm that she, too, belongs to the artificial and theatrical.

Yet, paradoxically, Kurrubi does not belong on earth. She appeals incessantly to the angel to take her back to heaven, yet her cries remain unanswered:

> KURRUBI. Trage mich in deinen Himmel zurück, Engel, vor das gewaltige Antlitz Gottes […] Ich bin von allen verlassen.
> .........................................................................
> KURRUBI *verzweifelt*. Nimm mich von dieser Erde, mein Engel, nimm mich zu dir!
> .........................................................................
> NEBUKADNEZAR. Der Engel entschwindet. Er sinkt zurück in seine gleichgültigen Sterne. Du bist allein. Der Himmel hat dich verlassen, die Menschen verstoßen.
> KURRUBI. *zusammengebrochen, leise*. Mein Engel, nimm mich zu dir, nimm mich zu dir, mein Engel.
> *Schweigen.* (249–50)

Kurrubi's presence on earth is an attestation of an unrepresentable God. No one is willing to accept her, yet her holy presence remains undisputed. Kurrubi cannot return to God because this God is part of the 'Andromedanebel' that is painted on the fixtures of the stage. Egon Karter states this most clearly in *Mit und über Dürrenmatt* (2001, 52):

> Der Engel, der als Geschenck Gottes fürn den Ärmsten der Menschen das Mädchen Kurrubi zur Erde bringt, habe […] keine Ahnung, was Gott mit diesem Mädchen eigentlich wolle; wir müssten leider scliessen, Gott wisse es auch nicht. Gottes Gnade sei nicht nur uns, sondern auch Gott unbegreiflich.

Mankind understands that she has been miraculously 'den Menschen gebracht' (169) by an unknown source, and that accepting her would mean accepting a divine presence. Sacrificing materially secure possessions such as power, riches, or orthodox theology for 'dieses Kleinod von einer Gnade' (190) is a responsibility that no one is willing to accept, for no one is able to see beyond immediate and rigid concepts:

> NEBUKADNEZAR *traurig*. Ich trachtete nach Vollkommenheit. Ich schuf eine neue Ordnung der Dinge. Ich suchte die Armut zu tilgen. Ich wünschte die Vernunft einzuführen. Der Himmel mißachtete mein Werk. Ich blieb ohne Gnade. (249)

In a last effort to eradicate a divine presence outside of the concepts he has built, Nebukadnezar orders her death:

> NEBUKADNEZAR. Geh mit dem Mädchen in die Wüste, Henker. Töte es. Verscharre es im Sand. (249)

Kurrubi's love for the least of men shows her unrelenting commitment to her mission and her uncompromising faith in the origin of this mission as existing behind the ambiguity and meaninglessness of the world. Kurrubi is aware that the king is unable to love because his seemingly fixed representation in fact entails its own negation: 'Du lebst nicht und bist nicht tot. Du bist ein Wesen und wesenlos' (244). The king's representation both exists and does not exist, like the 'Andromedanebel' that hangs above his world. Kurrubi, even when fleeing into the desert with Akki, still loves the king, albeit in his disguised form as the beggar who lost the language game:

> KURRUBI. Ich suche einen Bettler aus Ninive, einen Bettler, den ich liebe und den ich verloren habe. (250)

Because she believes that the beggar exists and because this beggar is the king, she believes in Nebukadnezar, who is both a beggar and a king. And because she remains convinced of its ultimate realization, she affirms her belief in God. Interestingly enough, in the third version of this play, written in 1980, the king's fatalistic sentence, 'Ich blieb ohne Gnade,' is left out.

Akki, however, believes in a possibility independent of conceptions and does not attempt to define or limit the world he lives in.

Dürrenmatt approves of this attitude, since he holds a similar stance, as we read in the 'Nachwort' to *Der Mitmacher* (1976a, 326): 'unter Antisemiten bin ich Jude, unter Anti-Christen bin ich Christ, unter Antimarxisten Marxist, unter Marxisten Antimarxist.' He realizes that an attempt on his part to do this would paradoxically result in an 'Endspiel' and 'Schach-Matt'. The play would then necessarily end with the king's last deterministic words, 'Nein. Nein', as the senseless gestures of his son, a grotesque image of the future, leave us only the vision of a dead God and a meaningless world. Instead, Akki discovers a break within the four seemingly impregnable borders of Babylon and commits himself to a path through the desert 'im Westen' (170). He is aware by now that Kurrubi's presence on earth is a testimony of an unrepresentable God. He also understands that he must actively embrace this grace that overcomes rigid signifiers and take Kurrubi with him into the unknown nothing of the desert: '*Finsternis. Die Kulissen fahren in die Höhe. Unbestimmt ist eine unermeßliche Wüste zu ahnen, eine gewaltige Weite, durch die Akki und Kurrubi fliehen*' (250).

The world of the stage, which, in the first three acts is technically and dramaturgically perfect, gives way in the concluding scene to another world 'hinter den Kulissen', as he writes in his short story 'Der Tunnel' (1952c, 141). In the same manner that the student in Dürrenmatt's 'Der Tunnel' is the only one able to perceive their train falling into a dark and endless abyss, so, too, does Akki have the ability to perceive the endlessness of what Dürrenmatt calls a '*unermeßliche Wüste*'. Although this unknown may appear to Akki as something that Dürrenmatt in 'Theaterprobleme' (1966c, 49) calls 'Schreckliches' and 'Ungeheuerliches', he nonetheless enters it:

AKKI. Weiter, mein Mädchen, weiter! Dem Sandsturm entgegen, der immer mächtiger heranheult und meinen Henkersmantel zerfetzt. (250)

A presence of the divine is discernible only after traditional institutions have been shown to hold neither permanence nor substance. Because of his distrust of earthly rules, whether of grammar, religion, or political ideology, Akki goes into the desert with only his faith to guide him.[11] One must have faith when experiencing a fall into what Kierkegaard (1953b) refers to as the 'Abgrund der Verzweiflung', an idea that cannot be conceptualized or rationalized. At this place, God is present. Paradoxically, however, Dürrenmatt writes in *Zusammenhänge* (1976c, 153), God seems here so absent

> daß wir nur an ihn glauben können, ohne Hoffnung, die geringste Stütze für unseren Glauben zu finden, es sei denn die, ihn unwahrscheinlicherweise erfahren zu haben, wobei diese Erfahrung einem anderen gegenüber durch nichts bewiesen werden kann.

Kierkegaard's (1953a) reference to the 'qualitativen Sprung' from objective logic and reasoning into a subjective existence is echoed by Dürrenmatt in *Zusammenhänge* (1976c, 186–87):

> Hinunterstarrend auf diese tote Welt, wird mir klar, daß der Gott, den die Wüste hervorbrachte, dieser unsichtbare Gott [...] eine Erfahrung der Wüste ist, nicht ein Schluß der Philosophie oder eine Konzeption, und daß, fehlt diese Erfahrung, uns die Sprache fehlt, von ihm zu reden, über ihn läßt sich nur schweigen [...]
> Der Gott der Wüste [...] läßt sich nur erleben in der Erschütterung, so daß den Glauben nicht ein Für-Wahr-Halten, sondern ein Erschüttertsein bedeutet, das durch nichts bewiesen werden kann und das auch nicht bewiesen werden muß.

Akki and Kurrubi flee beyond the confining borders of Babylon into an immeasurable 'Wüste' without names or concepts. Jacques Derrida, discussing the structure of metaphor in 'White Mythology' (1974, 9–10), notes that metaphor remains a metaphysical concept and cites Heidegger's *Der Satz vom Grund* (1957b) where he maintains that metaphor is 'a transposition into the non-sensible of the supposedly sensible': 'The notion of "transposition" and of metaphor', Heidegger asserts, rests on 'the distinction, not to say the separation' between the 'physical and the non-physical'. It is a basic feature of what is called 'metaphysics' and 'confers upon Western thought its essential characteristics' (25–26).

Akki and Kurrubi's flight serves as a passage into language and ultimately proclaims a new narrative. This path, however, can be taken only once the complete distrust in objective reality has been replaced by subjectivity. Dürrenmatt writes in *Über die Grenzen* 1990c, 89):

> Auch der Wissenschaftler muß natürlich glauben. Das heißt, er weiß, daß er etwas annehmen muß, das vielleicht einmal widerlegt werden wird. Er liefert also Information, weil ich sage, es können einem ganz andere Interpretationen möglich sein [...] Das, was man der Naturwissenschaft vorwirft, daß sie ständig sich irre, das ist natürlich gerade ihre Kraft. Indem sie sucht, widerlegt sie das wieder, was sie gefunden hat.

Akki must enter the desert in complete faith in 'die Gestalt einer Ungestalt, das Gesicht einer gesichtslosen Welt' (29). Implicit in the act of a turn toward the negative and unexpected is the power of another realm of life, as Dürrenmatt writes in 'Theaterprobleme' (1966c, 123):

> Wer das Sinnlose, das Hoffnungslose dieser Welt sieht, kann verzweifeln, doch ist diese Verzweiflung nicht eine Folge dieser Welt, sondern eine Antwort, die er auf diese Welt gibt, und eine andere Antwort wäre sein Nichtverzweifeln.

With Kierkegaardian faith, the individual can allow himself to fall into the abyss of nothingness with only the expectation that God is there.

Dürrenmatt refers to his subjective experience with the death of his mother in 1975 as an 'Erschütterung' that precipitates his own subjective oscillation between belief and doubt. He writes in *Zusammenhänge* (1976c, 188): 'und das Schwert ihres Glaubens lag immer noch zwischen ihr und mir, ihr Sieg und meine Niederlage, den Sohn von seiner Mutter trennend, den Sohn an seine Mutter bindend.' Such an experience speaks of a disturbing awakening to the need of a faith in a divine presence precisely within the rigidity of a reality whose unyielding conceptions and senseless paradoxes have lost their permanence.

Akki's entrance into the desert is an affirmation of endless life, an optimistic awakening to a new existence, a 'ride into the sunset'. Once in the desert, Akki experiences the presence of an unearthly world:

> Und ich liebe eine Erde, die es immer noch gibt, eine Erde der Bettler [...] an Möglichkeiten wunderbar, eine Erde, die ich immer aufs neue bezwinge [...]

von Macht bedroht und unbesiegt. Weiter denn, Mädchen, voran denn, Kind, dem Tod übergeben, und doch am Leben [...] und vor uns, hinter dem Sturm, den wir durcheilen, verfolgt von Reitern, beschossen mit Pfeilen, stampfend durch Sand, klebend an Hängen, verbrannten Gesichts, liegt fern ein neues Land, tauchend aus der Dämmerung, dampfend im Silber des Lichts, voll neuer Verfolgung, voll neuer Verheißung und voll von neuen Gesängen! (250–51)

This personal faith on the part of the individual occurs simultaneously with a personal acceptance of his position. Kierkegaard, in *Krankheit zum Tode* (1953b, 32), refers to this as a 'Kampf des Glaubens':

> Ob der so Kämpfende untergehen wird, beruht einzig und allein darauf, ob er Möglichkeit herbeischaffen wird, das heißt, ob er glauben wird. Und doch versteht er, daß menschlich gesprochen sein Untergang das Gewisseste von allem ist. Dies ist das Dialektische im Glauben [...] Der Glaubende sieht und versteht menschlich gesprochen seinen Untergang (in dem was ihm zustößt oder was er gewagt hat), aber er glaubt. Darum geht er nicht unter.

In the same manner, Kierkegaard writes about the self: 'Indem er über *etwas* verzweifelt, verzweifelt er eigentlich über *sich selbst* und will nun von sich selbst los' (38). Dürrenmatt was clearly influenced by this perception and speaks of this in *Über die Grenzen* (1990c, 101) in relation to the world: 'Bin ich der Gefangene im Labyrinth? [...] Darin steckt für mich auch der Begrif Kierkegaards vom Einzelnen, der sich selbst nie begegnen kann: Man ist im Grunde immer allein und in sich eingeschlossen.' Similarly, the student in Dürrenmatt's 'Der Tunnel' (1952c) progressively comes to terms with his pathetic earthly situation and realizes another part of existence that has in fact always been part of his reality:

> weil er nur auf diesen Augenblick hinlebte, der nun erreicht war, auf diesen Augenblick des Einbruchs, auf dieses plötzliche Nachlassen der Erdoberfläche, auf diesen abenteuerlichen Sturz ins Erdinnere. (153)

He eagerly and actively awaits, 'nicht ohne gespensterhafte Heiterkeit', an encounter with a divine presence: 'Gott ließ uns fallen, und so stürzen wir auf ihn zu' (157). The individual is therefore not locked inside of his own broken existence and committed to his own hell. Instead, in the words of Kierkegaard in *Die Tagebücher* (1962, 385), 'indem der Glaubende glaubt, ist das Absurde nicht das Absurde

– der Glaube verwandelt es.' Dürrenmatt keeps himself at a distance from the existentialism of Camus or Sartre, and his theater cannot take place, as Sartre said about his own theater, 'behind closed doors'. Whereas Camus's individual lives a limited and godless existence in hopelessness, Akki refuses to succumb to hopelessness in his confrontation with an absurd world. At the same time, he does not blindly believe, as did many of Dürrenmatt's 'mutige Menschen', that he can change the world. Instead, Akki makes a personal decision *not* to believe in anything predetermined, but rather to understand that he cannot change the world and instead must turn his own self around. Dürrenmatt, in an interview with Peter André Bloch (1980, 28), speaks of this turn that must occur:

> Der Mensch ist das Wesen mit dem Bewusstsein seiner Endlichkeit. Das Tier lebt in einem gewissen Sinne unendlich, es lebt im Moment, füllt ihn ganz aus; der Mensch hingegen lebt endlich, hat diese Einheit mit der Zeit verloren. Der Mensch ist das Tier mit der schlimmstmöglichen Wendung.

Knipperdollinck, a character in Dürrenmatt's play *Es steht geschrieben* (1947a), allows his own self to fill the void of his doubt with the grace of God. Stretched out and about to die on the wheel, he comes to terms with his self and begins to doubt. At this moment, he breaks free from the world of signifiers and turns his body. In this new position, he cries:

> Herr! Herr! [...]
> Sieh meinen Leib, der zerbrochen ist, und meine Glieder, die in dieses Holz gespannt sind,
> Das mich umgibt als meine Grenze, die Du mir gesetzt hast, damit ich mich selber erkenne!
> Ich habe alles von mir geworfen, als wäre es Feuer in meinen Händen, und Du hast keine meiner Gaben verschmäht.
> Nun breitest Du Dein Schweigen über mich, und die Kälte Deines Himmels tauchst Du in mein Herz wie ein Schwert!
> Senkrecht steigt meine Verzweiflung zu Dir, eine lodernde Flamme
> und die Qual, die mich zerfleischt,
> und der Schrei meines Mundes, der sich Dir entgegenwirft,
> und der nun zu Deinem Lobe verklingt,
> denn alles, was geschieht, offenbart Deine Unendlichkeit, Herr!
> Die Tiefe meiner Verzweiflung ist nur ein Gleichnis Deiner Gerechtigkeit,

Und wie in einer Schale liegt mein Leib in diesem Rad, welche Du jetzt mit Deiner Gnade bis zum Rande füllst! (158)

Realization of the presence of God occurs in the moment in which we become painfully aware of the borders that mark the limited space of our existence. At that moment, as we struggle to surpass the boundaries of our restrictive consciousness, we reach 'Erschütterung' and experience the void of existence. As we read in 'Theaterprobleme' (1966c, 63), at the place of the 'schlimmstmögliche Wendung' the stage is capable of assuming a manifestation, 'einen sich öffnenden Abgrund'.

The incongruencies, paradoxes, and turns that become apparent in the text and on the stage of *Ein Engel* leave open potentials that the audience is provoked to recognize. Dürrenmatt, most clearly in *Turmbau* (1990a), perceives that 'Gott sich nur im Glauben offenbart'. Philipp Burkhard (2003, 240) elucidates Dürrenmatt's understanding of faith, as it is found in 'Vinter:'

> Später, gegen Ende des Abschnitts, also in der allerletzten Passage der autobiographischen Darstellung der *Stoffe* überhaupt, als er nochmals auf das Geheimnis und die Unerklärlichkeit seines Glaubens zu sprechen kommt, legt Dürrenmatt den Entscheidungsmoment sogar auf den Zeitpunkt fest, 'als ich auf den Trolleybus sprang'. Diese Darstellung ist zweifellos als Allusion auf Kierkegaard zu lessen. Dürrenmatt suggeriert damit, die Entscheidung letztlich als 'Sprung' im Sinne Kierkegaards zu intrerpretieren: Als paradoxen 'Augenblick', in dem trotz der objektiven Unvernünftigkeit auf nicht rationalisierbare Weise eine Entscheidung für den subjektiven Glauben getroffen wird.

In a similar act of faith, in the 'Sprung', the spectator also may subjectively experience God within the desert of nothingness. It is impossible to accept as 'real' the God created by the Babylonian religion and simultaneously have faith that something divine yet inconceivable exists. Once inconsistencies and contradictions negate the permanent nature of established religious institutions in *Ein Engel*, an open end, into which Akki enters, becomes apparent.

Dürrenmatt's stage, and more specifically *Ein Engel*, does not expect a change from the audience. He asserts this in an interview with Bienek (1965, 109): 'Beunruhigen im besten, beeinflussen im seltensten Falle – verändern nie.' Dürrenmatt's statement about the task of the writer must be emphasized. In an interview with Peter André Bloch in *Schriftsteller in unserer Zeit* (1972, 36), he continues: 'Er [der Schriftsteller] hat selber keine Ahnung von der Wirkung seiner Werke, es ist wie in der Bergpredigt: man sät, aber man weiß nicht, was man erntet, man weiß nicht, wohin die Körner fallen.' The leap of faith is not a Brechtian call to action. 'Epic theater' stages an understandable, albeit politically and socially flawed, world that stimulates its audience to seek solutions via its intellect. The so-called Aristotelian theater, in contrast, assumes complete spectator identification with the action and characters, and it relies on emotion to reach the goal of complete identification with the stage – that is, a theatrical catharsis. In 'Sätze zum Theater' (1976b, 55), we read:

> Der Zuschauer des dramatischen Theaters sagt: Ja, das habe ich auch schon gefühlt. – So bin ich. – […] Das Leid dieses Menschen erschüttert mich, weil es keinen Ausweg für ihn gibt […] Der Zuschauer des epischen Theaters sagt: Das hätte ich nicht gedacht. – So darf man es nicht machen. – Das ist höchst auffällig, fast nicht zu glauben – das muß aufhören. – Das Leid dieses Menschen erschüttert mich, weil es doch einen Ausweg für ihn gäbe.

Dürrenmatt's spectator is now urged instead to recognize the inconsistency and hopelessness of the world in order to achieve a personal faith in another existence without absurdly searching for a change. Akki formulates this best in his 'Makame von der Waffe des Schwachen' when he emphasizes the necessity of an unheroic life:

> Die Welt zu bestehen, muß der Schwache sie erkennen, um nicht blind einen Weg zu gehen, der sich verliert, in eine Gefahr zu rennen, die zum Tode führt […] Heldentaten sind sinnlos, sie verraten die Ohnmacht des Schwachen. (221)

The spectator has the possibility to individualize his world and thus to arrive at a subjective freedom, not a social one. Whether he functions in the world of fascism, Marxism, or capitalism, the spectator now has the ability to achieve individuality independent of his social environment. It is ultimately the autonomy of the text and the stage that incites him to do so, as we read in *Theater-Schriften und Reden* (1966d, 124):

> Durch den Einfall, durch die Komödie wird das anonyme Publikum als
> Publikum erst möglich, eine Wirklichkeit, mit der zu rechnen, die aber auch zu
> berechnen ist. Der Einfall verwandelt die Menge der Theaterbesucher besonders
> leicht in eine Masse, die nun angegriffen, verführt, überlistet werden kann, sich
> Dinge anzuhören, die man sich sonst nicht so leicht anhören würde.

By means of the 'Einfall' presented on the stage, the audience is
readied to go 'hinter d[ie] Kulissen'.

Another factor that Dürrenmatt is aware of as he writes and
stages his plays is the impossibility of assuming a spectator's reactions. Since the audience is, according to Dürrenmatt in an interview
with Josef-Hermann Sauter (1982, 54), 'mehr oder weniger immer
genießend', the 'wissenschaftliche Publikum' that Brecht conceived of
is in fact 'eine große Illusion'. Dürrenmatt writes in the 'Nachwort' to
*Die Physiker* (1963c, 355) of the impossibility of forcing the audience
into a reaction or recognition: 'Die Dramatik kann den Zuschauer
überlisten, sich der Wirklichkeit auszusetzen, aber nicht zwingen, ihr
standzuhalten oder [sie] gar zu bewältigen.' Dürrenmatt's spectator is
not presented with a moral or asked to learn a lesson. Rather he is left
to undergo a personal 'Erschütterung', not as an imitation or as fear,
but as self-awareness. Irmgard Wirtz, in 'Die Verwandlungen des
Engels' (2000, 150), asserts this most poignantly:

> In der Engelskomödie ist die Gnade ein Angebot des Himmels, das die
> Menschen vor die freie Wahl stellt und zu Richtern macht. Das Gericht des
> Himmels wird [...] durch das Gericht der Menschen ersetzt. Aber nicht mehr
> wie beim frühen Barth, sondern vielmehr im Kierkegaardschen Sinne
> konzentriert sich die Gnadenproblematik auf den Aspekt der *Annahme* oder
> *Ablehnung* durch den Menschen.

The ending remains open to those who have this recognition. It is the
subjective consideration of the spectator, not the intentions of the
dramatist, that is ultimately capable of establishing the direct link between theater and reality. In the interview with Bienek (1965, 106),
Dürrenmatt states:

> Das Publikum stellt eigentlich die Verbindung zwischen Theater und Wirk-
> lichkeit her, findet seine Welt in der unsrigen, ob wir wollen oder nicht. Alles
> Moralische, Didaktische muß in der Dramatik unbeabsichtigt geschehen, nur

dem kann ich eine Antwort auf seine Fragen geben, der diese Antwort selber findet, nur dem Trost, der selber mutig ist: das ist die grausame menschliche Begrenztheit der Kunst. Sie ist an sich ohnmächtig, kein Trost, keine Religion, ein Zeichen nur, daß hin und wieder irgend jemand in der allgemeinen Verzweiflung nicht verzweifelte. Mehr als dieses Zeichen kann ich nicht geben.

As Knipperdollinck in *Es steht geschrieben* (1947a) dies on the wheel, he cries out to God: 'Herr, du schweigst, und ich brauche Antwort' (115). 'Der Schrei meines Mundes' that 'verklingt' in the early version, 'verröchelt' in the second, *Die Wiedertäufer* (1967a, 168). Knipperdollinck's tortured words in the first version are wrenched and broken in the same manner as his tortured body on the wheel. The same painful realization in the face of death, expressed now in the second version through wordless groans, discloses grace:

> BISCHOF. [...] Die Gnade, Knipperdollinck, zwischen blutigen Speichen hervorgekratzt, klagt mich an. (168)

Grace is exposed at the place between the dying man's last efforts at formulating concepts. The final revealing question is asked by the bishop, yet he receives no answer:

> Diese unmenschliche Welt muß menschlicher werden.
> Aber wie? Aber wie? *Vorhang.* (121)

The questions that at first appear to be merely rhetorical ones in a monologue expressing despair are in fact true ones asked of someone who does not answer. Dürrenmatt's essay entitled 'Selbstgespräch' (1988, 113–14) expresses a metaphysical encounter with a divine presence who suggests an answer to such a question:

> Ich kann mich nicht vorstellen. Ich bin nicht vorstellbar, ich bin nur denkbar, und denkbar ist auch das Unsinnige. Ich bin das Unsinnige. Ein Unsinn. Ich bin nicht ich, und ich bin ich. Ich existiere, und ich existiere nicht. Ich bin ein Punkt, eine Gerade, eine Fläche, ein Kubus, eine Kugel, ein n-dimensionaler Körper und nichts von allem, Nichts [...] Vielleicht ist alles nur eine Idee von mir, ein Einfall, der mir kam, kommt oder kommen wird, egal, wann auch immer, einmal eingefallen, in der Vorvergangenheit, in der Vergangenheit, in der Gegenwart, in der Zukunft, in der Nachzukunft, hinter jeder Unendlichkeit,

würde der Einfall ins Unermeßliche wachsen, wieder in sich zusammenstürzen und zu nichts werden: Das Endlose und das Nichts sind dasselbe[...].

This, of course, is also the sum of paradoxes to be found in Kurrubi's final words to Nebukadnezar: 'Du lebst nicht und bist nicht tot. Du bist ein Wesen und wesenlos [...] Du kannst mich nicht lieben, weil es dich nicht gibt' (244). Since all 'Wirklichkeit' is but mere construction, Dürrenmatt sees the brain as a primary point of departure for any conception, as a 'rein hypothetischen Punkt'. Clearly familiar with Kierkegaard's speculations of the 'I', he referred to it in his essay 'Das Hirn' in *Turmbau* (1990a, 261) as a 'mathematischen Punkt' that is capable of acquiring a level of subjectivity unknown to it before, 'ein Hirn im Hirn, ein Ineinander von Hirnen, ein "Ich" im "Ich"'. Once this point has been reached, Dürrenmatt's text asks a final question: 'Ist "Das Hirn" meine Fiktion, die ich schreibe, oder bin ich die Fiktion des Hirns [...]?' Although this question belongs to the 'Unentscheidbaren, aber Denkbaren' (261), it also compels us, the audience of the play *Ein Engel,* to become aware of subjective possibilities and to construct hypotheses, as Dürrenmatt states in his interview with Peter André Bloch (1980, 30):

Wir sind ebenso real wie das Ganze und gleichermassen hypothetisch. Ich bin für Sie ein Andromedanebel wie Sie für mich. Ich weiß, daß wir in einer Welt der Hypothesen leben [...] Ich bin eine Art Naiver, ich mache Hypothesen ins Leere hinaus [...] Ich bin ein Mensch, der in der Einsamkeit lebt [...] Ich erkenne, die Menschheit geht unter, es gibt eine Katastrophe [...] Wer sollte meinen Bildern glauben?

The theatrical 'Einfall' that has been of consequential momentum and the principal turning point in the play grows into the 'Unermeßliche', falls apart, and finally becomes 'nichts'. Since, however, 'das Endlose und das Nichts sind dasselbe', as we are told in 'Selbstgespräch', the 'Nichts' is negated, as were the stage representations of *Ein Engel*, and turns into the 'Endlose'. Although the audience is left with open questions as Akki goes farther into the emptiness of the desert, the last words of the play profess 'neue Gesänge' as a few survivors follow: '*einige Dichter folgen, durch den Sandsturm hüpfend*' (251).

Paradoxes, incongruencies, and turns that have been accumulating throughout the play as hypotheses finally join together in the openness of the end and ultimately imply the 'Sinn' as the manifest presence of God on the stage. Such thinking through contradiction and paradox allows that which cannot be articulated in words to be written. This 'Sinn' is also the sum of paradoxes and contradictions, the final disclosure of 'Zusammenhänge,' and revelation of a divine manifestation on the stage. Dürrenmatt's 'Andere' declares in the radio play *Nächtliches Gespräch mit einem verachteten Menschen* (1963b, 109):

Wäre der Mensch nur Leib, Herr, es wäre einfach für die Mächtigen; sie könnten ihre Reiche erbauen, wie man Mauern baut, Quader an Quader gefügt zu einer Welt aus Stein. Doch wie sie auch bauen, wie riesenhaft nun auch ihre Paläste sind, wie übermächtig auch ihre Mittel, wie kühn ihre Pläne, wie schlau ihre Ränke, in die Leiber der Geschändeten […] in dieses schwache Material ist das Wissen eingesenkt, wie die Welt sein soll, und die Erkenntnis, wie sie ist, die Erinnerung, wozu Gott den Menschen schuf, und der Glaube, daß diese Welt zerbrechen muß, damit sein Reich komme, als eine Sprengkraft, mächtiger denn jene der Atome, die den Menschen immer wieder umprägt, ein Sauerteig in seiner trägen Masse, der das sanfte Wasser die Felsen auseinanderzwängt und ihre Macht zu Sand zermahlt, der in einer Kinderhand zerrint.

# Chapter Six
# Conclusion

The starting point of the preceding study is the generally accepted notion that 'modernity' in Western civilization was accompanied by a secularization of society's institutions and a deterioration of religious tradition and moral values. This study also stresses the established idea that the modern era goes far beyond any previous age in its departure from traditional models of the past, its break with the traditional, religious ways of viewing the world, and its need to express the problem of coming to terms with the self.

This study reveals how a select group of modern German plays is able to intimate the presence of a divine entity on the stage by taking advantage of the communicative potential of silence. Evidence for the individual forms of this presence is collected by examining the various approaches to language in a historical context. This close analysis yields the thesis that the secularization and industrialization of the modern age have not necessarily made it impossible to portray the divine. On the contrary, these phenomena have provided playwrights with previously unexplored ways to suggest the visible presence of the divine on the stage.

Innumerable other studies and interpretations of these four plays promise to portray the authors or the works in a new and more authentic way, to shed greater light on them, or to reach new conclusions. Yet some of these studies provide us with but another lifeless, albeit often innovative, insight into the potential purpose the playwright has. Others attempt to show how these plays might have been understood in their time, but these efforts ultimately leave these works no less lifelessly suspended in time. Both groups have in common the problem that they leave unexplained why we sense a living entity on the stage when these plays are performed.

Chapter 1 examines how the pervasive sense of discontent in modern life stems from society's break with religious tradition as well as from its traditional reliance on language, that is, from the mounting skepticism about the ability of language to articulate anything of value, especially religious value. The Enlightenment was followed by the writings of Charles Darwin and other thinkers, whose works contributed intentionally or unintentionally to an increasingly widespread denial of the fundamental beliefs of Christianity. Then, in the last quarter of the nineteenth century, came Zarathustra's announcement of the death of God, which has come to be seen as symptomatic of the long development of the modern era's disillusionment with Western religion. This loss was paralleled by a fruitless search for a viable substitute in the later half of the nineteenth century, especially in Europe. By the *fin de siècle*, God had become more outdated and irrelevant than ever, above all in self-proclaimed 'modern' literature. This literature frequently documented its claim to 'modernity' by consciously distancing itself from traditional concepts of the divine.

The first chapter acquaints the reader with the central problem of literary modernity, that is, language's emerging limitations. One of the first writers who characterized the modern age by a stated or implied rejection of the metaphysical was Emile Zola. In his essay on the *Roman experimental* (1880), he proclaimed the death of metaphysical man and called for literature to become more scientific. In the last decades of the nineteenth century, subsequent Naturalist writers provided arguably the best evidence of a collapse in the traditional value structures of Western civilization when they chose as their recurrent themes the disintegration, enervation, and deterioration of moral and social structures, especially those associated with the Church and the bourgeoisie.

The predicament of modern writers soon became apparent. By breaking with religious tradition, they call the function of language into question. The 'Logos' proclaimed by John at the beginning of his Gospel has seemingly lost its relevance, authenticity, and authority. Another completely secular system is usurping its place. Works of literary modernity now reveal how the empty phrases and discursive inconsistencies of traditional values can no longer be accepted literally. They imply that language in the modern age has reached a condition described at the turn of the century as 'Sprachnot' (a want of language revealed in the deficiencies of linguistic constructions). In

210

short, we see how 'modern' writers lose their faith in the certainty that language is anchored in the timeless concept of the 'Logos'.

In this sense, Michel Foucault, in *The Order of Things* (1966, 304), provides a usable description of the emergence of modernity:

> The threshold between Classicism and modernity (though the terms themselves have no importance – let us say between our prehistory and what is still contemporary) has been definitely crossed when words cease to intersect with representations and to provide a spontaneous grid for the knowledge of things.

Writing on the original Fall in his essay, 'Über Sprache überhaupt und über die Sprache des Menschen', Walter Benjamin (1977d, 150) poignantly explains the predicament of language as it justifies the preceding study:

> Diese Erkenntnis der Sache ist aber nicht spontane Schöpfung, sie geschieht nicht aus der Sprache absolut uneingeschränkt und unendlich wie diese; sondern es beruht der Name, den der Mensch der Sache gibt, darauf, wie sie ihm sich mitteilt. Im Namen ist das Wort Gottes nicht schaffend geblieben, es ist an einem Teil empfangend, wenn auch sprachempfangend, geworden. Auf die Sprache der Dinge selbst, aus denen wiederum lautlos und in der stummen Magie der Natur das Wort Gottes hervorstrahlt, ist dies Empfängnis gerichtet.

Modern writers struggle with the religious problem when grammatical validity has replaced 'Logos', and 'God' has become but an 'empty word'. As a result, the only approach to Him seems for some writers to be by negation itself. Others employ self-conscious blasphemy. In either case, as the preceding study shows, these writers' attempts to express their feelings of despair in a desolate world without God characterize one of the most pressing predicaments of European intellectuals at the end of the nineteenth century.

The foregoing analysis posits the generally held view that by the close of the nineteenth century God has disappeared and traditional religious concepts have lost their value. However, while it accepts *arguendo* this generally accepted notion that modern German literature is being created in a climate of radical secularization and within the confines imposed by a conscious loss, or 'Sprachnot', it demonstrates that the resultant void is filled by intimations of the divine. Analysis of theatrical language, as well as of modern society's methods of communication, demonstrate that a divine presence asserts itself in certain works of modern literature at the very place where the linguistic breakdown occurs: within as well as outside the boundaries of language. Furthermore, by revealing this process, this new reading of some canonical works of modern literature encourages us to re-examine the previously accepted notions of 'modern' itself.

The introductory chapter singles out drama as the genre with the greatest potential for implying a divine presence with non-verbal means. Along with its shared ability to expose the falsity of the repressive moral and ideological institutions and values of society, drama is the only genre capable of suggesting the actual physical presence of the metaphysical. The basic problem of drama, especially since the innovations of Naturalists like Gerhart Hauptmann and Arno Holz, has been to determine whether the linguistic inadequacies reflect only the characters' lack of articulation or self-deception or whether they indicate fundamental shortcomings of all language. If an audience is made to recognize the collapse of all language, it becomes aware of a vacuum. This new awareness makes it uniquely receptive to the possibility that the divine is present on the stage.

The language and representations of the divine in Hugo von Hofmannsthal's *Jedermann* (1923), Wolfgang Borchert's *Draussen vor der Tür* (1949c), Bertolt Brecht's *Der gute Mensch von Sezuan* (1973b), and Friedrich Dürrenmatt's *Ein Engel kommt nach Babylon* (1954) are carefully analyzed. The philosophies of three leading theorists of language, Ludwig Wittgenstein, Martin Heidegger, and Walter Benjamin, provide the theoretical foundation for illuminating the suspension of signification of language and the ensuing potential for the sacred to assert itself within secular texts.

Chapter 2 reveals how Hugo von Hofmannsthal's *Jedermann* embodies the crisis of language, the 'Sprachnot' in *fin de siècle* Austria which occurs after the death of God had been intimated by many Naturalist writers and had already gained ground with the intellectuals of that time. In his plays and writings, Hofmannsthal displays many correspondingly pessimistic characteristics. In response to these, he strives in *Jedermann* for a possibility of attaining a new order and harmony. Obviously, the failure of language obviates the possibility of God's portraying Himself directly or indirectly, that is, by a voice

212

'from above'. But the play itself forces the audience to recognize the existence of an 'Augenblick' or a 'Vision einer Schöpfung'. We experience how the moment of 'Sprachskepsis' provides an awareness of the vacuum inherent in language. Once words begin to fail, we are able to catch a glimpse of how the text allows the spectator to attain such an 'Augenblick'. At the moment when language no longer functions as a tool for communication, we are forced to accept that this crisis of language produces a crisis of consciousness. Without this consciousness, we can no longer recognize the structural identity, formal consistency, and meaningful cohesion of the world and of life. Only when Jedermann retreats into complete silence can he achieve such recognition. For Jedermann, this moment lies outside of language. Yet paradoxically, it is attainable only through language. In other words, consciousness of the function of language must be present before the viewer is aware of the suggestion of something beyond or behind language. The awareness of the vacuum allows for the possibility of a uniquely supernatural interaction at the place where meaning and representation break down.

Chapter 3 examines Wolfgang Borchert's creation of *Draussen vor der Tür* at a moment in modern history when German society appeared to no longer believe in anything. Because of the economic and political misery and spiritual emptiness at the end of World War II, Germans readily turned to and accepted the idea of the death of God. 'Menschen zwischen Ruinen' became reality for many at this time in history, especially for those returning from the war. Crucial segments of society no longer saw any relevance in traditional religion and morals or in any social or political ideology. This is the world of the despair and isolation represented by Beckmann, the modern Everyman.

Our new reading of this seemingly nihilistic example of 'Trümmerliteratur' reveals the emergence of a second divine being on the stage. This revelation occurs as soon as the audience recognizes the insufficiency of the God portrayed on the stage. The spectator is made aware of the deficiency of language by the internal contradictions and negations characteristic of the crippled soldier's 'Sprachnot'. As previous interpretations would have us believe, this text does not merely serve Borchert as a vehicle to show his personal capitulation to life's

213

absurdity. Nor does it objectify his search for a new individual. Far from merely providing the suitable tone for bemoaning his own dis-illusionment, Borchert's Expressionist style, lyrical and rhetorical at the same time, provides stimulation to think positively by its use of traditional literary devices such as alliteration, assonance, and repe-tition.

If the spectators listen closely to the language but ignore its nihilistic statements and follow instead the actions, they perceive how the alliterations and the rhythms begin to make the entire work pulsate with new life. These musical elements as well as the negations, repe-titions, and inversions of the text could ultimately lead the spectators to relive Beckmann's experience. Through this new 'listening' and 'observing', the audience becomes aware of another dimension of the text, a new metanarrative. The text acquires a power and energy of its own. It becomes a new voice through which God could be revealing His presence and breaking down the doors of society. Unfortunately, spectators from a contemporary society, who are unfamiliar with the circumstances in Borchert's Germany and know only those since the 'Wirtschaftswunder', may have difficulty in emulating Borchert's and Beckmann's 'Vorstellungskraft', the ability to imagine.

Chapter 4 analyzes the emergence of the new dramatic doctrine. The anti-naturalistic attitude towards language implied in Hugo von Hofmannsthal's and Borchert's works was given a theoretical foun-dation by Brecht's concept of 'epic theater'. This chapter concedes that Brecht's theater is not committed totally to all aspects of modern theater, nor does it renounce all those of the traditional theater. Brecht's theater contains familiar elements of classical theater but insists on a break with the illusions of Aristotelian theater. In *Der gute Mensch von Sezuan*, Brecht criticizes conformity to the restrictions determined by linguistic rules and conventional forms and repre-sentations. This establishes that Brecht shares a distrust of language with other leading proponents of modern drama. In his portrayal of the capitalist ideology of oppression with its religious institutions, Brecht is clearly inducing the spectator to make the 'right' choice for Marxism.

This chapter relies on Brecht's new methods, especially the 'Verfremdungseffekt', that is, any device that deprives the stage of its illusionary qualities and leads to radical detachment and reorientation. Simultaneously, its use shows that *Der gute Mensch* goes far beyond simplistic rules and techniques. Despite Brecht's life-long assertions that 'epic' was a social category, not an aesthetic one, a close reading of the text leads the reader to the recognition that the language spoken on the stage, while liberated from all mimetic functions, remains a means to signify aspects of the real world. As such it becomes subject to the principle of absolute accountability. This work challenges the audience to confront the extent to which ideological uses of religious language and representations are merely failed attempts to bring about submission to conventional forms. The break with the authority of language and representations ultimately produces a caesura that does not allow any other ideology to bridge it. This space is the vacuum that becomes 'der Spielraum Gottes'.

Chapter 5 examines the apparently godless, senseless, and chaotic world of Friedrich Dürrenmatt. *Ein Engel kommt nach Babylon* takes place in a world in which life appears meaningless and hopeless, a world in which religious and state authorities subject the individual to ideological dogmas. Clearly, Dürrenmatt's concept of history reduces it to a series of senseless catastrophes. These he depicts in a series of grotesque and senselessness dramatic and linguistic contradictions and paradoxes. Yet here, too, the audience perceives distinct and elusive religious overtones.

A close reading of his text reveals how Dürrenmatt's techniques emphasize the individual's difficulty in comprehending and explaining his world. Most importantly, they expose the deceptive relationship between word and thing. As long as the individual struggles to comprehend his world, he remains restricted to its forms and structures. The individual's primary tools in this struggle, namely, language and material and religious representations, necessarily imprison the individual within the bounds of their limitations. Because Akki has no name or means, he has no place and, consequently, no goals within the structure: not being bound by a goal means not being bound by language. Just as Akki in *Ein Engel* has 'kein Geld und keinen Namen' (174), he is not bound to any restrictive terminology. Neither is Kurrubi, whose presence on earth is an attestation of an unrepresentable God. As a result of his distrust of earthly rules, whether of grammar, religion, or political ideology, Akki can wander off into the desert with only his faith to guide him. Ultimately, the spectator is able to recognize that one needs faith in order to experience a similar entry into what Kierkegaard refers to in 'Krankheit zum Tode' (1953b) as 'Verzweiflung'. Ultimately, the senselessness of the text and the stage allows Dürrenmatt's theater, as he writes in his 'Nachwort' to 'Porträt eines Planeten' (1980, 197), 'einen Sinn außerhalb der Sprache zu konzipieren'. This 'Sinn' represents the paradoxes and contradictions of the text and the final disclosure of a divine manifestation on the stage.

The significance of the preceding study lies in its demonstration of how these four 'modern' secular plays, each in its own distinct way, open up 'Gottes Spielraum' to their audiences. The plays were selected for study not only because they best respond to the modern dilemma of 'Sprachnot', but also because they do it by challenging audiences to engage in a reviewing and a reconstruction of the stage and the text. Such disassembling then reveals how words and representations, if extended to cover what was traditionally accepted for humanity, leave nothing to signify. Furthermore, the divine exists in these plays to the same degree that the audience is receptive to the negations on the stage. In other words, a spectator who still clings to traditional concepts of God and religious values will not even grasp the newness of these plays' approach and results. Induced by the style, themes, and content of the plays to think in terms of the divine, the spectators find themselves with no alternative but to consider a suddenly created vacuum as 'Gottes Spielraum'. By opening up 'Gottes Spielraum', this study shows how contemporary dramas often transcend the limitations imposed by a secularized age and the empty rhetoric of its values.

This is not to suggest, however, that as we close the door on our study of these four plays we are locking God within theatrical confines, leaving Him forever chained to a throne within His 'Spielraum'. On the contrary, these works provide the means for establishing a new paradigm that may well include much of modern literature. The preceding study examines these four 'modern' plays and their significance for 'modernity' in order to undo, paradoxically, that which imprisons them in their own time. What these plays accomplish is twofold. Not only do they offer the 'modern' spectator the possibility of escaping the secular and materialistic outlook of the age, they also take today's spectator beyond the complex dramatic presentation of a bygone world, of a sinful and materialistic Jedermann or a homeless and hopeless returning soldier. Each play possesses a timelessness that allows its spectators to view the action on the stage outside the historical confines that conditioned its genesis. In other words, whether we are viewing it in contemporary society or in 'modernity', the stage holds the potential to come to life for each spectator.

The relevance of these works for contemporary literature lies in the discrepancies and inconsistencies in the plays themselves. Each play is unique in its style, content, theme, and social criticism. In other words, intimations of the divine can be present in a literary work regardless of the time of its creation and the feeling or beliefs of its creator. Consequently, this original examination of the four canonical plays serves as an open door for future studies of works that have a similar potential. In short, this study provides evidence for the notion that the limitations imposed by language are not necessarily binding on all works of literature. Finally, it demonstrates that the presence of a 'Spielraum Gottes' cannot be ruled out even in the canonical works of secular literature.

# Notes

## Chapter One *Das Moderne*

1    Whereas G. W. F. Hegel understood Nature as 'das Anderssein des Geistes', Ludwig Feuerbach (1873) put nature in the place of God and knowledge and reason in the place of faith. To believe in the Church dogma was for him 'eine welthistorische Heuchelei: Homo homini deus'. David Strauss (1846) characterizes Christian dogma as myth and allegory in *Das Leben Jesu für das deutsche Volk.*

2    Zola contributed perhaps the most – more than Ibsen and Tolstoy – to the creation of a new literature in Germany, even though its blossoming lasted for only a brief period of time. See Ruprecht, E. 1962 and Nelson, B. 1992.

3    Sören Kierkegaard's 'Furcht und Zittern' in his *Philosophisch-Theologische Schriften* (1913, 129) already explains it in this way: 'Abraham schweigt – aber er *kann* nicht sprechen, darin liegt die Not und die Angst. Wenn ich mich nämlich, indem ich spreche, nicht verständlich machen kann, so spreche ich nicht, wenn ich gleich ununterbrochen Tag und Nacht spräche.'

4    See Paul Tillich, in Christofer Frey's *Systematische Theologie: Dogmatik* (1977, 173).

5    For more on the history of *Das Liebeskonzil*, see Brown, P. D. G. 1983.

6    Roy C. Cowen (1981, 838) in fact cites Panizza's remark that he does not believe in God: '1) Ich glaube an keinen persönlichen Gott irgend welcher Art, noch an persönliche Intelligenzen, welche, ohne Menschen von Fleisch und Blut zu sein fähig wären, auf unsere sinliche Existenz irgendwann oder irgendwoher inzuwirken.'

7    This point is brought home in Heidegger's *Über den Humanismus* (1947) and in 'Das Wesen der Sprache' in *Unterwegs zur Sprache* (1985), which contains his famous assertion 'die Sprache ist das Haus des Seins' (156). These essays develop and consolidate his thinking about the new linguistic relationship of experience.

8    For a detailed analysis of this issue, see Caputo, J. 1993.

9    In *Prismen* Theodor Adorno (1955, 294) observes about Benjamin's work: 'Seine Anschauung von Moderne als Archaik bewahrt nicht Spuren eines vorgeblich alten Wahren auf, sondern meint den realen Ausbruch aus der Traumbefangenheit der bürgerlichen Immanenz. Er läßt es nicht sowohl sich angelegen sein, die Totalität der bürgerlichen Gesellschaft nachzukonstruieren,

als vielmehr sie als Verblendentes, Naturhaftes, Diffuses unter die Lupe zu nehmen [...] So gedachte er der Entfremdung und Vergegenständlichung zu entgehen, in der die Betrachtung des Kapitalismus als System diesem sich anzugleichen droht.'

10   For a closer analysis of this issue, see Richard Wolin's *Walter Benjamin: An Aesthetic of Redemption* (1982).

11   Margarete Kohlenbach, in *Walter Benjamin: Self-Reference and Religiosity* (2002), writes of Benjamin's relationship to the spiritual. She argues: 'In spite of his unwillingness to use "directly theological" concepts, Benjamin cannot renounce theological principles, for what he calls the "experience" of remembrance is religious in kind. It may not actually imply the belief in any particular theological doctrine, as Horkheimer holds, but it certainly implies the general religious assumption that the life that was taken from those murdered was not their only and decisive one' (xi).

12   See, for example, the notion of history in Benjamin's 'Die Aufgabe des Übersetzers' (1987, 51–52): 'In völlig unmetaphorischer Sachlichkeit ist der Gedanke vom Leben und Fortleben der Kunstwerke zu erfassen [...] Vielmehr nur wenn allem demjenigen, wovon es Geschichte gibt und was nicht allein ihr Schauplatz ist, Leben zuerkannt wird, kommt dessen Begriff zu seinem Recht.'

13   Benjamin's essay 'Über den Begriff der Geschichte' (1977c) criticizes historicism through a linguistic notion of history.

# Chapter Two  Hofmannsthal's *Jedermann*

1    Karl Rosner explains how this 'Selbstgefühl' 'würzelte in einem österreichischen Heimatsgefühl, das schlicht und von natürlicher Einfalt war und keinen ausgleichenden Nenner finden konnte zu dem von überbetontem, beinahe herausforderndem Selbstgefühl getragenen Nationalstolz des jungen Reiches' in Wolfram Mauser, *Hugo von Hofmannsthal: Konfliktbewältigung und Werkstruktur* (1977, 83).

2    See Cowen, R. C. 1994, 68–111.

3    See Del Caro, A. 1982.

4    As Benjamin Bennet correctly states, there are probably as many explanations for Hofmannsthal's sudden turn from lyrics to drama as there are critics. He gives a number of examples: Peter Szondi in 'Lyrik und lyrische Dramatik in Hofmannsthals Frühwerk' (1978a) sees the years between *Der Tor und der Tod* and the longer plays as decisive. Bennet's position, in *Hugo von Hofmannsthal: The Theatres of Consciousness* (1988, 9) is that 'no turning point exists, that the

intertwining of problems in lyric and drama as forms is effective in all the early works'.

5    Hofmannsthal's transition/transformation was not merely a private affair. It was, as we have seen, part of a much wider intellectual crisis in Europe which left its imprint on the writings of Kafka, Musil, Rilke, Valéry, and T. S. Eliot, to name but a few.

6    See Arens, K. M. 1982.

7    Herder, J. G. 1978.

8    Schlegel, F. 1958.

9    Jean-Jacques Rousseau, 'Essai sur l'Origine des langues, ou il est parlé de la mélodie et de l'imitation musicale', in *Ecrits sur la musique,* 1967, 141–221.

10   In *Vorlesungen über die Aesthetik,* Hegel (1842–43) writes of the phenomenality of the linguistic sign which can, by an infinite variety of devices or turns, be aligned with phenomenality as knowledge and meaning of the signified toward which it is directed (468). The moment of the sublime, he argues, is the moment of separation between the order of discourse and the order of the sacred, 'die eine Substanz' (468). In the sublime, the substance 'becomes truly manifest' (479). In his essay 'Hegel on the Sublime', Paul de Man (1982) understands Hegel's language of negativity as a dialectical and recuperative moment that stresses the distance between the human discourse of the poets and the voice of the sacred. But, he continues, 'as long as this distance remains, as he puts it, a *relationship* (478, 481), however negative, the fundamental analogy between poetic and divine creation is preserved' (146). Precisely the obscurity of the idea of the true content of language, its separation as the result of placement and misunderstanding, situates Hegel's 'sublime' *behind* language.

11   Richard Alewyn, in *Über Hugo von Hofmannsthal* (1967), singles out 'das Unendliche' as Hofmannsthal's favorite word (91).

12   In *Hofmannsthal Blätter,* 1990, 291.

13   See Matthew 25:14–30; Luke 19:11–26.

14   See Lord Chandos in *Ein Brief* (von Hofmannsthal, H. 2000, 17).

15   Romans 1:17 reads: 'We live by faith, not by sight.'

16   James 2:17 reads: 'In the same way, faith by itself, if it is not accompanied by action, is dead.'

17   Timothy Bahti, analyzing Pindar's Pythian ode 8 in *Ends of the Lyric: Direction and Consequence in Western Poetry* (1996, 252) explains best the occurrence of such a *conversion*: 'The narratively and spiritually and cosmologically reversing structure of Dante's "Commedia" inverts as many of its elements and coordinates as it does – life and death, down and up, then and now, exile and home [...] – not without chiasmus but with and for the decisive pattern of conversion, and in no direction so much as the linear, future orientation of converting the example of one man's story into a narrative of universal exemplarity.'

221

# Chapter Three  Borchert's *Draußen vor der Tür*

1      Quoted by Jürgen Kocka, 1979, 115.
2      Speech and articulation progressed over the years from the ecstatic verses of the
       Expressionists, over a 'Neue Sachlichkeit' into a period that portrayed a being
       destroyed by external circumstances. The emotion of their language and their
       perspective toward circumstances was soon replaced by a certain cool, con-
       trolled distance. In contrast to Naturalism, the new writing implies an author's
       selective or ideologically determined relationship toward his understanding of
       reality: 'Der Begriff "Neue Sachlichkeit", zuerst 1925 von Gustav Friedrich
       Harlaub auf Objekte einer Kunstausstellung angewandt, unterstrich den Gegen-
       satz zur spekulativen expressionistischen und abstrahierenden Kunst […] Mit
       der moderneren Formel "expressiver Naturalismus" sollte die Verknüpfung der
       positivistischen Objektivität mit der durch den Expressionismus gewonnenen
       Subjektivität zum Ausdruck gebracht werden, und mit der Prägung "magischer
       Realismus" versuchte man, der Einbeziehung des Über- und Außerwirklichen
       gerecht zu werden' (Frenzel, H. A. und E. 1991, vol. 2, 568).
3      Hans Egon Holthusen in *Ja und Nein. Neue kritische Versuche* (1954) refers to
       *Draußen* as 'saurer Kitsch' (243) and in *Kritisches Verstehen* (1961) as 'ein
       schwaches oder doch unreifes Stück Nachkriegsliteratur' (250).
4      The total effect of the play has been felt by some critics to be negative or even
       nihilistic. Joseph Mileck (1959, 335) asserts that Beckmann 'argues hope into
       silence'. Wilhelm Duwe (1962, 430) believes Beckmann enters the river a
       second time.
5      Quoted by Ernst Schnabel (1946–47, 386).


# Chapter Four  Epic Theater

1      Brecht's insistence on the use of the 'V-Effekt' is aimed at the interests of a
       particular class by pointing to what is historically outmoded. He writes in
       *Schriften zum Theater* (1993, 358): 'Das Theater, das wir in unserer Zeit poli-
       tisch werden sahen, war vordem nicht unpolitisch gewesen. Es lehrte die Welt
       so anzuschauen, wie die herrschenden Klassen sie angeschaut haben wollten.
       Insofern diese Klassen unter sich uneinig waren, gab sich auch der Aspekt der
       Welt auf dem Theater unterschiedlich […] Die passive Haltung des Zuschauers,
       die der Passivität der überwiegenden Mehrheit des Volkes im Leben überhaupt

222

entsprochen hatte, wich einer aktiven, das heißt, dem neuen Zuschauer war die Welt als eine ihm und seiner Aktivität zur Verfügung stehende darzustellen.'

2    Quoted by Thomas Brandt, 1964, 172.

3    In *Grundlegung zur Metaphysik der Sitten,* Kant (1984a, 18) states: 'Es ist überall nichts in der Welt, ja überhaupt auch außerhalb derselben zu denken möglich, was ohne Einschränkung für gut könnte gehalten werden, als allein ein guter Wille.'


# Chapter Five  Dürrenmatt's *Ein Engel kommt nach Babylon*


1    Edward Diller (1971, 33) correctly asserts: 'Dürrenmatt has insisted on occasion that he regards the world as chaos and that an incomprehensible mass of forces acts upon man in unpredictable ways. As a result, men are not masters of their fate. All their relentless activity and fanatic insistence on improving society only compound the confusion of existence and expose their own impotence. Men cannot save their world, or even themselves for that matter'.

2    Wilder, 'Some Thoughts on Playwriting', in Frenz, H. 1965, 59–60.

3    'Einfall' means literally to 'fall into', that is, 'to recognize or to realize'.

4    Literary critics have divided Dürrenmatt's writing into distinct stages of development. Central to each stage is the notion of the individual as isolated in a world he cannot understand. Yet since the late 1950s and early 1960s, critics have characterized Dürrenmatt as having undergone a metamorphosis. This change has been described as a disavowal, first of the theater's socio-critical function and, second, of the religious orientation that played such an important role in his earlier stage works. As a result, Dürrenmatt's later works reveal a trend, on the one hand, toward an increasingly self-conscious, hermetic theater and, on the other, toward the growing preoccupation of his characters with the existential self.

5    Immanuel Kant, in *Kritik der reinen Vernunft* (1984b, 462), writes of this conflict between the sign and the signifier: 'Uns ist wirklich nichts gegeben, als die Wahrnehmung und der empirische Fortschritt von dieser zu anderen möglichen Wahrnehmungen. Denn an sich selbst sind die Erscheinungen, als bloße Vorstellungen, nur in der Wahrnehmung wirklich'. Reality cannot be reached through the logic of scientific thought.

6    Martin Esslin, in *Reflections: Essays on Modern Theater* (1971, 109) writes about Dürrenmatt: 'I mentioned that I had been criticized for not including him among the authors discussed in the *Theater of the Absurd.* "No", he replied, "I don't think I am on the same lines as Beckett or Ionesco. I would call my own theatre a 'theatre of paradox' because it is precisely the paradoxical results of

strict logic that interest me. Ionesco and Beckett attack language and logic as means of thought and communication. I am concerned with logical thought in its strictest application, so strict that it sets up its own internal contradictions."'

7 Dürrenmatt, *Ein Engel kommt nach Babylon: Eine fragmentarische Komödie in drei Akten: Zweite Fassung*, produced in 1957, is the version of the play that I will analyze here. The 'fragmentary' refers to Dürrenmatt's plan to write a trilogy. *Der Mitmacher* of 1973 could certainly be seen as a continuation of the theme. The first version appeared as *Ein Engel kommt nach Babylon: Eine Komödie in drei Akten*, 1954. The first act was left untouched later. The third version, with slight changes, appeared in 1980.

8 Dürrenmatt himself puts the word 'Wirklichkeit' in quotation marks.

9 Irmgard Wirtz (2000, 155) writes concerning Dürrenmatt's understanding of the angel: 'Dürrenmatt befürchtete, der Engel könne als lächerliche Figur missverstanden werden. Gemäss seinem Agendaeintrag von 1945 sollte der Engel das Staunen des Ausserirdischen vor dem Wunder der Schöpfung und nicht etwa die Blindheit des Göttlichen gegenüber der Nichtigkeit der Welt repräsentieren. Der Engel sei kein "weltfremder Idealist, somit so etwas wie ein himmlischer Trottel".' The angel must therefore be understood as a godly character who readily identifies himself with the earthly. Consequently, this forces the spectator to decide either to accept or reject his divinity.

10 Dürrenmatt's 'mutiger Mensch' Möbius in *Die Physiker* was accused by the critic Christian M. Jauslin of performing a 'Flucht vor der Verantwortung'. Though Akki's escape into the desert could be criticized in like manner, this criticism would not hold because staying and dying for his beliefs would make Akki a tragic martyr and place him either in the category of the tragic figures or of tragicomic ones, such as Ill, whose brave decision to die is an 'Endspiel' in itself.

11 This faith, however, cannot be an established belief. The more one tries to define faith the greater the possibility that it will become dogma or doctrine.

# Bibliography

Adorno, T. W. 1933. *Kierkegaard: Konstruktion des Ästhetischen*. Tübingen: Mohr Verlag.

—— 1955. *Prismen: Kulturkritik und Gesellschaft*. Berlin: Suhrkamp Verlag.

—— 1956. *Zur Metakritik der Erkenntnistheorie: Studie über Husserl und die phänomenologischen Antinomien*. Stuttgart: Kohlhammer Verlag.

—— 1965a. *Ästhetische Theorie*. Frankfurt am Main: Suhrkamp Verlag.

—— 1965b. *Noten zur Literatur I–III*. Frankfurt am Main: Suhrkamp Verlag.

—— 1966. *Negative Dialektik*. Frankfurt am Main: Suhrkamp Verlag.

—— 1973. *Versuch, das Endspiel zu verstehen*. Frankfurt am Main: Suhrkamp Verlag.

—— 1989. 'Culture Industry Reconsidered' in S. E. Bronner and D. M. Kellner (eds.), *Critical Theory and Society: A Reader*. New York: Routledge.

Alami, M. 1994. *Die Bildlichkeit bei Friedrich Dürrenmatt: Computergestützte Analyse und Interpretation mythologischer und psychologischer Bezüge*. Köln: Bohlau Verlag.

Albrecht, W. P. 1975. *The Sublime Pleasures of Tragedy: A Study of Critical Theory from Dennis to Keats*. Lawrence: University Press of Kansas.

Alewyn, R. 1967. *Über Hugo von Hofmannsthal*. Göttingen: Vandenhöck & Ruprecht.

Angermeyer, H. C. 1971. *Zuschauer im Drama: Brecht, Dürrenmatt, Handke*. Frankfurt am Main: Athenäum Verlag.

Apel, F. 1994. *Himmelssehnsucht: Die Sichtbarkeit der Engel in der romantischen Literatur und Kunst sowie bei Klee, Rilke und Benjamin*. Paderborn: Igel Verlag Literatur.

Arac, J. 1986. *Postmodernism and Politics*. Minneapolis: University of Minnesota Press.

Arato, A. 1978. 'Esthetic Theory and Cultural Criticism: Introduction' in A. Arato and E. Gebhardt (eds.), *The Essential Frankfurt School Reader*. New York: Urizen.

Arens, K. M. 1982. 'Linguistic Skepticism: Towards a Productive Definition', *Monatshefte* 74: 145–55.

Arnold, H. L. 1976. Interview in *Dürrenmatt: Gespräch mit Heinz Ludwig Arnold*. Zürich: Verlag der Arche.

—— ed. 2003a. *Text u. Kritik: Friedrich Dürrenmatt 50/51*.

—— 2003b. 'Frieden und Krieg – Dürrenmatts Passion', *Text u. Kritik: Friedrich Dürrenmatt* 50/51: 129–50.

Artaud, A. 1964. *Le Théatre et son double*. Paris: Gallimard.

Atkins, R. 1990. '"Und es ist kein Gott ausser Adolf Hitler": The Biblical Motifs in Brecht's *Arturo Ui* and Related Works as Political Counter-Propaganda', *The Modern Language Review* 85: 373–87.

Auerbach, E. 1959. *Mimesis: Dargestellte Wirklichkeit in der Abendländischen Literatur.* Bern: Francke Verlag.

—— 1967. *Gesammelte Aufsätze zur Romansichen Philologie.* Bern: Francke Verlag.

Augustine, Saint, Bishop of Hippo. 1914. *Les Confessions.* Paris: Flammarion.

Baden, H. J. 1963. *Der Verschwiegene Gott: Literatur und Glaube.* München: List Verlag.

—— 1971. *Poesie und Theologie.* Hamburg: Rauhes Haus.

Bahr, H. 1968. *Das Junge Österreich: Zur Überwindung des Naturalismus. Theoretische Schriften 1887–1907.* Stuttgart: W. Kohlhammer Verlag.

Bahti, T. 1992. *Allegories of History: Literary Historiography After Hegel.* Baltimore: Johns Hopkins University Press.

—— 1996. *Ends of the Lyrik: Direction and Consequence in Western Poetry.* Baltimore: Johns Hopkins University Press.

Baloch, H. 2001. 'Sine Fine Dicentes: Skizze zu Peter Handkes Religiöser Welt', *Ide: Informationen zur Deutschdidaktik* 4: 45–61.

Balthasar, H. U. von 1967a. 'Der Christ auf der Bühne' in *Spiritus Creator: Skizzen zur Theologie.* Einsiedeln: Johannes Verlag.

—— 1967b. *The God Question and Modern Man.* New York: The Seabury Press.

—— 1988. *Theo-drama: Theological Dramatic Theory* (trans. G. Harrison). San Francisco: Ignatius Press.

Bandera, C. 1994. *The Sacred Game: The Role of the Sacred in the Genesis of Modern Literary Fiction.* University Park: Pennsylvania State University Press.

Bänziger, H. 1992. *Kirchen ohne Dichter?: Zum Verhältnis von Literatur und institutionalisierter Religion.* Bern: Francke Verlag.

Barth, K. 1959. *Protestant Thought: From Rousseau to Ritschl: Being the Translation of Eleven Chapters of 'Die protestantische Theologie' im 19. Jahrhundert.* New York: Harper.

Barthes, R. 1953. *Le Degré Zéro de l'Ecriture.* Paris: Seuil.

—— 1975. *The Pleasure of the Text* (trans. R. Miller). New York: Hill and Wang.

—— 1977. 'The Struggle with the Angel' in S. Heath (ed. and trans.), *Image – Music – Text.* New York: Hill and Wang.

—— 1985. *The Responsibility of Forms: Critical Essays on Music, Art and Representation.* New York: Hill and Wang.

—— 1986. *The Rustle of Language.* New York: Hill and Wang.

—— 1989. 'Brecht and Discourse: A Contribution to the Study of Discursivity' in S. Mews (ed.), *Critical Essays on Bertolt Brecht* (trans. R. Howard). Boston: G. K. Hall.

Bateson, G. 1987. *Angels Fear: Towards an Epistemology of the Sacred.* New York: Macmillan.

Baudelaire, C. 1961a. 'Les paradis artificiels' in *Oeuvres Complètes.* Paris: Gallimard.

226

—— 1961b. 'Les Fleurs du mal' in *Oeuvres Complètes*. Paris: Gallimard.

Bauer, G. 1963. *Geschichtlichkeit: Wege und Irrwege eines Begriffs*. Berlin: De Gruyter Verlag.

—— 1969. *Zur Poetik des Dialogs: Leistung und Formen der Gesprächsführung in der neueren deutschen Literatur*. Darmstadt: Wissenschaftliche Buchgesellschaft.

—— 1988. *Sprache und Sprachlosigkeit im 'Dritten Reich'*. Köln: Bond Verlag.

Bedouelle, G.-T. 1994. *Les Lettres et le Sacrè: Littèrature, Histoire et Theologie*. Lausanne: L'age d'homme.

Behler, E. 1990. *Irony and the Discourse of Modernity*. Seattle: University of Washington Press.

Benjamin, W. 1950. *Berliner Kindheit um Neunzehnhundert*. Frankfurt am Main: Suhrkamp Verlag.

—— 1963. *Das Kunstwerk im Zeitalter seiner technischen Reproduzierbarkeit: Drei Studien zur Kunstsoziologie*. Frankfurt am Main: Suhrkamp Verlag.

—— 1973a. 'Der Autor als Produzent' in *Theorie der Politischen Dichtung: Neunzehn Aufsätze*. München: Nymphenburger Verlag.

—— 1973b. *Understanding Brecht*. London: New Left Books.

—— 1975. *Ursprung des deutschen Trauerspiels*. Frankfurt am Main: Suhrkamp Verlag.

—— 1977a. *Illuminationen: Ausgewählte Schriften*. Frankfurt am Main: Suhrkamp Verlag.

—— 1977b. 'Metaphysisch-geschichtsphilosophische Studien' in *Gesammelte Schriften* 2. Frankfurt am Main: Suhrkamp Verlag.

—— 1977c. 'Über den Begriff der Geschichte' in *Gesammelte Schriften* 1. Frankfurt am Main: Suhrkamp Verlag.

—— 1977d. 'Über Sprache überhaupt und über die Sprache des Menschen' in *Gesammelte Schriften* 2. Frankfurt am Main: Suhrkamp Verlag.

—— 1977e. 'Was ist das epische Theater?' in *Gesammelte Schriften* 2. Frankfurt am Main: Suhrkamp Verlag.

—— 1979. *Versuche über Brecht*. Frankfurt am Main: Suhrkamp Verlag.

—— 1984. *Passagen: Walter Benjamins Urgeschichte des neunzehnten Jahrhunderts*. München: W. Fink Verlag.

—— 1987. 'Die Aufgabe des Übersetzers' in R. Tiedermann and H. Schweppenhäuser (eds.), *Gesammelte Schriften: Supplement*. Frankfurt am Main: Suhrkamp Verlag.

Benn, G., F. Brock-Sulzer, and F. Furi, ed. 1962. *Der unbequeme Dürrenmatt*. Basel: Basilius Presse.

Bennet, B. ed. 1983. *Probleme der Moderne: Studien zur deutschen Literatur von Nietzsche bis Brecht*. Tübingen: Niemeyer Verlag.

—— 1988. *Hugo von Hofmannsthal: The Theatres of Consciousness*. Cambridge: Cambridge University Press.

Beutin, W. 1961. 'Bertolt Brecht' in K. Deschner (ed.), *Das Christentum im Urteil Seiner Gegner*. Wiesbaden: n.p.

Bentley, E. 1963. 'Epic Theater is Lyric Theater' in L. Shaw (ed.), *The German Theater Today*. Austin: University of Texas.

Bienek, H. 1965. 'Friedrich Dürrenmatt', interview in *Werkstattgespräche mit Schriftstellern*. München: dtv.

Bland, J. 1983. 'Up Against the Wall: The Ethical Limits of Rational Objectivity', *Science Fiction: A Review of Speculative Literature* 5.3: 96–101.

Bloch, E. 1974. *Das Prinzip Hoffnung*. Frankfurt am Main: Suhrkamp Verlag.

—— 1977. 'Nonsynchronism and the Obligation to its Dialectics', *New German Critique II* Spring (trans. M. Ritter).

Bloch, P. A. 1972. 'Gespräch mit Friedrich Dürrenmatt', interview in Peter André Bloch (ed.), *Der Schriftsteller in unserer Zeit*. Bern: Francke Verlag.

—— 1980. 'Dürrenmatt als Maler und Zeichner des Labyrinths und des Grotesken', interview in *Schweizer Monatshefte* 74: 6.

Bloom, H. 1989. *Ruin the Sacred Truth: Poetry and Belief from the Bible to the Present*. Cambridge: Harvard University Press.

Boehme, W., ed. 1987. *Zu dir Hin: Über mystische Lebenserfahrung: von Meister Eckhart bis Paul Celan*. Frankfurt am Main: Insel Verlag.

Bölsche, W. 1976. *Die naturwissenschaftlichen Grundlagen der Poesie*. Tübingen: Niemeyer Verlag.

Bonhoeffer, D. 1932. *Widerstand und Ergebung*. München: Kaiser.

Borchert, W. 1949a. 'Das ist unser Manifest' in *Das Gesamtwerk*. Hamburg: Rowohlt Verlag.

—— 1949b. 'Dann gibt es nur eins' in *Das Gesamtwerk*. Hamburg: Rowohlt Verlag.

—— 1949c. 'Draussen vor der Tür' in *Das Gesamtwerk*. Hamburg: Rowohlt Verlag.

—— 1949d. 'Generation ohne Abschied' in *Das Gesamtwerk*. Hamburg: Rowohlt Verlag.

—— 1949e. 'Die Hundeblume' in *Das Gesamtwerk*. Hamburg: Rowohlt Verlag.

—— 1949f. 'Im Mai, im Mai schrie der Kuckuck' in *Das Gesamtwerk*. Hamburg: Rowohlt Verlag.

—— 1949g. 'Der Kaffee ist undefinierbar' in *Das Gesamtwerk*. Hamburg: Rowohlt Verlag.

—— 1949h. 'Die lange Strasse lang' in *Das Gesamtwerk*. Hamburg: Rowohlt Verlag.

—— 1949i. 'Laternentraum' in *Laterne, Nacht und Sterne. Gedichte um Hamburg. Das Gesamtwerk*. Hamburg: Rowohlt Verlag.

—— 1949j. 'Nachlass' in *Das Gesamtwerk*. Hamburg: Rowohlt Verlag.

Both, W. 1979. *Vom religiösen Drama zur politischen Komödie: Friedrich Dürrenmatt 'Die Wiedertäufer' und 'Es steht Geschrieben'*. Frankfurt am Main: Peter Lang Verlag.

Boyd, G. N. 1973. *Religion in Contemporary Fiction: Criticism from 1945 to the Present*. San Antonio: Trinity University Press.

Brandt, T. 1964. 'Brecht und die Bibel', *PMLA* 79: 171–76.

Brecht, B. 1955. *Aufstieg und Fall der Stadt Mahagonny.* Berlin: Suhrkamp Verlag.

—— 1959. *Geschichten vom Herrn Keuner: Der verwundete Sokrates.* Hannover: Fackeltrager Verlag.

—— 1960a. *Die heilige Johanna der Schlachthöfe.* Berlin: Suhrkamp Verlag.

—— 1960b. *Kleines Organon für das Theater.* Frankfurt am Main: Suhrkamp Verlag.

—— 1966. *Über Theater.* Frankfurt am Main: Suhrkamp Verlag.

—— 1967. *Schriften zur Literatur und Kunst.* Frankfurt am Main: Suhrkamp Verlag.

—— 1971a. *Über Politik und Kunst.* Frankfurt am Main: Suhrkamp Verlag.

—— 1971b. *Über Realismus.* Frankfurt am Main: Suhrkamp Verlag.

—— 1973a. *Arbeitsjournal.* Frankfurt am Main: Suhrkamp Verlag.

—— 1973b. *Der gute Mensch von Sezuan.* Berlin: Suhrkamp Verlag.

—— 1974. *Schriften zur Politik und Gesellschaft.* Frankfurt am Main: Suhrkamp Verlag.

—— 1990. 'Hauspostille' in *Die Gedichte von Bertolt Brecht in einem Band.* Berlin: Suhrkamp Verlag.

—— 1993. *Schriften zum Theater 1–3. Gesammelte Werke.* Frankfurt am Main: Suhrkamp Verlag.

—— 1993. 'Anmerkungen zur Oper *Aufstieg und Fall der Stadt Mahagonny*' in *Schriften zum Theater 1–3. Gesammelte Werke.* Frankfurt am Main: Suhrkamp Verlag.

Breslin, C. 1961. 'Philosophy or Philology: Auerbach and Aesthetic Historicism', *Journal of the History of Ideas* 22: n.p.

Brinker, C., ed. 1995. *Contemplata Aliis Tradere: Studien zum Verhältnis von Literatur und Spiritualität.* Bern: Peter Lang Verlag.

Broch, H. 1974. *Hofmannsthal und seine Zeit.* Frankfurt am Main: Suhrkamp Verlag.

Brooks, C. 1963. *The Hidden God: Studies in Hemmingway, Faulkner, Yeats, Eliot and Warren.* New Haven: Yale University Press.

Brown, P. D. G. 1983. *Oskar Panizza: His Life and Works.* New York and Bern: Peter Lang.

Browning, D. S. 1987. *Religious Thought and the Modern Psychologies: A Critical Conversation in Theology of Culture.* Philadelphia: Fortress Press.

Bruce, S., ed. 1992. *Religion and Modernization: Sociologists and Historians Debate the Secularization Thesis.* Oxford: Oxford University Press.

Buck-Morss, S. 1977. *The Origin of Negative Dialectics: Theodor W. Adorno, Walter Benjamin, and the Frankfurt Institute.* Hassocks: Harvester Press.

Bulthaup, P., ed. 1975. *Materialien zu Benjamins Thesen 'Über den Begriff der Geschichte': Beiträge und Interpretationen.* Frankfurt am Main: Suhrkamp Verlag.

Burgess, G. 1984. 'Wirklichkeit, Allegorie und Traum in "Draussen vor der Tür": Beckmanns Weg zur Menschlichkeit' in Rudolf Wolff (ed.), *Wolfgang Borchert: Werk und Wirkung.* Bonn: Bouvier Verlag.

—— 2003. *The Life and Works of Wolfang Borchert*. New York: Camden House.

Burkard, P. 2003. 'Eine Lebensgeschichte als Geschichte von ungeschriebenen Stoffen? Friedrich Dürrenmatts paradoxes Projekt der 'Stoffe' im literature-geschichtlichen Kontext der Autobiografie', *Text u. Kritik: Friedrich Dürrenmatt* 50/51.

—— 2004. *Dürrenmatts 'Stoffe': Zur literarischen Transformation der Erkenntnistheorien Kants und Vaihingers im Spätwerk*. Tübingen: Francke Verlag.

Burke, K. 1967. *Language as Symbolic Action: Essays on Life, Literature, and Method*. Berkeley: University of California Press.

Cage, J. 1968. *Silence*. New York: n.p.

Camus, A. 1942. *Le mythe de Sisyphe: Essais sur l'absurde*. Paris: Gallimard.

—— 1987. *American Journals* (trans. H. Levick). New York: Panagon.

Caputo, J. 1993. *Demythologizing Heidegger*. Bloomington, Ind.: Indiana University Press.

Carroll, D. 1975. 'Mimesis Reconsidered: Literature, History, Ideology', *Diacritics* 5.2: n.p.

Cauquelin, A. 1997. *Le Voleur d'Anges*. Paris: L'Harmattan.

Centre Freudien Romand d'Etudes Cliniques et Littéraires, 1989. *Analytica: La Psychose dans le Texte*. Paris: Navarin.

Cesar, J. 1992. *Walter Benjamin on Experience and History: Profane Illumination*. San Francisco: Mellen Research University Press.

Cloeren, H.-J., ed. 1971. *Philosophie als Sprachkritik im 19. Jahrhundert*. Stuttgart: Problemata Frommann-Holzboog Verlag.

Coward, R. 1986. *Language and Materialism: Developments in Semiology and the Theory of the Subject*. London: Routledge.

Cowen, R. C. 1973. *Der Naturalismus: Kommentar zu einer Epoche*. München: Winkler Verlag.

—— 1981. *Dramen des deutschen Naturalismus: Von Hauptmann bis Schönherr*. München: Winkler Verlag.

—— 1994. 'Der Naturalismus' in H. J. Piechotta, R. W. Wuthenow and S. Rothemann (eds.), *Die literarische Moderne in Europa*, 1. Opladen: Westdeutscher Verlag.

Creegan, C. 1989. *Wittgenstein and Kierkegaard: Religion, Individuality and Philosophical Method*. London: Routledge.

Crowther, P. 1993. *Critical Aesthetics and Postmodernism*. New York: Oxford University Press.

Cunningham, V. 1994. *In the Reading Goal: Postmodernity, Texts and History*. Blackwell: Oxford.

Daiches, D. 1984. *God and the Poets: The Gifford Lectures*. Oxford: Clarendon Press.

Darboven, A.-M. 1957. *Wolfgang Borchert, der Rufer in einer Zeit der Not*. Hannover: Norddeutsche Verlagsanstalt.

Del Caro, A. 1982. 'Reception and Impact: The First Decade of Nietzsche in Germany', *Orbis Litterarum* 37: 32–46.

Deloria, V. 1979. *The Metaphysics of Modern Existence*. San Francisco: Harper Row.

De Man, P. 1971. *Blindness and Insight: Essays in the Rhetoric of Contemporary Criticism*. New York: Oxford University Press.

—— 1972. 'Literature and Language: A Commentary', *New Literary History* 4: 181–92.

—— 1979. *Allegories of Reading: Figural Language in Rousseau, Nietzsche, Rilke, and Proust*. New Haven: Yale University Press.

—— 1982. 'Hegel on the Sublime' in Mark Krupnick (ed.), *Displacement*. Bloomington: Indiana University Press.

—— 1984. *The Rhetoric of Romanticism*. New York: Columbia University Press.

—— 1986. *The Resistance to Theory*. Minneapolis: University of Minnesota Press.

Derrida, J. 1967a. *De la grammatologie*. Paris: Minuit.

—— 1967b. *L'Ecriture et la Différence*. Paris: Seuil.

—— 1972. *Marges de la Philosophie*. Paris: Minuit.

—— 1973. *Speech and Phenomena and other Essays on Husserl's Theory of Signs*. Evanston: Northwestern University Press.

—— 1974. 'White Mythology: Metaphor in the Text of Philosophy', *New Literary History: A Journal of Theory and Interpretation* 6: 5–74.

—— 1978. *Spurs: Nietzsche's Styles / Eperons: Les Styles de Nietzsche*. Chicago: University of Chicago Press.

—— 1981. *Dissemination*. Chicago: University of Chicago Press.

—— 1989. *Of Spirit: Heidegger and the Question*. Chicago: University of Chicago Press.

—— 1998. *Resistances of Psychoanalysis*. Stanford: Stanford University Press.

Deschner, K., ed. 1961. *Das Christentum im Urteil seiner Gegner*. Wiesbaden: n.p.

Dettweiler, R. 1989. *Breaking the Fall: Religious Readings of Contemporary Fiction*. Basingstoke: Macmillan.

Diller, E. 1967. 'Friedrich Dürrenmatt's Theological Concept of History', *German Quarterly* 40: 363–71.

—— 1971. 'Friedrich Dürrenmatt's Chaos and Calvinism', *Monatshefte* 63: 28–40.

—— 1997. *Dissent and Marginality: Essays on the Borders of Literature and Religion*. Basingstoke: Macmillan Press.

Duchesne, J. 1996. *Histoire Chrétienne de la Littèrature*. France: Flammarion.

Dürrenmatt, F. 1947a. *Es steht geschrieben*. Basel: B. Schwabe Verlag.

—— 1947b. 'Anmerkung' in *Es steht geschrieben*. Basel: B. Schwabe Verlag.

—— 1952a. 'Der Folterknecht' in *Die Stadt. Prosa I–IV*. Zürich: Verlag der Arche.

—— 1952b. *Die Stadt. Prosa I–IV*. Zürich: Verlag der Arche.

—— 1952c. 'Der Tunnel' in *Die Stadt. Prosa I–IV*. Zürich: Verlag der Arche.

—— 1952d. 'Weihnacht' in *Die Stadt. Prosa I–IV*. Zürich: Verlag der Arche.

—— 1954. *Ein Engel kommt nach Babylon*. Zürich: Verlag der Arche.

—— 1957a. 'Der Besuch der alten Dame' in *Komödien I*. Zürich: Verlag der Arche.

—— 1957b. 'Romulus der Grosse' in *Komödien I*. Zürich: Verlag der Arche.

—— 1958. *Das Versprechen*. Zürich: Verlag der Arche.

—— 1960. *Der Blinde. Ein Drama.* Zürich: Verlag der Arche.

—— 1963a. 'Frank der Fünfte' in *Komödien II und Frühe Stücke.* Zürich, Verlag der Arche.

—— 1963b. 'Nächtliches Gespräch mit einem verachteten Menschen' in *Gesammelte Hörspiele.* Zürich: Verlag der Arche.

—— 1963c. 'Die Physiker' in *Komödien II und Frühe Stücke.* Zürich, Verlag der Arche.

—— 1966a. *Die Ehe des Herrn Mississippi.* Zürich: Verlag der Arche.

—— 1966b. 'Gespräch mit Friedrich Dürrenmatt' in Deutsche Akademie der Künste (ed.), *Sinn und Form, Beiträge zur Literatur.* Berlin: Rütten & Loening Verlag.

—— 1966c. 'Theaterprobleme' in *Theater-Schriften und Reden.* Zürich: Verlag der Arche.

—— 1966d. *Theater-Schriften und Reden.* Zürich: Verlag der Arche.

—— 1967a. *Die Wiedertäufer: Eine Komödie in zwei Teilen.* Zürich: Verlag der Arche.

—— 1967b. 'Dramaturgische Überlegungen zu den Wiedertäufern', in *Die Wieder-täufer: Eine Komödie in zwei Teilen.* Zürich: Verlag der Arche.

—— 1968. *König Johann: Nach Shakespeare.* Zürich: Verlag der Arche.

—— 1970. 'Die Stadt' in *Sätze aus Amerika.* Zürich: Verlag der Arche.

—— 1972. *Theater-Schriften und Reden II: Dramatisches und Kritisches.* Zürich: Verlag der Arche.

—— 1976a. 'Nachwort' to *Der Mitmacher: Ein Komplex: Text der Komödie, Dra-maturgie, Erfahrungen, Berichte, Erzählungen.* Zürich: Verlag der Arche.

—— 1976b. 'Sätze zum Theater', *Text u. Kritik* 50/51 May: 1–18.

—— 1976c. *Zusammenhänge: Essay über Israel, eine Konzeption.* Zürich: Verlag der Arche.

—— 1977. 'Über Toleranz', *Schweizer Monatshefte: Zeitschrift für Politik, Wirt-schaft, Kultur* 57: 107–20.

—— 1979. *Albert Einstein: Ein Vortrag.* Zürich: Diogenes Verlag.

—— 1980. 'Nachwort' to 'Porträt eines Planeten' in *Werkausgabe in dreißig Bänden.* Zürich: Diogenes Verlag.

—— 1981. *Labyrinth: Stoffe I–III.* Zürich: Diogenes Verlag.

—— 1986a. *Der Auftrag, oder vom Beobachten des Beobachters der Beobachter: Novelle in 24 Sätzen.* Zürich: Diogenes Verlag.

—— 1986b. 'Pilatus' in *Aus den Papieren eines Wärters: Frühe Prosa.* Zürich: Dio-genes Verlag.

—— 1988. 'Selbstgespräch' in *Versuche.* Zürich: Diogenes Verlag.

—— 1989. *Durcheinandertal.* Zürich: Diogenes Verlag.

—— 1990a. *Turmbau: Stoffe IV–IX.* Zürich: Diogenes Verlag.

—— 1990b. 'Vinter' in *Turmbau: Stoffe IV–IX.* Zürich: Diogenes Verlag.

—— 1990c. *Über die Grenzen.* Zürich: Verlag der Arche.

—— 1991. *Abschied vom Theater.* Göttingen: Wallstein Verlag.

—— 1992. *Gedankenfuge.* Zürich: Diogenes Verlag.

—— 1996. *Dürrenmatt-Gespräche*. Zürich: Diogenes Verlag.

Duwe, W. 1962. *Deutsche Dichtung des 20. Jahrhunderts: Vom Naturalismus zum Surrealismus*. Zürich: O. Fussli Verlag.

*Ecrivains et le Sacré, Les*. 1989. Paris: Belles Lettres.

Edschmid, K. 1919. *Über den Expressionismus in der Literatur und die neue Dichtung*. Berlin: n.p.

Elias, N. 1989. *Studien über die Deutschen: Machtkämpfe und Habitusentwicklung im 19. und 20. Jahrhundert*. Frankfurt am Main: Suhrkamp Verlag.

Eliot, T. S. 1950. 'Religion and Literature' in *Selected Essays*. New York: Harcourt, Brace.

—— 1957. *On Poetry and Poets*. New York: Farrar, Strauss, Cudahy.

Esslin, M. 1963. 'Dürrenmatt – Merciless Observer', *Plays and Players* March: n.p.

—— 1971. *Reflections: Essays on Modern Theater*. New York: Doubleday.

Feher, F. 1985. 'Lukacs, Benjamin, Theatre', *Theatre Journal* 37.4: 415–25.

Feuerbach, L. 1973. *Das Wesen des Christentums*. Berlin: Akademie Verlag.

Ficker, K. 1965. 'Some Biblical Protoypes in Wolfgang Borchert's Stories', *German Quarterly* 32: 172–78.

—— 1972. *To Heaven and Back: The New Morality in the Plays of Friedrich Dürrenmatt*. Lexington: University Press of Kentucky.

—— 1979. 'The Christ-Figure in Borchert's "Draussen vor der Tür"', *Germanic Review* 54: 165–69.

Fiddes, P. 1991. *Freedom and Limit: A Dialogue between Literature and Christian Doctrine*. Basingstoke: Macmillan.

Fischer, J. M. 1978. *Fin de Siècle*. München: Winckler Verlag.

Fischlin, D., ed. 1994. *Negation, Critical Theory and Postmodern Textuality*. Boston: Kluwer Academic Publishers.

Foucault, M. 1966. *Les Mots et les Choses: Une Archéologie des Sciences Humaines*. Paris: Gallimard.

Fradkin, I. 1965. 'Brecht, die Bibel, die Aufklärung und Shakespeare', *Kunst und Literatur: Zeitschrift für Fragen der Aesthetik und Kunsttheorie* 13: 156–217.

Frank, M. 1980. *Das Sagbare und das Unsagbare: Studien zur neuesten französischen Hermeneutik und Texttheorie*. Frankfurt am Main: Suhrkamp Verlag.

Frenz, H. 1965. *American Playwrights on Drama*. New York: Hill and Wang.

Frenzel, H. A. and E. 1991. *Daten deutscher Dichtung*. Chronologischer Abriss der Deutschen Literaturgeschichte, 2 vols. München: dtv.

Frey, C. 1973. *Reflexion und Zeit: Ein Beitrag zum Selbstverständnis der Theologie in der Auseinandersetzung vor allem mit Hegel*. Gütersloh: Gütersloher Verlagshaus.

—— 1977. *Systematische Theologie: Dogmatik*. Gütersloh: Verlagshaus Mohn.

—— 1990. *Theologische Ethik*. Düsseldorf: Neukirchener Verlag.

Frisby, D. 1986. *Fragments of Modernity: Theories of Modernity in the Work of Simmel, Kracauer and Benjamin*. Cambridge, Mass.: MIT Press.

Frohlich, A. M., ed. 1991. *Engel: Texte aus der Weltliteratur*. Zürich: Manesse Verlag.

Frye, N. 1991. *The Double Vision: Language and Meaning in Religion*. Toronto: University of Toronto Press.

Gadamer, H. G. 1960. *Wahrheit und Methode: Grundzüge einer philosophischen Hermeneutik*. Tübingen: Mohr Verlag.

—— 1986. *Wer bin ich und wer bist du? Eine Kommentar zu Paul Celans Gedichtefolge 'Atemkristall'*. Frankfurt am Main: Suhrkamp Verlag.

Garidis, A. 1996. *Les Anges du Désir. Figures de l'Ange au XXe Siècle*. Paris: Albin Michel.

Georgen, P. 1982. *'Produktion' als Grundbegriff der Anthropologie: Bertolt Brecht und seine Bedeutung für die Theologie*. Frankfurt am Main: Fischer Verlag.

Giles, S. 1992. 'Post-Structuralist Brecht? Representation and Subjectivity in "Der Dreigroschenprozess"', *Das Brecht-Jahrbuch* 17: 147–63.

Gilman, S. L. 1976. *Nietzschean Parody: An Introduction to Reading Nietzsche*. Bonn: Bouvier Verlag.

—— 1991. *Inscribing the Other*. Lincoln: University of Nebraska Press.

—— 1992. *The Visibility of the Jew in the Diaspora: Body Imagery and its Cultural Context*. Syracuse: Syracuse University Press.

Girard, R. 1987. *Das Heilige und die Gewalt* (trans. E. Mainberger-Ruh). Zürich: Benziger Verlag.

Goethe, J. W. von 1970. *Aus Meinem Leben: Dichtung und Wahrheit*. 2 vols. Berlin: Akademie Verlag.

Goll, Y. 1917. 'Appell an die Kunst', *Die Aktion* VI: 45–46.

Gossman, L. 1990. *Between History and Literature*. Cambridge: Harvard University Press.

Graff, G. 1987. *Professing Literature: An Institutional History*. Chicago: University of Chicago Press.

Gray, R. T. 1986. 'Aphorism and Sprachkrise in Turn-of-the-Century Austria', *Orbis Litterarum* 41.4: 332–54.

Grenzmann, W. 1964. *Dichtung und Glaube: Probleme und Gestalten der Deutschen Gegenwartsliteratur*. Frankfurt am Main: Athenäum Verlag.

Grimm, R. 1979a. *Brecht und Nietzsche oder Geständnisse eines Dichters: Fünf Essays und ein Bruchstück*. Frankfurt am Main: Suhrkamp Verlag.

—— 1979b. 'Kant, Kopernikus und einige ihrer Zeitgenossen: Zwei Beispiele für Nietzsche als Erblasser Brechts', *Nietzsche Studien: Internationales Jahrbuch für Nietzsche-Forschung* 8: 389–95.

Grimminger, R. 1991. 'Offenbarung und Leere: Nietzsche, Freud, Paul de Man', *Merkur* 45.5: 387–402.

Grohotolsky, E. 1984. *Ästhetik der Negation: Tendenzen des Deutschen Gegenwartsdramas*. Königstein: Forum Academicum.

Gruber, B., ed. 1997. *Erfahrung und System. Mystik und Esoterik in der Literatur der Moderne*. Opladen: Westdeutscher Verlag.

Guidry, G. A. 1989. *Language, Morality and Society: An Ethical Model of Communication in Fontane and Hofmannsthal.* Berkley: University of California Press.

Gumtau, H. 1969. *Wolfgang Borchert.* Berlin: Colloquium Verlag.

Gunn, G. 1979. *The Interpretation of Otherness: Literature, Religion and the American Imagination.* New York: Oxford University Press.

Gustafson, S. E. 1992. 'Kleist, Freud and Kirsteva: "Die heilige Cäcilie oder die Gewalt der Musik" and the Unspeakable Abyss', *Seminar* 28.2: 110–30.

Habermas, J. 1972. 'Bewusstmachende oder rettende Kritik – die Aktualität Walter Benjamins' in S. Unseld (ed.), *Zur Aktualität Walter Benjamins.* Frankfurt am Main: Suhrkamp Verlag.

—— 1974. *Strukturwandel der Öffentlichkeit. Untersuchungen zu einer Kategorie der bürgerlichen Gesellschaft.* Neuwied und Berlin: Luchterhand Verlag.

—— 1986. *Der philosophische Diskurs der Moderne.* Frankfurt am Main: Suhrkamp Verlag.

Haikola, L. 1977. *Religion as Language Game.* Lund: Gleerup.

Haller, R., and F. Stadler, eds. 1988. *Mach, Ernst: Werk und Wirkung.* Wien: Verlag Hölder.

Hart Nibbrig, C. L. 1974. *Ja und Nein: Studien zur Konstitution von Wertgefügen in Texten.* Frankfurt am Main: Suhrkamp Verlag.

—— 1981. *Rhetorik des Schweigens: Versuch über den Schatten literarischer Rede.* Frankfurt am Main: Suhrkamp Verlag.

—— 1989. *Ästhetik der letzten Dinge.* Frankfurt am Main: Suhrkamp Verlag.

—— 1995. *Übergänge: Versuch in sechs Anläufen.* Frankfurt am Main: Insel Verlag.

Hassan, I. 1967. *The Literature of Silence.* New York: Knopf.

Hauptmann, G. 1922. 'Vor Sonnenaufgang' in *GW Centenar-Ausgabe IX.* Berlin: Fischer Verlag.

Hebbel, F. 1965. 'Mein Wort über das Drama' in *Werke III.* München: C. Hanser Verlag.

Hegel, G. W. F. 1907. *Phänomenologie des Geistes.* Leipzig: F. Meiner Verlag.

Heidegger, M. 1842–43. *Vorlesungen über die Aesthetik.* Berlin: Duncker und Humblot Verlag.

—— 1949. *Sein und Zeit.* Tübingen: Neomarius Verlag.

—— 1951. *Kant und das Problem der Metaphysik.* Frankfurt am Main: Klostermann Verlag.

—— 1953. *Einführung in die Metaphysik.* Tübingen: Niemeyer Verlag.

—— 1957a. *Identität und Differenz.* Pfullingen: Neske Verlag.

—— 1957b. *Der Satz vom Grund.* Pfullingen: Neske Verlag.

—— 1968. *Über den Humanismus.* Frankfurt am Main: Klostermann Verlag.

—— 1970. *Phänomenologie und Theologie.* Frankfurt am Main: Klostermann Verlag.

—— 1971. *Erläuterungen zu Hölderlins Dichtung.* Frankfurt am Main: Klostermann Verlag.

—— 1976a. 'Was ist Metaphysik?' *Wegmarken*. Frankfurt am Main: Klostermann Verlag.

—— 1976b. *Wegmarken*. Frankfurt am Main: Klostermann Verlag.

—— 1978. *Metaphysische Anfangsgründe der Logik im Ausgang von Leibniz*. Frankfurt am Main: Klostermann Verlag.

—— 1983a. *Die Grundbegriffe der Metaphysik. Welt, Endlichkeit, Einsamkeit: Gesamtausgabe*, Vol. 29/30. Frankfurt am Main: Klostermann Verlag.

—— 1983b. 'Holzwege' in *Gesamtausgabe*, Vol. 13. Frankfurt am Main: Klostermann Verlag.

—— 1984. 'Grundfragen der Philosophie' in *Gesamtausgabe*, Vol. 45. Frankfurt am Main: Klostermann Verlag.

—— 1985. 'Unterwegs zur Sprache' in *Gesamtausgabe*, Vol. 12. Frankfurt am Main: Klostermann Verlag.

—— 1989. 'Beiträge zur Philosophie' in *Gesamtausgabe*, Vol. 65. Frankfurt am Main: Klostermann Verlag.

Herder, J. G. 1978. *Abhandlung über den Ursprung der Sprache: Text, Materialien, Kommentar*. München: Hanser Verlag.

Hewitt, M. A. 1995. *Critical Theory of Religion*. Minneapolis: Fortress Press.

Hillebrand, B. 1978. *Nietzsche und die deutsche Literatur*. Tübingen: Niemeyer Verlag.

Hinck, W. 1980. *Handbuch des deutschen Dramas*. Düsseldorf: Bagel Verlag.

Hirsch, R. 1982. 'Jedermann: Ein überfordertes Weltgedicht?' *Hofmannsthal Blätter* 26: 81–85.

Hofer, W. 1954. 'Toward a Revision of the German Concept of History' in H. Kohn (ed.), *German History: Some New German Views*. London: George Allen & Unwin.

Hofmannsthal, H. von 1923. *Jedermann: Das Spiel vom Sterben des Reichen Mannes*. Berlin: Fischer Verlag.

—— 1929. *Buch der Freunde*. Leipzig: Insel Verlag.

—— 1953a. *Briefe der Freundschaft (1897–1919)*. Düsseldorf: E. Diederichs Verlag.

—— 1953b. 'Die Briefe des Zurückgekehrten' in *Reitergeschichte. Erzählungen und Aufsätze*. Frankfurt am Main: Fischer Verlag.

—— 1955. *Gedichte*. Wiesbaden: Insel Verlag.

—— 1956. *Österreichische Aufsätze und Reden*. Wien: Bergland Verlag.

—— 1979a. 'Corona' in *Gesammelte Werke in zehn Einzelbänden*. Frankfurt am Main: Fischer Verlag.

—— 1979b. 'Die Idee Europa' in *Reden und Aufsätze II, 1914–1924. Gesammelte Werke in zehn Einzelbänden*. Frankfurt am Main: Fischer Verlag.

—— 1979c. 'Der Tor und der Tod' in *Gesammelte Werke in zehn Einzelbänden*. Frankfurt am Main: Fischer Verlag.

—— 1980a. 'Ad me ipsum' in *Reden und Aufsätze III, 1925–1929: Aufzeichnungen 1889–1929. Gesammelte Werke in zehn Einzelbänden*. Frankfurt am Main: Fischer Verlag.

—— 1980b. 'Aufzeichnungen aus dem Nachlass 1894' in *Reden und Aufsätze III, 1925–1929: Aufzeichnungen 1889–1929. Gesammelte Werke in zehn Einzelbänden.* Frankfurt am Main: Fischer Verlag.

—— 1980c. *Reden und Aufsätze III, 1925–1929: Aufzeichnungen 1889–1929. Gesammelte Werke in zehn Einzelbänden.* Frankfurt am Main: Fischer Verlag.

—— 1980d. 'Das Schrifttum als geistiger Raum der Nation' in *Reden und Aufsätze III, 1925–1929: Aufzeichnungen 1889–1929. Gesammelte Werke in zehn Einzelbänden.* Frankfurt am Main: Fischer Verlag.

—— 1980e. 'Wert und Ehre deutscher Sprache' in *Reden und Aufsätze III, 1925–1929: Aufzeichnungen 1889–1929. Gesammelte Werke in zehn Einzelbänden.* Frankfurt am Main: Fischer Verlag.

—— 1990. 'Letter to Elsa Bruckmann-Cantacuzène' in *Hofmannsthal Blätter* 4 (Spring): 290–292.

—— 2000. *Ein Brief.* Frankfurt am Main: Insel Verlag.

Holthusen, H. E. 1954. *Ja und Nein: Neue kritische Versuche.* München: P. Piper Verlag.

—— 1961. *Kritisches Verstehen: Neue Aufsätze zur Literatur.* München: P. Piper Verlag.

Hoppe, M. 1968. *Literatentum, Magie und Mystik im Frühwerk Hugo von Hofmannsthals.* Berlin: de Gruyter Verlag.

Horkheimer, M. 1968a. 'Gedanke zur Religion' in *Kritische Theorie I: Eine Dokumentation.* Frankfurt am Main: Fischer Verlag.

—— 1968b. *Kritische Theorie I: Eine Dokumentation.* Frankfurt am Main: Fischer Verlag.

—— 1968c. *Zur Kritik der instrumentellen Vernunft: Aus den Vorträgen und Aufzeichnungen seit Kriegsende.* Frankfurt am Main: Fischer Verlag.

Horkheimer, M., and T. W. Adorno. 1969. *Dialektik der Aufklärung: Philosophische Fragmente.* Frankfurt am Main: Fischer Verlag.

Huber, M., and G. Lauer, ed. 1996. *Bildung und Konfession: Politik, Religion und Literarische Identitätsbildung 1850–1918.* Tübingen: M. Niemeyer Verlag.

Iggers, G. G. 1968. *The German Conception of History: The National Tradition of Historical Thought from Herder to the Present.* Middletown: Wesleyan University Press.

Innes, C. D. 1981. *Holy Theater: Ritual and the Avant Garde.* Cambridge: Cambridge University Press.

Iser, W., and S. Budick, eds. 1989. *Languages of the Unsayable: The Play of Negativity in Literature and Literary Theory.* New York: Columbia University Press.

Jacobs, C. 1978. *The Dissimulating Harmony: The Image of Interpretation in Nietzsche, Rilke, Artaud, and Benjamin.* Baltimore: Johns Hopkins University Press.

Jaeschke, W. 1990. *Reason in Religion: The Foundations of Hegel's Philosophy of Religion.* Berkley: University of California Press.

Jameson, F. 1971. *Marxism and Form: Twentieth-Century Dialectical Theories of Literature*. Princeton: Princeton University Press.

Jannidis, F. 1996. *Das Individuum und sein Jahrhundert*. Tübingen: Niemeyer Verlag.

Jaron, N., R. Möhrmann and H. Müller. 1986. *Berlin – Theater der Jahrhundertwende: Bühnengeschichte der Reichshauptstadt im Spiegel der Kritik*. Tübingen: M. Niemeyer Verlag.

Jasper, D. 1984. *Images of Belief in Literature*. New York: St. Martin's Press.

—— 1989. *The Study of Literature and Religion: An Introduction*. Basingstoke: Macmillan.

—— 1990. *European Literature and Theology in the Twentieth Century: Ends of Time*. London: Macmillan.

—— 1992. *Postmodernism, Literature and the Future of Theology*. Basingstoke: Macmillan.

—— 1993. *Rhetorik, Power and Community: An Exercise in Reverse*. Basingstoke: Macmillan.

Jauss, H. R. 1973. 'Geschichte der Kunst und Historie' in *Literaturgeschichte als Provokation*. Frankfurt am Main: Suhrkamp Verlag.

Jens, W. 1985. *Dichtung und Religion: Pascal, Gryphius, Lessing, Hölderlin, Novalis, Kierkegaard, Dostojewski, Kafka*. München: Kindler Verlag.

Jens, W., and H. Küng. 1991. *Literature and Religion. Pascal, Gryphius, Lessing, Hölderlin, Novalis, Kierkegaard, Dostoyevsky, Kafka*. New York: Paragon House.

Jesse, H. 1986. 'The Young Bertolt Brecht and Religion', *Communications from the International Brecht Society* 15.2: 17–27.

—— 1996. 'Die Kritik am Zusammenspiel von Religion und Kapital', *Communications from the International Brecht Society* 25: 48–53.

Jossua, J.-P. 1994. *Pour une Histoire religieuse de l'Expérience Littéraire: Dieu aux XIXe et XXe siècles*. Paris: Beauchesne.

Kano, K. 1985. 'Über die Seelenrettung bei Wolfgang Borchert', *Language and Culture* 7: 51–66.

Kant, I. 1984a. *Grundlegung zur Metaphysik der Sitten*. Erlangen: H. Fischer Verlag.

—— 1984b. *Kritik der reinen Vernunft*. München: Franklin Bibliothek.

—— 1996. *Religion and Rational Theology*. Cambridge: Cambridge University Press.

Karter, E. 2001. *Mit und über Friedrich Dürrenmatt: Essay*. Basel: Opinio Verlag.

Keele, A. F. 2003. *In Search of the Supernatural: Pre-existence, Eternal Marriage, and Apotheosis in German Literary, Operatic, and Cinematic Texts*. Münster: Agenda.

Kermode, F. 1979. *The Genesis of Secrecy: On the Interpretation of Narrative*. Cambridge, Mass.: Harvard University Press.

Kettels, V. 1971. 'Friedrich Dürrenmatt at Temple University', *Journal of Modern Literature* 1: 89–108.

Kierkegaard, S. 1953a. 'Furcht und Zittern' in *Gesammelte Werke* (trans. E. Hirsch). Düsseldorf: Eugen Diederichs Verlag.

—— 1953b. 'Krankheit zum Tode' in *Gesammelte Werke* (trans. E. Hirsch). Düsseldorf: E. Diederichs Verlag.

—— 1962. *Die Tagebücher.* Düsseldorf: E. Diederichs Verlag.

—— 1967. *Sören Kierkegaard's Journals and Papers* (ed. and trans. H. V. Hong and E. H. Hong). Bloomington: Indiana University Press.

Klarmann, A. F. 1952. 'Wolfgang Borchert: The Lost Voice of a New Germany', *Germanic Review* xxvii: n.p.

—— 1960. 'Friedrich Dürrenmatt and the Tragic Sense of Comedy', *The Tulane Drama Review* 4 May: n.p.

Klotz, V. 1960. *Geschlossene und offene Form im Drama.* München: C. Hanser Verlag.

Knapp, G., and G. Labroisse, ed. 1981. *Facetten: Studien zum 60. Geburtstag Friedrich Dürrenmatts.* Bern: Peter Lang Verlag.

Knauer, B., ed. 1997. *Das Buch und die Bücher: Beiträge zum Verhältnis von Bibel, Religion und Literatur.* Würzburg: Königshausen & Neumann.

Knopf, J. 1981. 'Sprachmächtigkeiten' in G. Knapp (ed.), *Facetten: Studien zum 60. Geburtstag Friedrich Dürrenmatts.* Berne: Peter Lang Verlag.

Knust, H. 1985. 'Brecht's Galileo-Evangelium', *Euphorion* 79.2: 207–225.

Kocka, J. 1979. 'Restauration oder Neubeginn? Deutschland 1945–1949' in C. Stern and H. A. Winkler (eds.), *Wendepunkte deutscher Geschichte 1848–1945.* Frankfurt: Fischer Verlag.

Koelle, L. 1997. *Paul Celans pneumatisches Judentum: Gott-Rede und menschliche Existenz nach der Shoah.* Mainz: Matthias Grünewald-Verlag.

Kohlenbach, M. 2002. *Walter Benjamin: Self-Reference and Religiosity.* New York: Palgrave Macmillan.

Kolb, D. 1990. *Postmodern Sophistication: Philosophy, Architecture and Tradition.* Chicago: University of Chicago Press.

Koller, A. 2000. *Wolfgang Borcherts 'Draußen vor der Tür'.* Marburg: Tectum Verlag.

Koopmann, H., and W. Woesler, eds. 1984. *Literatur und Religion.* Freiburg: Herder Verlag.

Köpke, W. 1984. 'In Sachen Wolfgang Borchert' in R. Wolff (ed.), *Wolfgang Borchert: Werk und Wirkung.* Bonn: Bouvier Verlag.

Kosselleck, R. 1979. *Vergangene Zukunft: Zur Semantik Geschichtlicher Zeiten.* Frankfurt am Main: Suhrkamp Verlag.

Kracauer, S. 1969. *History: The Last Things Before the Last.* New York: Oxford University Press.

Krättli, A. 2003. 'Dürrenmatts Abschied vom Theater', *Text u. Kritik* 50/51: 222–33.

Krupnick, M., ed. 1982. *Displacement. Derrida and After.* Bloomington: Indiana University Press.

Kühn, J. 1975. *Gescheiterte Sprachkritik: Fritz Mauthners Leben und Werk.* Berlin: n.p.

Kuna, F. 1970. 'The Expense of Silence: Sincerity and Strategy in Hofmannsthal's "Chandos Letter"', *Publications of the English Society* 40: 69–94.

Kunert, G., ed. 1989. *Dichter Predigen: Reden aus der Wirklichkeit.* Stuttgart: Radius Verlag.

Kupfer, A. 1996a. *Göttliche Gifte: Kleine Kulturgeschichte des Rausches seit dem Garten Eden.* Stuttgart: Metzler Verlag.

—— 1996b. *Die künstlichen Paradiese: Rausch und Realität seit der Romantik.* Stuttgart: Metzler Verlag.

Kurz, P. K. 1996. *Gott in der modernen Literatur.* München: Koesel Verlag.

Kuschel, K.-J. 1985. *Weil wir uns auf dieser Erde nicht ganz zu Hause fühlen: 12 Schriftsteller über Religion und Literatur.* München: Piper Verlag.

Labat, S. 1997. *La Poésie de l'Extase et le Pouvoir Chamanique du Langage.* Paris: Maisonneuve et Larose.

*Languages of Visuality: Crossings between Science, Art, Politics and Literature.* 1996. Detroit: Wayne State University Press.

Larsen, N. 1990. *Modernity and Hegemony: A Materialist Critique of Aesthetic Agencies.* Minneapolis: University of Minnesota Press.

Ledbetter, M. 1989. *Virtuous Inventions: The Religious Dimension of Narrative.* Atlanta: Scholars Press.

Leitch, V. B. 1983. *Deconstructive Criticism: An Advanced Introduction.* New York: Columbia University.

Lenz, S. 1982. '"Ich habe nichts über den Krieg aufgeschrieben": Ein Gespräch mit Heinrich Böll und Hermann Lenz', interview in *Über Phantasie: Siegfried Lenz, Gespräche mit Heinrich Böll, Günter Grass, Walter Kempowski, Pavel Kohout.* Hamburg: Hoffmann und Campe.

Lichtenberg, G. C. 1954. *Aphorismen.* Bern: A. Scherz Verlag.

Lissa, Z. 1970. 'Ästhetische Funktionen des musikalischen Zitats' in J. Znak (ed.), *Sign, Language, Culture / Signe, Langage, Culture.* The Hague: Mouton.

*Literature and Theology: National Conference on Literature and Religion Newsletter.* 1987–98. Oxford: Oxford University Press.

Lobsien, E. 1988. *Das literarische Feld: Phänomenologie der Literaturwissenschaft.* München: Wilhelm Fink Verlag.

Longinus, C. 1939. *Du Sublime.* Paris: Les Belles Lettres.

Lukacs, G. 1953. *Deutsche Realisten des 19. Jahrhunderts.* Berlin: n.p.

Lundin, R. 1993. *The Culture of Interpretation: Christian Faith and the Postmodern World.* Grand Rapids: William Eerdmans Publishing.

Mach, E. 1922. *Die Analyse der Empfindungen und das Verhältnis des Physischen zum Psychischen.* Jena: Gustav Fischer Verlag.

Macho, T. H. 1987. *Todesmetaphern: Zur Logik der Grenzerfahrung.* Frankfurt am Main: Suhrkamp Verlag.

Madsen, D. 1996. *Allegory in America: From Puritanism to Postmodernism*. Basingstoke: St. Martin's Press.

Maeterlinck, M. 1913. 'Le silence' in *Le Trésor des Humbles*. Paris.

Magris, C. 1975. 'Der Zeichen Rost: Hofmannsthal und "Ein Brief"', *Sprachkunst* 6: 53–74.

Malekin, P., and R. Yarrow. 1997. *Consciousness, Literature and Theatre: Theory and Beyond*. London: Macmillan Press.

Mallard, W. 1977. *The Reflection of Theology in Literature: A Case Study in Theology and Culture*. San Antonio: Trinity University Press.

Marcuse, H. 1966. *Eros and Civilization: A Philosophical Inquiry into Freud*. Boston: Beacon Press.

Marquard, O. 1973. *Schwierigkeiten mit der Geschichtsphilosophie*. Frankfurt am Main: Suhrkamp Verlag.

Martens, G. 2003. *Wege der Lyrik in der Moderne*. Würzburg: Königshausen & Neumann Verlag.

Martin, J. A. 1990. *Beauty and Holiness: The Dialogue between Aesthetics and Religion*. Princeton: Princeton University Press.

Marx, K., and F. Engels. 1957. *Werke*. Berlin: Dietz Verlag.

Massey, I. 1970. *The Uncreating Word: Romanticism and the Object*. Bloomington: Indiana University Press.

Matz, W. 1989. 'Hofmannsthal und Benjamin', *Akzente* 36.1: 43–65.

Mauranges, J.-P. 1976. 'L'Image de l'Amerique dans l'Oeuvre de Dürrenmatt: Une Perspective Theologique?', *Seminar: A Journal of Germanic Studies* 12: 156–73.

Mauser, W. 1961. *Bild und Gebärde in der Sprache Hofmannsthals*. Wien: Bohlhaus Verlag.

—— ed. 1971–87. *Hofmannsthal-Forschungen*. Freiburg im Breisgau: Schadel und Wehle Verlag.

—— 1977. *Hugo von Hofmannsthal: Konfliktbewältigung und Werkstruktur*. München: Fink Verlag.

Mauthner, F. 1918. *Erinnerungen*. München: G. Müller Verlag.

—— 1922. *Der Atheismus und seine Geschichte im Abendlande*. Stuttgart: Deutsche Verlagsanstalt.

—— 1967. *Beiträge zu einer Kritik der Sprache*. Hildesheim: Olms Verlag.

Mayer, H. 1967. *Zur deutschen Literatur der Zeit*. Reinbeck: Rowohlt Verlag.

McCole, J. 1993. *Walter Benjamin and the Antinomies of Tradition*. Ithaca: Cornell University Press.

McKinney, L. D. 1992. 'Weeping in the Night: Reading Beyond Language in the "Caucasian Chalk Circle"', *Modern Drama* 35: 530–37.

McLellan, D. 1987. *Marxism and Religion*. New York: Harper & Row.

McRae, R. G. 1985. *Philosophy and the Absolute: The Modes of Hegel's Speculation*. Dordrecht: Martinus Nijhoff Publishers.

Meinecke, F. 1946. *Die deutsche Katastrophe: Betrachtungen und Erinnerungen.* Zürich: Aero-Verlag.

—— 1954. 'Ranke and Burckhard' in H. Kohn (ed.), *German History: Some New German Views.* London: George Allen & Unwin.

—— 1959. *Die Entstehung des Historismus*, Vol. 3 (ed. C. Hinrichs). München: R. Oldenbourg Verlag.

Mennemeier, F. N. 1975. *Modernes deutsches Drama II.* München: Fink Verlag.

Mensching, G. 1926. *Das Heilige Schweigen: Religionsgeschichtliche Versuche und Vorarbeiten.* Giessen: n.p.

Mèredieu, F. de 1992. *Antonin Artaud: les Couilles de l'Ange.* Paris: Blusson.

Merkl, P. and N. Smart, ed. 1983. *Religion and Politics in the Modern World.* New York: New York Press.

Metz, J. B. 1980. *Faith in History and Society: Toward a Practical Fundamental Theology* (trans. David Smith). N.p.

Mileck, J. 1959. 'Wolfgang Borchert: "Draussen vor der Tür": A Young Poet's Struggle with Guilt and Despair', *Monatshefte* LI: n.p.

Miller, H. 1977a. 'The Linguistic Moment in "The Wreck of the Deutschland"' in T. D. Young (ed.), *The New Criticism and After.* Charlottesville: University of Virginia Press.

—— 1977b. 'Nature and the Linguistic Moment' in U. C. Knoepflmacher and G. B. Tennyson (eds.), *Nature and the Victorian Imagination.* Berkeley: University of California Press.

Mills, K. 1996. *Justifying Language: Paul and Contemporary Literary Theory.* Basingstoke: St. Martin's Press.

Mingels, A. 2003. *Dürrenmatt und Kierkegaard: Die Kategorie des Einzelnen als gemeinsame Denkform.* Köln: Böhlhau Verlag.

Morrison, K. F. 1988. *'I am You': The Hermeneutics of Empathy in Western Literature, Theology and Art.* Princeton: Princeton University Press.

Mortimer, A. 1984. *Contemporary Approaches to Narrative.* Tübingen: G. Narr Verlag.

Mosès, S. 1990. 'Geschichte und Subjektivität – Zur Konstitution der historischen Zeit bei Walter Benjamin' in G. Buhr, F. A. Kittler, and H. Turk (eds.), *Das Subjekt der Dichtung: Festschrift für Gerhard Kaiser.* Würzburg: Königshausen & Neumann Verlag.

Motte, M. 1996. *Auf der Suche nach dem verlorenen Gott: Religion in der Literatur der Gegenwart.* Mainz: Matthias-Grünewald-Verlag.

Müller, B. 1966. 'Der Verlust der Sprache: Zur linguistischen Krise in der Literatur', *Germanisch-Romanische Monatsschrift* 16: 225–43.

Müller, H.-H. 2003. 'Bertolt Brecht's Frühe Lyrik: Eine Skizze' in G. Martens (ed.), *Wege der Lyrik in die Moderne: Beiträge eines deutsch-polnischen Symposiums.* Würzburg: Königshausen & Neumann Verlag.

Murphy, R. 1980. *Brecht and the Bible: A Study of Religious Nihilism and Human Weakness in Brecht's Drama of Morality and the City*. Chapel Hill: University of North Carolina Press.

Nägele, R. 1966. 'Die Sprachkrise und ihr dichterischer Ausdruck bei Hofmannsthal', *Germanisch-Romanische Monatsschrift* 16: 225–43.

—— 1986. 'The Scene of the Other: T. W. Adorno's Negative Dialectic in the Context of Poststructuralism' in J. Arac (ed.), *Postmodernism and Politics*. Minneapolis: University of Minnesota Press.

—— 1987. *Reading after Freud: Essays on Goethe, Hölderlin, Habermas, Nietzsche, Brecht, Celan, Freud*. New York: Columbia University Press.

—— 1988. *Benjamin's Ground: New Reading on Walter Benjamin*. Detroit: Wayne State University Press.

—— 1991. *Theater, Theory, Speculation: Walter Benjamin and the Scenes of Modernity*. Baltimore: Johns Hopkins University Press.

—— 1997. *Echoes of Translation: Reading Between Texts*. Baltimore: Johns Hopkins University Press.

Näger, R. 2004. 'Body Politics: Benjamin's Dialectical Materialsism between Brecht and the Frankfurt School' in *The Cambridge Companion to Walter Benjamin*. Cambridge: Cambridge University Press.

Nelson, B. 1992. *Naturalism in the European Novel: New Critical Perspectives*. New York: Berg.

Nelson, D. 1975. 'To Live or Not to Live: Notes on Archetypes and the Absurd in Borchert's "Draussen vor der Tur"', *German Quarterly* 48: 343–54.

Nieli, R. 1987. *Wittgenstein: From Mysticism to Ordinary Language: A Study of Viennese Positivism and the Thought of Ludwig Wittgenstein*. Albany: State University of New York Press.

Nietzsche, F. 1988a. 'Also Sprach Zarathustra' in G. Colli and M. Montinari (eds.), *Sämtliche Werke: Kritische Studien Ausgabe*. Berlin: dtv.

—— 1988b. 'Ecce Homo' in G. Colli and M. Montinari (eds.), *Sämtliche Werke: Kritische Studien Ausgabe*. Berlin: dtv.

—— 1988c. 'Die Geburt der Tragödie. Oder: Griechenthum und Pessimismus. Neue Ausgabe mit dem Versuch einer Selbstkritik' (1886) in G. Colli and M. Montinari (eds.), *Sämtliche Werke: Kritische Studien Ausgabe*. Berlin: dtv.

—— 1988d. 'Unzeitgemässe Betrachtungen' in G. Colli and M. Montinari (eds.), *Sämtliche Werke: Kritische Studien Ausgabe*. Berlin: dtv.

—— 1988e. 'Unzeitgemässe Betrachtungen II' in G. Colli and M. Montinari (eds.), *Sämtliche Werke: Kritische Studien Ausgabe*. Berlin: dtv.

—— 1988f. 'Über Wahrheit und Lüge im aussermoralischen Sinne' in G. Colli and M. Montinari (eds.), *Sämtliche Werke: Kritische Studien Ausgabe*. Berlin: dtv.

Noble, C. 1978. *Text u. Kritik: Sprachskepsis über Dichtung der Moderne*.

Nolte, E. 1992. *Martin Heidegger: Politik und Geschichte im Leben und Denken*. Berlin: Propyläen Verlag.

Norbert, J., R. Möhrmann and H. Müller. 1986. *Berlin-Theater der Jahrhundertwende*. Tübingen: Max Niemeyer Verlag.

Norris, C. 1988. *Paul de Man: Deconstruction and the Critique of Aesthetic Ideology*. New York: Routledge.

Nossack, H. E. 1981. *Der Untergang. Hamburg 1943*. Hamburg: E. Kabel Verlag.

'Nu' in *Das Grimmsche Worterbuch: Untersuchungen zur lexikographischen Methodologie*. 1987. Stuttgart: S. Hirzel Verlag.

Obad, V. 1992. 'Zwei "Heilige Experimente" der deutschsprachigen Dramatik: Fritz Hochwälders "Das heilige Experiment" und Friedrich Dürrenmatts "Es steht geschrieben"', *Sprachkunst* 23: 233–43.

O'Brien, G. M. 1977. 'Ernst Mach and a Trio of Austrian Writers: Hofmannsthal, Andrian, Musil', *International Fiction Review* 4: 64–67.

Oppel, H. 1972. *Die Suche nach Gott in der amerikanischen Literatur der Gegenwart*. Mainz: Akademie der Wissenschaft und Literatur.

Pabst, H. 1977. *Brecht und die Religion*. Graz: Verlag Styria.

Panizza, O. 1896. *Das Liebeskonzil. Eine Himmelstragödie in fünf Aufzügen*. Zürich: Verlags-Magazin.

Pascal, B. 1954. 'Pensées' in J. Chevalier (ed.), *Oeuvres completes de Pascal*. Paris: Gallimard.

Peignot, C. 1997. *Le Nombre, Langage de Dieu. Essai sur la Symbolique des Nombres*. Paris: Courrier du Livre.

Pestalozzi, K. 1958. *Sprachskepsis und Sprachmagie im Werk des jungen Hofmannsthals*. Zürich: Atlantis Verlag.

Pestalozzi, K., and M. Stern. 1991. *Basler Hofmannsthal-Beiträge*. N.p.: Königshausen & Neumann Verlag.

Pfister, M. 1977/91. *The Theory and Analysis of Drama*. Cambridge: n.p.

Phillips, D. Z. 1991. *From Fantasy to Faith: The Philosophy of Religion and Twentieth Century Literature*. Houndsmill: Macmillan.

Piechotta, H. J. 1994. 'Die Differenzfunktion der Metapher in der Literatur der Moderne' in H. J. Piechotta, R.-R. Wuthenow and S. Rothemann (eds.), *Die literarische Moderne in Europa*. Opladen: Westdeutscher Verlag.

Pieper, I. 2000. *Modernes Welttheater: Untersuchungen zum Welttheatermotiv zwischen Katastrophenerfahrung und Welt-Anschauungsversuchen bei Walter Benjamin, Karl Kraus, Hugo von Hofmannsthal und Else Lasker-Schüler*. Berlin: Duncker & Humblot Verlag.

Poizat, M. 1991. 'La Voix du Diable' in *La Jouissance Lyrique Sacrée*. Paris: Métailié.

Pörtner, P. 1960. *Literatur-Revolution, 1919–1925, I*. Darmstadt: H. Luchterhand Verlag.

Poyatos, F. 1983. *New Perspectives in Nonverbal Communication. Studies in Cultural Anthropology, Social Psychology, Linguistics, Literature and Semiotics*. Oxford: Pergamon Press.

Raddatz, Fritz. 1985. 'Ich bin der finsterste Komödienschreiber, den es gibt. Ein ZEIT-Gespräch mit Friedrich Dürrenmatt', interview in *Die Zeit* 34, 16–18.

Renard, J.-C. 1987. *L'Expérience intérieure de Georges Bataile ou la Négation du Mystère*. Paris: Seuil.

Rocker, S. 1995. *Hegel's Rational Religion: The Validity of Hegel's Argument for the Identity in Content of Absolute Religion and Absolute Philosophy*. Cranbury, NJ: Associated University Press.

Roelke, T. 1994. *Dramatische Kommunikation: Modell und Reflexion bei Dürrenmatt, Handke and Weiss*. Berlin: W. de Gruyter Verlag.

Rohse, E. 1983. *Der frühe Brecht und die Bibel: Studien zum Augsburger Religions-unterricht und zu den Versuchen des Gymnasiasten*. Göttingen: Vandenhoeck & Ruprecht Verlag.

Röllecke, H. 1996. 'Hofmannsthal: Jedermann' in *Interpretationen des 20. Jahrhunderts*, Vol. 1. Stuttgart: Reclam Verlag.

Roloff, V. 1973. 'Reden und Schweigen' in *Münchner Romanistische Arbeiten*. München: Fink Verlag.

Rolshoven, P.-E. K.-J., ed. 1982. *Le Sacré: Aspects et Manifestations*. Tübingen: Gunter Narr Verlag.

Ronse, H. 1966. 'Littérature et Silence', *Synthèses* 236–7: 41–48.

Rorty, R. 1984. 'The Historiography of Philosophy: Four Genres' in R. Rorty, J. B. Shneewind, and Q. Skinner (eds.), *Philosophy in History*. Cambridge: Cambridge University Press.

Rosefeldt, P. 1995. *The Absent Father in Modern Drama*. New York: Peter Lang.

Rousseau, J.-J. 1967a. 'Essai sur l'Origine des langues, ou il est parlé de la mélodie et de l'imitation musicale', in *Ecrits sur la musique*. Paris: Le Graphe.

Rousseau, J.-J. 1967b. *Oeuvres completes*. Paris: Editions Seuil.

——— 1990. 'Considérations sur le gouvernement de Pologne' in *Discours sur l'économie politique*. Paris: Flammarion.

Rudiger, G. 2001. *Traces of Transcendency: Religious Motifs in German Literature and Thought*. München: Ludicium.

Rupp, G. 1981. 'Zweiter Weltkrieg im Drama. Literarhistorische und schulerische Lebenswelt am Beispiel von Wolfgang Borchert, Gunther Weisenborn und Carl Zuckmayer' in H. Müller-Michaels (ed.), *Deutsche Dramen: Interpretationen zu Werken von der Aufklärung bis zur Gegenwart*, Vol. 2. Königstein: Athenäum Verlag.

Ruprecht, E., ed. 1962. *Literarische Manifeste des Naturalismus, 1880–1882*. Stuttgart: Metzler Verlag.

Rusterholz, P. 1995. 'Theologische und Philosophische Denkformen und ihre Funktion für die Interpretation und Wertung von Texten Friedrich Dürrenmatts' in C. Brinker, U. Herzog, N. Largier, and P. Michel (eds.), *Contemplata Aliis Tradere: Studien zum Verhältnis von Literatur und Spiritualität*. Bern: Peter Lang Verlag.

245

—— ed. 2000. *Die Verwandlung der 'Stoffe' als Stoff der Verwandlung: Friedrich Dürrenmatts Spätwerk.* Berlin: E. Schmidt Verlag.

Sartre, J. P. n.d. 'Qu'est-ce que la Littérature? Situation de l'ecrivain en 1947', *Situations II* 14.

Sauter, J-H. 1982. 'Friedrich Dürrenmatt', interview in Josef-Hermann Sauter (ed.), *Interviews mit Schriftstellern: Texte und Selbstaussagen.* Leipzig: Gustav-Kiepenheuer Verlag.

Schaeffer, J.-M. 1994. 'La Religion de l'Art: Un Paradigme philosophique de la Modernité', *Revue Germanique International: Histoire et Théories de l'Art: de Winckelmann à Panofsky* 2: 195–207, 258–59.

Schaffler, H. and H. Schaffler. 1975. *Studien zum ästhetischen Historismus.* Frankfurt am Main: Suhrkamp Verlag.

Schenkel, M. 1984. *Lessings Poetik des Mitleids im bürgerlichen Treuerspiel* Miss Sara Sampson*: Poetisch-poetologische Reflexionen mit Interpretationen zu Pirandello, Brecht, und Handke.* Bonn: Bouvier Verlag.

Schlegel, F. 1975. 'Über die Sprache und Weisheit der Inder' in E. Behler and U. Struc-Oppenberg (eds.), *Studien zur Philosophie und Theologie: Kritische Friedrich Schlegel Ausgabe,* Vol. 8. München: F. Schöningh Verlag.

Schlueter, J. 1979. *Metafictional Characters in Modern Drama.* New York: Columbia University Press.

Schmidt, A. 1975. *Wolfgang Borchert: Sprachgestaltung in seinem Werk.* Bonn: Bouvier Verlag.

Schnabel, E. 1946–47. 'Eine Injektion Nihilismus', *Hamburger akademische Rundschau* I.9: n.p.

Schnitzler, A. 1985. *Aphorismen und Notate: Gedanken über Leben und Kunst.* Leipzig: Gustav Kiepenheuer Verlag.

Schnurre, W. 1989. 'Schriftsteller und Öffentlichkeit', *Sprache im technischen Zeitalter* 27.12: n.p.

Scholem, G. 1972. 'Walter Benjamin und sein Engel' in S. Unseld (ed.), *Zur Aktualität Walter Benjamins.* Frankfurt am Main: Suhrkamp Verlag.

Schorske, C. 1961. 'Politics and the Psyche in Fin-de-Siècle Vienna: Schnitzler and Hofmannsthal', *American Historical Review* 46.4: n.p.

Schulte, V. 1987. *Das Gesicht einer gesichtslosen Welt: Zu Paradoxie und Groteske in Friedrich Dürrenmatts dramatischem Werk.* Frankfurt am Main: Peter Lang Verlag.

Sebald, W. G., ed. 1988. *A Radical Stage: Theatre in Germany in the 1970s and 80s.* Oxford: Berg.

Simmel, G. 1989. *Philosophie des Geldes.* Frankfurt am Main: Suhrkamp Verlag.

Sohlich, W. 1993. 'The Dialectic of Mimesis and Representation in Brecht's *Life of Galileo',* *Theatre Journal* 45.1: 49–64.

Sölle, D. 1996. *Das Eis der Seele spalten: Theologie und Literatur in Sprachloser Zeit.* Mainz: Matthias-Grünewald-Verlag.

Sörging, J. and A. Mingels. 2004. *Dürrenmatt im Zentrum: 7. Internationales Neuenburger Kolloquium 2000*. Frankfurt am Main: Peter Lang Verlag.

Spender, S. 1952. *The Man Outside*. Norfolk: n.p.

Spinoza, B. de 1981. *Ethics* (trans. George Eliot). Salzburg: Institut für Anglistik und Amerikanistik, Universität Salzburg.

Spörl, U. 1997. *Gottlose Mystik in der deutschen Literatur um die Jahrhundertwende*. Paderborn: Schöningh Verlag.

Sprinzen, D. 1988. *Camus: A Critical Examination*. Philadelphia: Temple University Press.

Spycher, P. 1981. 'Friedrich Dürrenmatts Israel-Essay: Religiöse Konzeption und Glaubensbekanntnis' in Gerhard Knapp (ed.), *Facetten: Studien zum 60. Gerburtstag Friedrich Dürrenmatts*. Bern: Peter Lang Verlag.

Standish, P. 1992. *Beyond the Self: Wittgenstein, Heidegger and the Limits of Language*. Brookfield, VT: Avebury.

Stark, J. 1997. *Wolfgang Borchert's Germany: Reflections of the Third Reich*. Lanham: University Press of America.

Strauss, D. 1846. *Das Leben Jesu für das deutsche Volk*. Leipzig: Brockhaus Verlag.

Strathausen, C. 2003. *The Look of Things: Poetry and Vision around 1900*. Chapel Hill: University of North Carolina Press.

Stromsik, J. 1981. 'Apokalypse Komisch' in Gerhard Knapp (ed.), *Facetten: Studien zum 60. Gerburtstag Friedrich Dürrenmatts*. Bern: Peter Lang Verlag.

Stubbe, E. 1995. *Die Wirklichkeit der Engel in Literatur, Kunst und Religion*. Münster: Lit Verlag.

Sun, W. 1997. 'Post-Brechtian Theatre in the Age of Media: A Cross-Cultural Overview', *Communications from the International Brecht Society* 26.1: 52–57.

Sussman, H. 1982. *The Hegelian Aftermath: Readings in Hegel, Kierkegaard, Freud, Proust, and James*. Baltimore: Johns Hopkins University Press.

Suvin, D. 1995. 'On "Haltung", Agency, and Emotions in Brecht: Prolegomena'. *Communications from the International Brecht Society* 24.1: 65–77.

Szondi, P. 1978a. 'Lyrik und lyrische Dramatik in Hofmannsthals Frühwerk' in *Schriften II*. Frankfurt am Main: Suhrkamp Verlag.

—— 1978b. *Theorie des Modernen Dramas. Schriften I*. Frankfurt am Main: Suhrkamp Verlag.

Tadie, A., ed. 1994. *Permanent Things: Toward the Recovery of a More Human Scale at the End of the Twentieth Century*. Grand Rapids: William B. Eerdmans.

Tessin, T., ed. 1995. *Philosophy and the Grammar of Religious Belief*. New York: St. Martin's Press.

Thielicke, H. 1983. *Glauben und Denken in der Neuzeit: Die grossen Systeme der Theologie und Religionsphilosophie*. Tübingen: n.p.

Tollini, F. 2003. 'The Song of Nevercome Day in Brecht's "The Good Person of Setzuan"', *Communications from the International Brecht Society* 32 (June): 74–75.

Tomczuk, D. 2000. 'Babylon als Sinnbild für die Grossstadt aller Zeiten: Die Raumkozeption in "Ein Engel kommt nach Babylon" von Friedrich Dürrenmatt', *Lubelskie Materialy Neofilolgiczne* 24: 89–99.

Troeltsch, E. 1922. 'Die Krisis des Historismus', *Die Neue Rundschau* 33:n.p.

—— 1924. *Der Historismus und seine Überwindung.* Berlin: R. Heise Verlag.

Vilas-Boas, G. 2003. 'Die undurchschaubare Unsicherheit: Dürrenmatts labyrinthische Welt' in *Sentimente, Gefühle, Empfindungen: zur Geschichte und Literatur des Affektiven von 1770 bis heute.* Würzburg: Königshausen & Neumann Verlag.

Vormweg, H. n.d. 'Literatur war ein Asyl', *Literaturmagazin* 7: n.p.

Wagner-Egelhaaf, M. 1989. *Mystik der Moderne: Die Visionäre Ästhetik der deutschen Literatur im 20. Jahrhundert.* J. B. Metzler Verlag.

Waldmann, G. 1964. 'Dürrenmatts paradoxes Theater: Die Komödie des christlichen Glaubens', *Wirkendes Wort: Deutsche Sprache in Forschung und Lehre* 14: 22–35.

Warren, W., ed. 1982. *The Secular Mind: Transformations of Faith in Modern Europe.* New York: Holmes and Meyer.

Weber, E. 1980. *Friedrich Dürrenmatt und die Frage nach Gott: Zur theologischen Relevanz der frühen Prosa eines merkwürdigen Protestanten.* Zürich: Theologischer Verlag.

Wehler, H.-U. 1984. 'Historiography in Germany Today' in J. Habermas (ed.), *Observations on the Spiritual Situation of the Age* (trans. A. Buchwalter). Cambridge, Mass.: MIT Press.

Weiler, G., ed. 1970. *Mauthner's Critique of Language.* Cambridge: Cambridge University Press.

—— 1986. *Fritz Mauthner. Sprache und Leben.* Salzburg: Residenz.

Weimar, K. 1956. 'No Entry, No Exit: A study of Borchert with some notes on Sartre' in *Modern Language Quarterly* 8: 153–165.

Weisman, F. 1967. *Wittgenstein und der Wiener Kreis.* Oxford: Blackwell.

Whalley, F. 2002. *The Elusive Transcendent: The Role of Religion in the Plays of Frank Wedekind.* Oxford: Peter Lang.

Whitton, K. 1974. 'Afternoon Conversation with an Uncomfortable Person', *New German Studies* 2: n.p.

—— 1990. *Dürrenmatt: Reinterpretation in Retrospect.* New York: Berg.

Wilder, T. 1957. *Three Plays.* New York: Harper.

Wilson, L. 1972. 'Beckmann, der Ertrinkende', *Akzente* 19: 466–79.

Wirsching, J. 1973. 'Friedrich Dürrenmatt. "Der Tunnel": Eine theologische Analyse', *Der Deutschunterricht: Beiträge zu seiner Praxis und wissenschaftlichen Grundlegung* 25(1): 103–17.

Wirtz, I. 2000. 'Die Verwandlung des Engels' in P. Rusterholz and I. Wirtz (eds.), *Die Verwandlung der 'Stoffe' als Stoff der Verwandlung: Friedrich Dürrenmatts Spätwerk.* Berlin: Erich Schmidt Verlag.

Wittgenstein, L. 1960a. 'Philosophische Untersuchungen' in *Schriften*. Frankfurt am Main: Suhrkamp Verlag.

—— 1960b. 'Traktatus logico-philosophicus' in *Schriften*. Frankfurt am Main: Suhrkamp Verlag.

—— 1966. *Lectures and Conversations on Aesthetics, Psychology, and Religious Belief* (ed. Cyril Barrett). Berkeley: University of California Press.

—— 1969. *Briefe an Ludwig von Ficker.* Salzburg: Miller Verlag.

—— 1980. *Culture and Value* (trans. P. Winch). Chicago: University of Chicago Press.

—— 1984. *Philosophische Bemerkungen.* Frankfurt am Main: Suhrkamp Verlag.

Wittschier, S. M. 1998. *Mein Engel Halte Mich Wach: das Engelbild in der zeitgenossischen Literatur.* Wurzburg: Echter Verlag.

Wodak, R., ed. 1989. *Language, Power and Ideology: Studies in Political Discourse.* Amsterdam: Benjamins.

Wohlfarth, I. 1978. 'On the Messianic Structure of Walter Benjamin's Last Reflections' in S. Weber and H. Sussman (eds.), *Glyph 3*. Baltimore: Johns Hopkins University Press.

Wolin, R. 1982. *Walter Benjamin: An Aesthetic of Redemption.* New York: Columbia University Press.

Wright, E. 1989. *Postmodern Brecht: A Re-Presentation.* London: Routledge.

Wright, T. R. 1988. *Theology and Literature.* Oxford: Blackwell.

Wunberg, G. 1971. *Die literarische Moderne: Dokumente zum Selbstverständnis der Literatur um die Jahrundertwende.* Frankfurt am Main: Athenäum Verlag.

Wurfgaft, B. A. 2002. 'Language at its Core: Ethical and Religious Subjects in Levines and Benjamin', *Sinn und Form: Beiträge zur Literatur* 54.4: 473–84.

Yarrow, R. 1985. 'Consciousness, the Fantastic and the Reading Process' in R. Collins and H. Pearce (eds.), *The Scope of the Fantastic*. Westport, Conn.: Greenwood.

—— 1986. '"Neutral" Consciousness in the Experience of Theater', *Mosaic* 33.3a.

Zola, E. 1902. *Le Roman expérimental.* Paris: E. Fasquelle.

# Index

# Studies in Modern German Literature

Peter D. G. Brown
*General Editor*

22  Joachim Warmbold, *Germania in Africa: Germany's Colonial Literature.* 1989.

23  Ernst Schürer, *Franz Jung: Leben und Werk eines Rebellen.* 1994.

24  David B. Dickens, *Negative Spring: Crisis Imagery in the Works of Brentano, Lenau, Rilke, and T.S. Eliot.* 1989.

25  Ernest M. Wolf, *Magnum Opus: Studies in the Narrative Fiction of Thomas Mann.* 1989.

26  Roger Gerhild Brueggemann, *Das Romanwerk von Ingeborg Drewitz.* 1989.

27  Margaret Devinney, *The Legends of Gertrud von Le Fort: Text and Audience.* 1989.

28  Jürgen Kleist, *Das Dilemma der Kunst. Zur Kunst- und Künstlerproblematik in der deutschsprachigen Prosa nach 1945.* 1989.

29  Frederick Amrine (ed.), *Goethe in the History of Science: Bibliography, 1776–1949. Volume I.* 1996.

30  Frederick Amrine (ed.), *Goethe in the History of Science: Bibliography, 1950–1990. Volume II.* 1996.

32  Christina E. Brantner, *Robert Schumann und das Tonkünstler-Bild der Romantiker.* 1991.

33  Brenda Keiser, *Deadly Dishonor: The Duel and the Honor Code in the Works of Arthur Schnitzler.* 1990.

34  Claus Reschke, *Life as a Man: Contemporary Male-Female Relationships in the Novels of Max Frisch.* 1990.

35  Bernhard H. Decker, *Gewalt und Zärtlichkeit. Einführung in die Militärbelletristik der DDR 1956–1986.* 1990.

36  Kathy Brzovic, *Bonaventura's "Nachtwachen": A Satirical Novel.* 1990.

37  Jozef A. Modzelewski, *Das Pandämonium der achtziger Jahre. Kurzprosa des Jahres 1983.* 1990.

38  Jürgen Fröhlich, *Liebe im Expressionismus. Eine Untersuchung der Lyrik in den Zeitschriften "Die Aktion" und "Der Sturm" von 1910–1914.* 1991.

39  Richard A. Weber, *Color and Light in the Writings of Eduard von Keyserling.* 1990.

40  Ingeborg C. Walther, *The Theater of Franz Xaver Kroetz.* 1990.

41  Ralph W. Büchler, *Science, Satire and Wit: The Essays of Georg Christoph Lichtenberg.* 1990.

42  Peter J. Schroeck, *Character Transition in the Writings of Hans Erich Nossack.* 1991.

43  William Grange, *Partnership in the German Theatre: Zuckmayer and Hilpert, 1925–1961.* 1991.

44  Mary Rhiel, *Re-Viewing Kleist: The Discursive Construction of Authorial Subjectivity in West German Kleist Films.* 1991.

45  Hülya Ünlü, *Das Ghasel des islamischen Orients in der deutschen Dichtung.* 1991.

46  Russel Christensen, *The Virility Complex: A Casebook of National Socialist Practice.* Forthcoming.

47 Klaus-Jürgen Röhm, *Polyphonie und Improvisation. Zur offenen Form in Günter Grass' "Die Rättin"*. 1992.

48 Kevin G. Kennedy, *Der junge Goethe in der Tradition des Petrarkismus.* 1995.

49 Thomas Mann, *Thomas Mann – Félix Bertaux: Correspondence 1923–1948. Edited by Biruta Cap.* 1993.

50 Ilse-Rose Warg, *"Doch ich krümm mich um alles, was lebt". Wolfdietrich Schnurres lyrisches Schaffen.* 1993.

51 Muriel W. Stiffler, *The German Ghost Story as Genre.* 1993.

52 Roger F. Cook, *The Demise of the Author: Autonomy and the German Writer, 1770–1848.* 1993.

53 Gisela Moffit, *Bonds and Bondage: Daughter-Father Relationships in the Father Memoirs of German-Speaking Women Writers of the 1970s.* 1993.

55 Margo R. Bosker, *Sechs Stücke nach Stücken. Zu den Bearbeitungen von Peter Hacks.* 1994.

56 Calvin N. Jones, *Negation and Utopia: The German Volksstück from Raimund to Kroetz.* 1993.

57 Alan John Swensen, *Gods, Angels, and Narrators: A Metaphysics of Narrative in Thomas Mann's "Joseph und seine Brüder".* 1994.

58 Karl-Heinz Finken, *Die Wahrheit der Literatur. Studien zur Literaturtheorie des 18. Jahrhunderts.* 1993.

59 Marina Foschi Albert, *Friedrich Schlegels Theorie des Witzes und sein Roman "Lucinde".* 1995.

60 Johann Wolfgang Goethe, *Correspondence between Goethe and Schiller 1794–1805: Translated by Liselotte Dieckmann.* 1994.

61 Timothy Torno, *Finding Time: Reading for Temporality in Hölderlin and Heidegger.* 1995.

62 Steven Fuller, *The Nazis' Literary Grandfather: Adolf Bartels and Cultural Extremism, 1871–1945.* 1996.

63 Cordelia Stroinigg, *Sudermann's "Frau Sorge": Jugendstil, Archetype, Fairy Tale.* 1995.

64 Jean H. Leventhal, *Echoes in the Text: Musical Citation in German Narratives from Theodor Fontane to Martin Walser.* 1995.

66 Cordula Drossel-Brown, *Zeit und Zeiterfahrung in der deutschsprachigen Lyrik der Fünfziger Jahre. Marie Luise Kaschnitz, Ingeborg Bachmann und Christine Lavant.* 1995.

67 Marianne & Martin Löschmann, *Einander verstehen. Ein deutsches literarisches Lesebuch.* 1997.

68 Caroline Kreide, *Lou Andreas-Salomé. Feministin oder Antifeministin? Eine Standortbestimmung zur wilhelminischen Frauenbewegung.* 1996.

69 Fredric S. Steussy, *Eighteenth-Century German Autobiography: The Emergence of Individuality.* 1996.

70 Aminia M. Brueggemann, *Chronotopos Amerika bei Max Frisch, Peter Handke, Günter Kunert und Martin Walser.* 1996.

71 Norgard Klages, *Look Back in Anger: Mother-Daughter and Father-Daughter Relationships in Women's Autobiographical Writings of the 1970s and 1980s.* 1995.

72 Romey Sabalius, *Die Romane Hugo Loetschers im Spannungsfeld von Fremde und Vertrautheit.* 1995.

73 Bianca Rosenthal, *Pathways to Paul Celan: A History of Critical Responses as a Chorus of Discordant Voices.* 1995.

74 Lilian Ramos, *Peter Rosegger: Pedagogue of Passion.* Forthcoming.

75 Sandra L. Singer, *Free Soul, Free Woman? A Study of Selected Fictional Works by Hedwig Dohm, Isolde Kurz, and Helene Böhlau.* 1995.

76 Brigitta O'Regan, *Self and Existence: J.M.R. Lenz's Subjective Point of View.* 1997.

77 Elke Matijevich, *The "Zeitroman" of the Late Weimar Republic.* 1995.

78 Vera B. Profit, *Menschlich. Gespräche mit Karl Krolow.* 1996.

79 Schürer/Keune/Jenkins (eds.), *The Berlin Wall: Representations and Perspectives.* 1996.

80 Frank Schlossbauer, *Literatur als Gegenwelt. Zur Geschichtlichkeit literarischer Komik am Beispiel Fischarts und Lessings.* 1998.

81 Cara M. Horwich, *Survival in "Simplicissimus" and "Mutter Courage".* 1997.

82 Catherine O'Brien, *Women's Fictional Responses to the First World War: A Comparative Study of Selected Texts by French and German Writers.* 1997.

83 Heather I. Sullivan, *The Intercontextuality of Self and Nature in Ludwig Tieck's Early Works.* 1997.

85 Jean Wotschke, *From the Home Fires to the Battlefield: Mothers in German Expressionist Drama.* 1998.

86 Ellen M. Nagy, *Women in Germanics, 1850–1950.* 1997.

87 Mary R. Strand, *I/You: Paradoxical Constructions of Self and Other in Early German Romanticism.* 1998.

88 Hildegard F. Glass, *Future Cities in Wilhelminian Utopian Literature.* 1997.

89 Irene B. Compton, *Kritik des Kritikers. Bölls "Ansichten eines Clowns" und Kleists "Marionettentheater".* 1998.

90 Heide Witthoeft, *Von Angesicht zu Angesicht. Literarische Spiegelszenen.* 1998.

91 Peter Yang, *Theater ist Theater. Ein Vergleich der Kreidekreisstücke Bertolt Brechts und Li Xingdaos.* 1998.

92 Hartmut Heep (ed.), *Unreading Rilke: Unorthodox Approaches to a Cultural Myth.* 2001.

93 Wendy Wagner, *Georg Büchners Religionsunterricht 1821–1831. Christlich-Protestantische Wurzeln sozialrevolutionären Engagements.* 2000.

94 Kevin F. Yee, *Aesthetic Homosociality in Wackenroder and Tieck.* 2000.

95 Gary Schmidt, *The Nazi Abduction of Ganymede: Representations of Male Homosexuality in Postwar German Literature.* 2003.

96 Susan Ray, *Beyond Nihilism: Gottfried Benn's Postmodernist Poetics.* 2003.

97 W. Scott Hoerle, *Hans Friedrich Blunck: Poet and Nazi Collaborator, 1888–1961.* 2003.

98 Olivia G. Gabor, *The Stage as "Der Spielraum Gottes".* 2006.

99 Jared Poley, *Decolonization in Germany: Weimar Narratives of Colonial Loss in Foreign Occupation.* 2005.

100 Marc Falkenberg, *Rethinking the Uncanny in Hoffmann and Tieck.* 2005.

101 Erika M. Nelson, *Reading Rilke's Orphic Identity.* 2005.

102 Forthcoming.

103 Bennett Irving Enowitch, *Eros and Thanatos: A Psycho-Literary Investigation of Walter Vogt's Life and Works.* 2005.

104 Forthcoming.

105 Dirk Wendtorf, *Adoleszente Wehrmachtssoldaten in der Nachkriegsjugendliteratur: Opfer oder Täter? Autobiografische Erklärungsansätze zur Motivation adoleszenter Soldaten.* 2006.